Library Of

Rev. Patrick M. Connolly

Understanding the Book of Amos

D1474065

NCMC
BS
1585.2
.H375
1991

Understanding the Book of Amos

Basic Issues
in Current Interpretations

Gerhard F. Hasel

BAKER BOOK HOUSE
Grand Rapids, Michigan 49516

Copyright 1991 by
Gerhard F. Hasel

Printed in the United States of America

Library of Congress Cataloging-in-Publication Data

Hasel, Gerhard F.
   Understanding the book of Amos : basic issues in current interpretations /
Gerhard F. Hasel.
        p.   cm.
   Includes bibliographical references and index.
   ISBN 0-8010-4353-0
        1. Bible. O.T. Amos—Criticism, interpretation, etc.—History—20th
century. I. Title.
   BS1585.2.H375   1991
   224'. 806 '09045—dc20   ˙90-21256
                                                                              CIP

CONTENTS

ABBREVIATIONS

AA	Alttestamentliche Abhandlungen
ABR	*Australian Biblical Review*
AJBI	Annual of the Japanese Biblical Institute
Ang	*Angelicum*
ArOr	*Archiv orientální*
AsSeign	*Assemblées du Seigneur*
ASTI	*Annual of the Swedish Theological Institute*
AUSS	*Andrews University Seminary Studies*
BAR	*Biblical Archaeologist Reader*
BARev	*Biblical Archaeology Review*
BASOR	*Bulletin of the American Schools of Oriental Research*
BeO	*Bibbia e oriente*
BETL	Bibliotheca Ephemeridum Theologicarum Lovaniensium
Bib	*Biblica*
BiL	*Bibel und Leben*
BiOr	*Bibliotheca Orientalis*
BIOSCS	*Bulletin of the International Organization for Septuagint and Cognate Studies*
BN	*Biblische Notizen*
BO	*Bibliotheca Orientalis*
BR	*Biblical Research*
BS	*Biblische Studien*
BT	*The Bible Translator*
BTB	*Biblical Theology Bulletin*
BZ	*Biblische Zeitschrift*

CAH	*Cambridge Ancient History*
CBQ	*Catholic Biblical Quarterly*
CTM	*Concordia Theological Monthly*
CuBi	*Cultura biblica*
CurTM	*Currents in Theology and Mission*
DBS	*Dictionnaire Biblique Supplement*
ECarm	*Ephemerides Carmeliticae*
ErIsr	Eretz Israel
EstBib	*Estudios bíblicos*
ETL	*Ephemerides théologicae lovanienses*
ETR	*Etudes théologiques et religieuses*
EvTh	*Evangelische Theologie*
ExpTim	*Expository Times*
Foi Vie	*Foi et Vie*
GTT	*Gereformeerd theologisch Tijdschrift*
HAR	*Hebrew Annual Review*
HS	*Hebrew Studies*
HTR	*Harvard Theological Review*
HUCA	*Hebrew Union College Annual*
IDB	*Interpreter's Dictionary of the Bible*
IDB (Sup)	*Interpreter's Dictionary of the Bible* (Supplementary Volume)
IEJ	*Israel Exploration Journal*
Int	*Interpretation: A Journal of Bible and Theology*
ISBE	*International Standard Bible Encyclopedia*
ITQ	*Irish Theological Quarterly*
JANES	*Journal of the Ancient Near Eastern Society*
JANESCU	*Journal of the Ancient Near Eastern Society of Columbia University*
JAOS	*Journal of the American Oriental Society*
JBL	*Journal of Biblical Literature*
JCS	*Journal of Cuneiform Studies*
JETS	*Journal of the Evangelical Theological Society*
JNES	*Journal of Near Eastern Studies*
JNSL	*Journal of Northwest Semitic Languages*
JQR	*Jewish Quarterly Review*
JSOT	*Journal for the Study of the Old Testament*
JSS	*Journal of Semitic Studies*

J Th So Africa	Journal of Theology for Southern Africa
JTS	Journal of Theological Studies
Kairos	Kairos: Zeitschrift für Religionswissenschaft und Theologie
KD	Kerygma und Dogma
LB	Linguistica Biblica
LP	Liber pontificalis
LU VITOR	Lumen Vitor
NedTTS	Nederlands theologisch tijdschrift
NorTT	Norsk Teologisk Tidsskrift
NovT	Novum Testamentum
NTT	Nieuw theologisch Tijdschrift
N Z Sys Th	Neue Zeitschrift für systematische Theologie und Religionsphilosophie
OLZ	Orientalistische Literaturzeitung
Or	Orientalia
OrAnt	Oriens antiquus
OTE	Old Testament Essays
OTS	Oudtestamentische Studiën
PAAJR	Proceedings of the American Academy for Jewish Research
PEGLBS	Proceedings, Eastern Great Lakes and Midwest Biblical Societies
PEQ	Palestine Exploration Quarterly
Per Rel St	Perspectives in Religious Studies
Proof	Prooftexts: A Journal of Jewish Literary History
RArch	Revue archéologique
RB	Revue biblique
REJ	Revue des études juives
Rel	Religion
RelSRev	Religious Studies Review
ResQ	Restoration Quarterly
RevEx	Review and Expositor
RevScRel	Revue des sciences religieuses
RivB	Rivista biblica
RoB	Religion och Bibel
RSR	Recherches de science religieuse
RTK	Roczniki Teol.-Kanoniczne

RTL	*Revue théologique de Louvain*
SBFLA	*Studii biblici franciscani liber annuus*
SBLSP	*SBL Seminar Papers*
ScEs	*Science et esprit*
SDB	See *DBS*
SEÅ	*Svensk exegetisk Årsbok*
Semeia	*Semeia: An Experimental Journal for Biblical Criticism*
SH	*Seckauer Hefte*
SJTh	*Scottish Journal of Theology*
SR	*Studies in Religion*
StTh	*Studia Theologica*
SWJT	*Southwestern Journal of Theology*
TBT	*The Bible Today*
TDOT	*Theological Dictionary of the Old Testament*
ThZ	*Theologische Zeitschrift*
TLZ	*Theologische Literaturzeitung*
TQ	*Theologische Quartalschrift*
TRE	*Theologische Realenzyklopädie*
TRu	*Theologische Rundschau*
TTZ	*Trierer Theologische Zeitschrift*
TWAT	*Theologisches Wörterbuch zum Alten Testament*
TZ	*Theologische Zeitschrift*
UF	*Ugarit-Forschungen*
USQR	*Union Seminary Quarterly Review*
VT	*Vetus Testamentum*
VTS	*Vetus Testamentum Supplements*
WD	*Wort und Dienst*
WO	*Die Welt des Orients*
ZAW	*Zeitschrift für evangelische Ethik*
ZDPV	*Zeitschrift des deutschen Palästina-Vereins*
ZEE	*Zeitschrift für evangelische Ethik*
ZSTh	*Zeitschrift für systematische Theologie*
ZTK	*Zeitschrift für Theologie und Kirche*

INTRODUCTION

The prophet Amos, whose book is in the heart of the Old Testament, is one of the so-called classical prophets of ancient Israel. These prophets addressed Israel, God's people, as a whole and not just a person or a group of people within the nation. Amos' book of nine chapters is dated by its internal information to the first half of the eighth century B.C. The man Amos is a colorful and powerful preacher. His work is one of exquisite literary art and sublime poetry, full of variety and yet carefully structured.

The Book of Amos is the oldest and thus earliest of the "writing prophets" in the Hebrew Bible. Bible students have recognized for centuries that for this reason alone, aside from many others, it is of utmost importance for readers and students of Scripture. Our understanding of prophecy and how it functioned in biblical times is to a significant degree shaped by the oracles and invectives, the predictions and accusations, and the pleadings and calls to repentance provided by Amos. In this sense a study of the Book of Amos serves as a type or paradigm—if not a microcosm—for the study of all of the prophetic writings of the Old Testament.

John S. Holladay, a keen student of Old Testament prophecy and prophetic writings, notes, "The explosive emergence of the so-called 'writing prophets' in the history of Israel is one of the great historical mysteries of Old Testament scholarship."[1] This is indeed so. To understand Amos means to understand and to have a key to Old Testament prophecy. An unraveling of Amos and his prophetic message contributes toward the lifting of this mystery.

The Book of Amos is one of the most fascinating books of the Old Testament. With its nine succinct chapters and its 149 verses it is by no means a long book. But its content grips the reader's attention. Amos employs numerous literary techniques, using the surprise effect with great skill, reversing popular religious expectations, stunning his audience with revealing exposés, and holding out no hope whatever for Israel as a nation in view of the impending Assyrian political-military threat.

Amos' prophetic call "from following the flock" and the command through a divine imperative, "Go prophesy to my people Israel" (7:15), took place probably somewhere between 780 and 760 B.C. This was the first half of "the greatest of centuries" of Israel, according to Philip J. King.[2] It was "a kind of Golden Age," as Martin Noth once said,[3] and more precisely "the Silver Age of Israelite history" during which "Israel reached the summit of its material power and economic prosperity as well as the apogee of its territorial expansion."[4]

Israel and Judah were smug and complacent. On the whole things had gone very well for both nations on every side. Yahweh, however, called prophets such as Amos, Hosea, Isaiah, and Micah to give messages of warning, repentance, and a call to return to the Lord, pointing to a revival of true religion and morality joined to genuine Yahweh worship. Rituals of the cult could not substitute for a moral lifestyle. The covenant of God required "devotion, not

1. John S. Holladay, "Assyrian Statecraft and the Prophets of Israel," *HTR* 63 (1970): 29.

2. Philip J. King, "The Eighth, the Greatest of Centuries?" *JBL* 108 (1989): 3–15.

3. Martin Noth, *The History of Israel*, 2d ed. (New York: Harper & Row, 1960), 250.

4. Shalom M. Paul, *Amos: A Commentary on the Book of Amos* (Minneapolis: Fortress, 1991), 1.

devotions."[5] For Amos religion is a lifestyle, and decadence cancels all religious activities. What happens in everyday life is what brings meaning to religious practice.

Amos was sent at a time when the threat of the mighty and cruel Assyrians, who were in the process of building a vast empire in the ancient Near East, was felt throughout the entire region. The Assyrians made no secret of the cruelty they could inflict on those who did not yield to them or opposed them. By the time the Neo-Assyrian period (9th–7th cents. B.C.) was in full swing, the Assyrian Empire had reached its zenith. Countries, cities, and peoples that did not submit to Assyrian rule were punished by total destruction. Not only were cities and villages leveled by the conquering Assyrian armies, but fields and orchards were totally annihilated so that any people who may have escaped would starve to death. The Assyrians introduced the wholesale deportation of peoples. The ghastly record of impaling prisoners on stakes, of tearing out the tongues of prisoners, of cutting off ears and noses, of gouging out eyes, and of flaying prisoners alive by cutting off pieces of skin is preserved in its total starkness on the reliefs carved in stone in the palaces of Assyrian kings from Nineveh. There are pictures of the dismemberment of opponents and the beheading of prisoners of war in order to count the enemy conquered.[6] In one report Shalmaneser III (858–824 B.C.) boasts, "A pyramid (pillar) of heads I erected in front of the city."[7] Ashurnasirpal II (883–859 B.C.) also leaves a record of his cruelty: "I flayed many nobles as had rebelled against me [and] draped their skins over the pile [of corpses]; some I spread out within the pile, some I erected on stakes upon the pile. . . . I flayed many right through my land [and]

5. S. Spiegel, *Amos versus Amaziah*, Essays in Judaism 3 (New York: Jewish Theological Seminary, 1957), 43.

6. See James B. Pritchard, ed., *The Ancient Near East*, vol. 1, *An Anthology of Texts and Pictures* (Princeton, N.J.: Princeton University Press, 1973); Erika Bleibtreu, "Grisly Assyrian Record of Torture and Death," *BARev* 17/1 (1991): 52–61.

7. D. D. Luckenbill, *Ancient Records of Assyria and Babylonia* (Chicago: University of Chicago Press, 1926), vol. 1, sec. 599.

draped their skins over the walls."[8] Tiglath-pileser III
(744–727 B.C.) engaged in several campaigns in Syria-
Palestine and held the major place of Assyrian kings in the
eighth century B.C. His successor, Shalmaneser V, finally
besieged Samaria and ultimately destroyed the kingdom of
Israel with its capital in 723/22 B.C.[9] Sargon II (722–705
B.C.), however, claims he took the city and, therefore, the
year 722 is often taken as the year of the fall of Samaria.
Most survivors were led into captivity. The ten-tribe kingdom of Israel that came into existence in 931 B.C. when the
Davidic empire was split came to an end.

Amos was thus a prophet of the eleventh hour! Could
the Lord save his apostate people Israel? Could the people
count on their Lord when they did not practice what he
had asked of them? The people thought so, but Amos (and
the Lord) did not!

This book provides the serious reader and student of the
Old Testament with an introduction in the form of a survey
and review of the unusually rich amount of thought, study,
and research that has gone into the Book of Amos in modern times. It includes a comprehensive select bibliography
of works written over the last three decades on the Book of
Amos. We have found more than eight hundred (!) publications written since 1969 on this short book.[10] There are
diachronic approaches using all forms of modern historical-
critical research, and synchronic ones. There are also important new literary approaches that seem to point in the
direction of a paradigm change.

The approach to Amos in this volume is to focus on
major issues. The first chapter briefly surveys the content of

8. A. K. Grayson, *Assyrian Royal Inscriptions*, pt. 2, *From Tiglath-pileser I to Ashur-nasir-apli II* (Wiesbaden: O. Harrassowitz, 1976), 124.

9. This is the date given by Edwin R. Thiele, *The Mysterious Numbers of the Hebrew Kings*, 3d ed. (Grand Rapids: Zondervan, 1983), 137.

10. For further bibliography on the earlier period and partially but incom-
pletely overlapping with our period, see Adrian van der Wal, *Amos: A Classified
Bibliography*, 3d ed. (Amsterdam: Free University Press, 1986). The select bibliography cites over 350 items not listed by van der Wal.

the book and depicts the major stages in its interpretation over the span of about the last hundred years. Chapters 2 through 4 deal with the issues of Amos' vocation before he was called to his prophetic ministry, what kind of prophetic task he was called to, and whether his home and background are to be sought in Judah in the south or Galilee in the north. Chapter 5 treats the complexities, authenticity, and purpose of the famous "oracles against the nations," the first of this kind of literature in the Hebrew Bible. This discussion is followed with the matters of Amos' use of Israelite traditions, themes, and motifs (chap. 6) and the debate about the "intellectual" background of Amos on the basis of which much modern scholarship has attempted to explain his message (chap. 7). The following two chapters treat the nature of the so-called hymnic doxologies (chap. 8) and the composition of Amos with an emphasis on the new trends in the literary study of the book (chap. 9). Chapter 10 is devoted to the rich and diverse literature on Amos and his social criticism and its relevance for liberation theology. The concluding chapter addresses major theological emphases of the book, particularly the "day of the Lord/Yahweh" and whether Amos' message holds out a future hope (a remnant), and the meaning of the puzzling conclusion of the book (9:11–15) and how this passage has been handled by modern scholars.

We will present opposing opinions and raise questions to stimulate thinking and to point to divergent issues. Regardless of one's own position or preferences, we are all enriched by the work that has been done on Amos. Despite the bewildering volume of material available, the last word has by no means been said about this exciting book and this challenging prophet.

It is hoped that this volume will assist in leading more serious readers of the Bible to find their way through the rich thought expressed in Amos and thus gain a foundation for further investigation.

The content of this book is a significant enlargement and reworking of materials presented in papers to the Society of

Biblical Literature at its annual meeting in Anaheim, California, in November 1989, under the title, "Amos in Contemporary Scholarship: Issues and Problems," and to the Midwest Branch of the Society of Biblical Literature, American Oriental Society, and American Society of Oriental Research Conference, February 18–19, 1990, at the University of Wisconsin, Madison, Wisconsin, on the topic of eschatology in the Book of Amos.

I wish to express my appreciation to my secretary, Mrs. Betty Jean Mader, for her profound assistance in technical matters pertaining to the production of this volume and to Reinaldo Siqueira, a doctoral student in Old Testament Studies, for his assistance in collecting various materials for the select bibliography.

1

AMOS IN THE STAGES OF MODERN INTERPRETATION

The Book of Amos, a "minor prophet"[1] usually accepted as the earliest of the "writing prophets,"[2] consists of only 9 chapters, 146 verses,[3] and 2,042 words.[4] Yet there are not too many themes of the Old Testament that Amos does not draw on; others he mentions for the first time. Amos is the first prophet who condemns not only Israel and Judah, but also the surrounding nations. Later Old Testament prophets follow up on this indictment and

1. The designation "minor prophet" derives from Jewish tradition. It is used for the book of the Twelve Prophets, that is, the short or small prophetic books outside of the long ones such as Isaiah, Jeremiah, and Ezekiel.

2. The designation "writing prophets" is employed to distinguish the prophets of the Old Testament who produced books that have become part of the canon of the Old Testament from those prophetic figures known in the Old Testament (such as Nathan) who did not leave their messages in written form.

3. According to the Massorah of the Hebrew MSS.

4. This is the count by G. E. Weil, "Analyse automatique quantifiee en critique textuelle biblique: Limite des analyses statistiques," *College de l'ALLC, Tel-Aviv. Bulletin of the Association for Literary and Linguistic Computing* 8 (1980): 34, as cited by

condemnation of the foreign nations, but Amos is the first
of the prophets of the Hebrew Bible to provide such oracles.
The expression "the day of the Lord/Yahweh" appears for
the first time in the Book of Amos. Does he invent this idea
or is it one that is already in existence?[5] Does Amos take this
popular idea of the people of Israel and turn it against them?
If so, what motivates him to reverse popular eschatology?

Amos' message, in its canonical form, is eschatological in
nature. Various scholars dispute this to the present.[6] What
kind of eschatology does the book reveal? Where does it come
from? Did Amos invent eschatology? Or is eschatology super-
imposed upon an earlier noneschatological message?

On what grounds or foundations does Amos base his
message of judgment? Is he indebted to the covenant? Is it
based in the cult? Is it rooted in circles of popular wisdom?
Does it derive from all of these and/or from other sources
and traditions?[7]

The incisive criticism of society in the Book of Amos is
unparalleled in the entire Old Testament.[8] Amos' invectives
against the rich and his defense of the poor, the widow, and
the orphan stand as an unequalled testimony in Israelite
faith. Amos has received much attention in our time
because he is a useful and power-driven agent for third
world, black, and feminist liberation theologies. Where does
his social criticism derive from? What is its aim? Is it
directly applicable to modern situations, or does it stand in
need of "translation"?

---

and independently counted by Francis I. Andersen and David Noel Freedman,
Amos: A New Translation with Introduction and Commentary (New York: Doubleday,
1989), 25. According to A. Even-Shoshan, *A New Concordance of the Old Testament*
(Jerusalem: Kiryat Sefer, 1985), xxxviii, there are 2,053 words with 7,800 signs.
Since there is no tradition about the word count, words in Hebrew seem to have
unclear definitions, and there are differing orthographic conventions regarding
the boundaries of words, either of the figures may be regarded as correct, depend-
ing on the variation of word boundaries and definitions.

5. See chap. 11.
6. See chap. 11.
7. See chaps. 6 and 7.
8. See chap. 10.

The Book of Amos seems to have a distinct structure.[9] The heading or superscription of the book (1:1) introduces the prophet,[10] dates his ministry, gives his place of origin,[11] and provides information about the source of the prophet's message.

Amos' motto or revelatory theme appears to be 1:2. Some have taken this verse to stand for the whole book, while other scholars see it as an introduction to 1:3–2:16 or take it as part of the introductory superscription.

The first major section of the book (1:3–2:16) consists of the so-called Oracles Against the Nations (OAN). As we shall see later,[12] modern scholars have suggested that either none—or at best only four—of the eight oracles derive from the prophet Amos himself. The other oracles are said to come from various reconstructed stages of the supposedly long development of the book. Other scholars argue for the genuineness of all OAN. Whatever scholarly position is taken, it is clear that these oracles are prophecies of doom for the nations involved, concluding with Judah and Israel.

A second major section of the book is 3:1–6:14, which contains a variety of prophetic words and visions. Amos 3:1–2 affirms Israel's election and the responsibilities deriving from it. It also presents the guilt incurred. Amos 3:3–8 seems to present certain causes and resultant effects. Amos 3:9–4:3 contains proclamations regarding Israel and Samaria. Amos 4:4–5 is a warning about cultic sacrilege. Amos 4:6–13 describes plagues, and is marked by the refrain, "Yet you did not return to me," which climaxes in a threat (v. 12) and a doxology (v. 13).[13] Amos 5:1–27 contains various exhortations for the northern kingdom of Israel and the southern kingdom of Judah. The sayings regarding the "remnant of Joseph" (5:15) and "the day of Yahweh" (5:18–20) seem to be the two hingepins of the

9. See chap. 9.
10. See chap. 2.
11. See chap. 4.
12. See chap. 5.
13. See chap. 8.

book in terms of the relationship of hope for the future and doom for the nation. Amos 6:1–14 contains a number of prophetic invectives and judgments with warnings.

The remaining part of the book (7:1–9:15) contains visions (7:1–9; 8:1–9:6), a biographical report (7:10–17) with the famous statement, "I was/am no prophet, and I was/am no son of a prophet,"[14] and prophecies of salvation (9:7–15).[15] The authorship of the latter section is customarily denied to the prophet in modern historical-critical scholarship, but this position has found powerful defenders in that group and among other scholars.

Modern scholarship on Amos has vascillated or, better stated, has moved along several clearly demarcated lines and stages of development. This is true even if it is suggested that "every aspect of the book [of Amos] and its author—or authors?—produces dissonance."[16] In the period before the historical-critical method became predominant in Amos studies among many scholars (i.e., in the precritical period that reached well into the latter part of the nineteenth century), the entire Book of Amos was held to be written by the prophet Amos of Tekoa himself with the possible exception of 7:10–17, which contains a third-person report and which some exegetes thought may have been written by someone other than the prophet himself (perhaps a student or an eyewitness). Nevertheless even this section was considered to come from the time of Amos.

This assessment was radically altered when Julius Wellhausen argued that the Book of Amos contains both genuine sayings of Amos and later additions from editors. William R. Harper, in his well-known commentary (1905) on Amos in the International Critical Commentary series, harvested the opinions of Wellhausen and others and joined these historical-critical scholars in the search for the histori-

---

14. See chap. 3.
15. See chap. 11.
16. Stanley N. Rosenbaum, *Amos of Israel: A New Interpretation* (Macon, Ga.: Mercer University Press, 1990), 1.

cal Amos and the *ipsissima verba,* the "very words," of the
real Amos of the eighth century. In this first phase of modern critical research the prophet Amos was considered as the
earliest exponent of a new phase of the religion of ancient
Israel characterized by "ethical monotheism." The two great
exponents in the English-speaking world of these new
developments were George A. Smith and William R. Harper.

A second major phase developed in the 1930s, when
form criticism had matured and the traditio-historical
method was developed by Martin Noth, Albrecht Alt, and
Gerhard von Rad in Germany and various representatives
in Scandinavia.[17] In contrast to the first phase, where
source criticism was the major occupation followed by form
criticism's interest in oral tradition, the traditio-historical
phase of the historical-critical method showed that Amos
was in continuity with historically reconstructed ancient
traditions of Israel. Amos was not an innovator at all; he
was not "an isolated individual of great creativity."[18] Thus
the assessment of today is rather the opposite of a previous
generation of scholars.[19] J. Alberto Soggin states that Amos'
"thought is not speculative, nor it is original and creative."[20]
His conclusion is countered by the new and extensive commentary of Shalom M. Paul, who asserts that "deeply
rooted in earlier traditions, Amos, with his *innovative ideas,*
distinctive literary style,and polemics against popular current beliefs, inaugurated a new epoch in the religious life

17. Pivotal for a survey of this new methodology and its developments are
Douglas A. Knight, *Rediscovering the Traditions of Israel: The Development of the
Traditio-Historical Research on the Old Testament,* Society of Biblical Literature
Dissertation series, 9 (Missoula: Scholars, 1973). An invaluable recent contribu-
tion from the point of view of Scandinavian scholarship is provided by Knud
Jeppesen and Benedict Otzen, eds., *The Productions of Time: Tradition History in Old
Testament Scholarship* (Sheffield: Almond, 1984).

18. Brevard S. Childs, *Introduction to the Old Testament as Scripture* (Philadelphia:
Fortress, 1979), 398.

19. See chap. 7.

20. J. Alberto Soggin, *Introduction to the Old Testament,* rev. ed. (Philadelphia:
Westminster, 1980), 244.

of Israel."[21] Evidently it depends how much is assigned to Amos and how much is assigned to later editors.

The results of traditio-historical research on Amos is well summarized by Werner H. Schmidt:

> The book of Amos, then, reached its present form through a gradual process of growth, as the words and visions of Amos himself were supplemented by the third-person account (7:10–17), perhaps also by sayings from a circle of friends or disciples whose existence is a matter of inference ("the school of Amos"), and finally by later additions. This development of the book took place in the southern kingdom (see 1:1f.; 2:4f.; 7:10; etc.), from which Amos had come and to which he was sent back (7:12).[22]

From the point of view of methodology it does not matter whether there are only three major stages of development in the book (as Robert Coote suggests), or six (as Hans W. Wolff maintains), or eight (as Susamu Jozaki holds).[23] Rolf Rendtorff affirms along this line of traditio-historical investigation that "the careful analysis reveals that the present collection [in the Book of Amos] reveals that it has undergone a longer history in which one can distinguish several stages."[24]

This bird's eye view of several stages of interpretation of Amos in the last one hundred years of research reveals that we are engaged in a *Methodenstreit* (battle of methods). In an analysis of Wolff's hypothesis of multilayered redactions of

21. Shalom M. Paul, *Amos: A Commentary on the Book of Amos* (Minneapolis: Fortress, 1991), 7, emphasis added.

22. Werner H. Schmidt, *Old Testament Introduction* (New York: Crossroad, 1984), 196.

23. See chap. 9. Robert Coote, *Amos among the Prophets: Composition and Theology* (Philadelphia: Fortress, 1981), 1–10; Hans Walter Wolff, *Joel and Amos: A Commentary on the Books of the Prophet Joel and Amos* (Philadelphia: Fortress, 1977), 106–14; Susamu Jozaki, "The Secondary Passages of the Book of Amos," *Kwansei Gakuin University Annual Studies* 4 (1956): 25–100.

24. Rolf Rendtorff, *Das Alte Testament. Eine Einführung* (Neukirchen-Vluyn: Neukirchener Verlag, 1983), 232.

Amos, John Bright cautiously but incisively states the limitations of this form-critical and redaction-critical analysis: "But do the tools at our disposal really allow us anything like the precision in describing this process that we find here? In so small a book as Amos do we have a broad enough field of evidence to entitle us to say that this stylistic tract, this line of thought, this formal characteristic, could have been employed by the prophet, but must be assigned to some later stratum of the tradition?"[25] These form-critical and redaction-critical limitations are also noted by John H. Hayes.[26] Shalom M. Paul seriously questions "this scissors-and-paste method" of Wolff and his followers.[27]

At the forefront of other recent literary approaches to the Book of Amos is the most recent and, to my knowledge, the most extensive commentary ever published on the Book of Amos. Francis I. Andersen and David Noel Freedman published, after two decades of research, their 979-page *Amos: A New Translation with Introduction and Commentary* in the Anchor Bible series (1989). In contrast to the approaches of previous interpreters, they are "interested in looking once more at the available text of the book of Amos." They are concerned with the book's literary form as a finished, although not necessarily perfect, product than with the numerous and diverse ingredients that were used in its composition.[28] They insist that "insofar as we can speak about the *book* of Amos, we can recognize one master hand. If not Amos himself, then at least an editor unified the text who must have been very close to his teacher and whose contribution was to arrange and integrate the prophecies that Amos himself produced."[29] For Andersen and Freedman, it "practically amounts to the same thing"[30]

25. John Bright, "A New View of Amos," *Int* 25 (1971): 357.
26. John H. Hayes, *Amos, His Time and His Preaching: The Eighth Century Prophet* (Nashville: Abingdon, 1988), 39.
27. Paul, *Amos*, 6.
28. Andersen and Freedman, *Amos*, 3.
29. Ibid., 5.
30. Ibid., 143.

whether Amos himself or someone very close to him produced the book.

Along a similar line John H. Hayes has produced a commentary on Amos, independent of the previous one, that
uses the approach of a "close reading," which is opposed to
the position that the Book of Amos "is the product of a long
editorial process during which the material was shaped,
reinterpreted, and augmented in various stages of redaction. None of these conclusions can withstand close
scrutiny; all should be discarded as interpretive assump-
tions."[31] Stanley N. Rosenbaum concludes in a similar fash-
ion that "there is no compelling reason . . . for assuming the
present text [of the Book of Amos] to be anything but
largely authentic and the work of its traditional author."[32]
Shalom M. Paul adds his voice to these in his new
Hermeneia series commentary on Amos.[33] These representative voices are typical of those who move beyond the
usual historical-critical paradigm of biblical research. It is
not possible at this time to engage in a discussion of various literary, structuralist, "close-reading," or semiotic methods. It is certain that the new trend begun in the last few
years of the 1980s will be a powerful force in the future.
There will be more and more studies of the biblical writings
based on more recent paradigms and methodologies. It is
evident beyond the shadow of a doubt that there are a plurality of methods used in the study of the Book of Amos—
which raises the matter of priority of methods and priority
of synchronic and diachronic approaches.[34] The future will

31. Hayes, *Amos*, 13.
32. Rosenbaum, *Amos of Israel*, 84. In the view of Rosenbaum, Amos 3:7 is not
original. The hymn-fragments are "probably" not original in the sense that they
are quoted from another source, and he is not sure about the authenticity of 5:25
and 9:13 (p. 83). Everything else in the book is from Amos.
33. Paul, *Amos*, 5–30.
34. An instructive survey of trends in Old Testament studies is provided by L.
Alonso Schöckel, "Trends: Plurality of Methods, Priority of Issues," in *Congress
Volume Jerusalem 1986*, ed. J. A. Emerton (Leiden: E. J. Brill, 1988), 285–92; Alan
Cooper, "On Reading the Bible Critically and Otherwise," in *The Future of Biblical
Studies: The Hebrew Scriptures*, eds. Richard Elliot Friedman and H. G. M.
Williamson (Atlanta, Ga.: Scholars, 1987), 61–79; Jon D. Levenson, "The Hebrew

also determine whether a combination of the synchronic and historical-critical diachronic approaches is a viable one. At the moment there is no single master paradigm that has shown this to be done successfully.

This concise summary of stages, trends, and issues reveals to the student of the Book of Amos that there is no such thing as a purely objective or scientific study of the book. We hope to inform both scholar and clergyperson, student and layperson, who may or may not have the technical tools or the inordinate amount of time to keep abreast of directions in the interpretation of the Book of Amos. We emphasize particularly the most recent decades of research. The 1960s to the present are chosen somewhat arbitrarily because they are watershed years. During this time the most significant historical-critical commentaries of this century (Hans W. Wolff and others) based on form-critical and traditio-historical methodologies (the diachronic approach of historical reconstruction) were published. The latter part of the 1980s is again a watershed period, with the publication of commentaries (Andersen and Freedman and others) that move in a radically different direction. The same is true of the commentaries by John H. Hayes, G. V. Smith, and D. K. Stuart, not to speak of the "new interpretation" of Stanley N. Rosenbaum, who claims that Amos was not simple, was not a shepherd, and, most forcefully, was not a Judean. Amos' hometown of Tekoa is to be located in the northern kingdom of Israel and, therefore, a totally new understanding of Amos has to be posited.[35] These new directions continue with full force and will have a lasting impact on the understanding of Amos as the earliest Old Testament "writing prophet."

Bible, the Old Testament, and Historical Criticism," in *Future of Biblical Studies*, 19–59; Wesley A. Kort, *Story, Text, and Scripture: Literary Interests in Biblical Narrative* (University Park: Pennsylvania State University Press, 1988); Frank McDonnell, ed., *The Bible and the Narrative Tradition* (New York/Oxford: Oxford University Press, 1986); Lynn M. Poland, *Literary Criticism and Biblical Hermeneutics: A Critique of Formalist Approaches*, AAR Academic series, 48 (Chico, Calif.: Scholars, 1985).

35. Rosenbaum, *Amos of Israel*, 29–50.

The Book of Amos has attracted an extraordinary amount of scholarly study in the last few decades.[36] This may be best illustrated by a comparison of the bibliographical entries in the most comprehensive bibliography published to date on the Book of Amos. The third enlarged edition of Adrian van der Wal's *Amos: A Classified Bibliography,* which appeared in 1986, contains approximately 1,600 books and articles. It covers the period from 1800 to June 1986. Our own collection of published materials for the period of 1960s to the present consists of over 800 items, of which over 350 are not found in the bibliography of van der Wal.[37] During these three decades over 60 commentaries on Amos have appeared. This means that in the last three decades more than 40 percent of all commentaries published since 1800 are on Amos! This explosion of publications establishes the fact that commentaries, dissertations, monographs, books, and articles on the Book of Amos form an extensive library in their own right. It becomes nearly impossible for any serious student or scholar to keep abreast of or to remain informed about the multiplicity of approaches and variety of trends that are employed in recent Amos studies.

The Book of Amos evidently is not a neglected book in the area of scholarly study of the Old Testament. It will be

36. Surveys of Amos studies are provided by James L. Mays, "Words about the Words of Amos," *Int* 13 (1959): 259–72; Page H. Kelley, "Contemporary Study of Amos and Prophetism," *RevEx* 63 (1966): 375–85; J. J. M. Roberts, "Recent Trends in the Study of Amos," *ResQ* 13 (1970): 1–16; John F. Craghan, "The Prophet Amos in Recent Literature," *BTB* 2 (1972): 242–61; L. Monloubou, "Prophètes d'Israël: Amos," *DBS* 8 (1972): 706–24; C. J. Pfeifer, "Amos the Prophet: The Man and His Book," *TBT* 19 (1981): 295–300; A. S. van der Woude, "Three Classical Prophets: Amos, Hosea, and Micah," in *Israel's Prophetic Traditions: Essays in Honor of Peter R. Ackroyd,* eds. Richard Coggins, Anthony Phillips, and Michael Knibb (Cambridge: Cambridge University Press, 1982), 32–57. One may wish to add the book by A. G. Auld (*Amos* [Sheffield: JSOT, 1986]).

37. Aside from van der Wal's bibliography, we have consulted the major commentaries published since 1969: *OTA, IZBG, Elenchus bibliographicus Biblicus,* and P.-E. Langevin, ed., *Biblical Bibliography* (Quebec: University of Laval Press, 1972–85).

impossible to mention every item that has been written in the last three decades of study on Amos. The present horizon of the study of Amos indicates that we are in the midst of a paradigm change[38] in Amos studies, if not of prophecy in the Old Testament as a whole.[39] The following chapters will indicate the ways in which this change is manifested.

38. For the language of paradigm change, see Thomas S. Kuhn, *The Structure of Scientific Revolutions*, 2d ed. (Chicago: University of Chicago Press, 1972). For the debate about paradigm change, see Gary Gutting, ed., *Paradigms and Revolutions: Applications and Appraisals of Thomas Kuhn's Philosophy of Science* (Notre Dame: University of Notre Dame Press, 1980).

39. So Ferdinand E. Deist, "The Prophets: Are We Heading for a Paradigm Shift?" in *Prophet und Prophetenbuch. Festschrift für Otto Kaiser zum 65. Geburtstag*, eds. Volkmar Fritz, Karl-Friedrich Pohlmann, and Hans-Christoph Schmitt (Berlin/New York: W. de Gruyter, 1989), 1–18.

2

AMOS'
PROFESSIONS
BEFORE HIS CALL

The probable professions of Amos before his call to prophetic ministry have received much attention. It is believed that as his sociocultural background is grasped or reconstructed we have a key, if not *the* key, to his message. Amos must have some socioeconomic, literary, intellectual, religious, and/or other connections with his contemporaries that can provide a possible clue or clues for his rise as prophet and preacher. This, in turn, may help us find the roots of prophetism in general, or at least the roots of the prophetic nature of Amos.

The question of Amos' professions before his call to prophetic ministry may not be important at all for some exegetes for reasons that will soon become apparent. Julius Morgenstern already in 1941 engaged in extensive reconstruction of the text of the Book of Amos by means of deletions, rearrangements, and revisions. He seems to be "unsurpassed in the history of Amos studies"[1] in creating by means of these reconstructions a single sermon that the historical Amos supposedly preached in Bethel at one time in a thirty-minute period. After this one-time preaching stint at the Bethel sanctuary, Amos returned to his native Tekoa in Judah. This incident allegedly comprises Amos' full prophetic ministry.[2]

John H. Hayes believes that "Amos' preaching at Bethel probably lasted only a single day at the least and a few days at the most."[3] Stanley N. Rosenbaum, however, suggests that Amos delivered his message in a "fit of passion" at a single occasion in a short "twenty-minute harangue," after which he went into exile in the south.[4] These scholars argue for a rather short stint of prophetic ministry for the historical Amos. The assumption seems to be that Amos preached out of the background of his professional life experience and the political climate of his time as a citizen of the kingdom of Judah (or, for Rosenbaum, the kingdom of Israel).

These suggestions are not at all as minimalist as Helmer Ringgren reported at the 1986 Jerusalem Congress of the International Organization for the Study of the Old Testament. He knew "at least one scholar who is prepared to write off the entire book [of Amos], with the exception of two or three verses, as a Deuteronomistic composition."[5] Ringgren may have had the views of Volkmar Fritz in mind: "The prophet Amos is thus to be demonstrated only in the two first visions of 7:1–6 and in the sayings of the announcement of a catastrophe that will come upon the

1. Francis I. Andersen and David Noel Freedman, *Amos: A New Translation with Introduction and Commentary* (New York: Doubleday, 1989), 12.

2. J. Morgenstern, *Amos Studies*, vol. 1 (Cincinnati: Hebrew Union College Press, 1941).

3. John H. Hayes, *Amos, His Time and His Preaching: The Eighth Century Prophet* (Nashville: Abingdon, 1988).

4. Stanley N. Rosenbaum, *Amos of Israel: A New Interpretation* (Macon, Ga.: Mercer University Press, 1990), 76, 100.

5. H. Ringgren, "Israelite Prophecy: Fact or Fiction?" *Congress Volume Jerusalem 1986*, ed. J. A. Emerton (Leiden: E. J. Brill, 1988), 204.

people in 3:12aba and 5:3."[6] If this extreme position could be sustained, then the question of the function, nature, and purpose of the man Amos as prophet would elude us nearly entirely. As Rosenbaum notes, "modern critical schools necessarily splinter biblical books to such a degree that the portion left to the 'original' author is usually too small to provide a sound basis for investigating the personal history, sense of history, or place in history."[7] What is particularly enlightening in all of this are the contradictory results rendered by practitioners of the same historical-critical methodologies. Rolf Rendtorff can state with confidence, "The Book of Amos provides a very clear profile of the prophet."[8] Is it surprising that Hayes turns his back on form criticism?[9] Andersen and Freedman maintain that "the major discipline of form criticism now seems to have reached its limits without solving its problems, and it has become so preoccupied with the parts that it misses—or even denies the existence of—the whole."[10]

Modern historical-critical reconstructions that use form criticism, tradition criticism, and redaction criticism have no room for any *ipsissima verba* of Amos. While some who oppose a very radical redating and reconstructing of the Book of Amos may admit that "there can be no proof that what we have is Amos' ipsissima verba,"[11] others may feel that if Amos' words were collected and put down in writing within a reasonably short period of time after their presentation that we may be quite sure we have the *ipsissima verba* of Amos.

6. Volkmar Fritz, "Amosbuch, Amos-Schule und historischer Amos," in *Prophet und Prophetenbuch. Festschrift für Otto Kaiser zum 65. Geburtstag*, eds. Volkmar Fritz, Karl-Friedrich Pohlmann, and Hans-Christoph Schmitt (Berlin/New York: W. de Gruyter, 1989), 42. Evidently Fritz goes far beyond his critical colleagues in assigning nearly the whole book to the so-called school of Amos, a group of followers whose work extended over centuries.

7. Rosenbaum, *Amos of Israel*, 4.

8. Rolf Rendtorff, *Das Alte Testament. Eine Einführung* (Neukirchen-Vluyn: Neukirchener Verlag, 1983), 232.

9. Hayes, *Amos*, 38–39.

10. Andersen and Freedman, *Amos*, 4.

11. Ibid., 5.

It is interesting to note that scholars who use traditio-historical and redaction-critical methods arrive at widely varying conclusions. Is the amount of subjectivity involved too great to render them useful and reliable, or is the evolutionary reconstruction of the religion of Israel the cause of such widely divergent pictures?[12]

In one branch of modern scholarship much emphasis is placed on the allegedly complex literary traditions that formed the present books of the prophets. An attempt is made to reconstruct the process along sociocultural lines.[13] Scholars taking this approach often have little interest in the prophet himself as a vehicle of divine revelation with a unique relationship to deity and a special message. Notable exceptions to these trends among recent major commentators include Douglas Stuart, Gary V. Smith, David A. Hubbard, Thomas J. Finley, Stanley N. Rosenbaum, and Shalom M. Paul.

Certain contemporary scholars seem to place equal authority in the suggested successive stages of the formation of the canonical writings, the Book of Amos not excluded. While we can provide only the briefest discussion of this issue in this chapter, there is a direct bearing on the professions of Amos. Tradition critics acknowledge that the canonical form of the text is recognized as authoritative and that, therefore, the reconstructed earlier versions of biblical books do not seem to have either canonical or normative status. Brevard Childs has been the champion of the authoritative status of the final canonical form of the biblical text in recent years. His "canonical approach" has left an indelible mark on modern scholarship on both continents.

---

12. For one such recent reconstruction, see Bernhard Lang, *Monotheism and the Prophetic Minority*, Social World of Biblical Antiquity series, 1 (Sheffield: Almond, 1983), 13–56.

13. See among various approaches the ones by Robert Carroll, *When Prophecy Failed: Cognitive Dissonance in the Prophetic Tradition of the Old Testament* (New York: Seabury, 1979); Robert R. Wilson, *Prophecy and Society in Ancient Israel* (Philadelphia: Fortress, 1980); idem, *Sociological Approaches to the Old Testament* (Philadelphia: Fortress, 1984); David L. Petersen, *The Role of Israel's Prophets* (Sheffield: JSOT, 1981).

While this corrective to form-critical and traditio-historical trends in historical-critical biblical scholarship does not deny earlier stages in the tradition-building process, neither does it allow these stages to have binding, canonical status.[14] Those who wish to sidestep Childs' concerns, or who believe that little of the Book of Amos derives from the prophet Amos himself, will be confronted by the concern of James M. Ward in his essay with the anxious title, "The Eclipse of the Prophet in Contemporary Prophetic Studies."[15] He notes with some sense of alarm that in contemporary study the prophet himself is no longer of real interest. Thus the focus of traditio-historical and redaction-critical study, by virtue of the very nature of the methodologies used, can no longer be interested in the biblical figures known as the prophets. The primary or exclusive focus is on the various hypothetical tradition-building stages and redactional activities of various tradents.[16]

It is along these lines that James A. Sanders' enterprise of "canonical criticism" makes its impact.[17] Sanders' criticism, which is not to be confused or equated with the "canonical approach" of Childs,[18] is to be understood as an advancement of the debate on the function and role of the canon of the Bible within the framework of the methodologies used in modern historical-critical scholarship. Sanders summarizes his own methodology as follows:

14. See Childs' massive *Introduction to the Old Testament as Scripture* (Philadelphia: Fortress, 1979); idem, *Old Testament Theology in a Canonical Context* (Philadelphia: Fortress, 1986).

15. James M. Ward, "The Eclipse of the Prophet in Contemporary Prophetic Studies," *USQR* 42 (1988): 97–104.

16. The collection of essays edited by James Luther Mays and Paul J. Achtemeier (*Interpreting the Prophets* [Philadelphia: Fortress, 1987]) provides a useful overview of some of these trends.

17. Among the many publications of James A. Sanders the following deserve to be mentioned: *Torah and Canon* (Philadelphia: Fortress, 1986); "Biblical Criticism and the Bible as Canon," *USQR* 32 (1977): 157–65; *Canon and Community: A Guide to Canonical Criticism* (Philadelphia: Fortress, 1984); and *From Sacred Story to Sacred Text: Canon as Paradigm* (Philadelphia: Fortress, 1987).

18. Sanders, *From Sacred Story to Sacred Text*, 155–74.

Canonical criticism sees validity in all the subdisciplines of
biblical criticism and views them all as complementary, but
moves on beyond tradition and redaction criticism and
focuses on the periods of intense canonical process, after the
last individual geniuses [redactors] had done their work
when the several believing communities either found life-
giving value in this or that literature received, or did not.[19]

Canonical criticism places emphasis on the various stages
of the tradition-building process and sees canonical authority at each level in that process as the believing communities
found "life-giving value" in each developmental stage. These
stages are the levels of redactions that function as canonical
levels for the communities out of which they arise and for
which they carry authority.[20] This means that there are multiple canonical authorities with no stage or level having normative and final canonical authority. The emphasis is on the
function of canon and not on canon as a final closure of a
text that only in *this* one final form has canonical authority.

If this approach is applied to the Book of Amos it means
that any of the reconstructed stages—whether three, six, or
more[21]—have equal canonical authority for the respective
believing communities that they are made to address or
that contributed to these stages. In short, canonical criticism
renders canonical authority on any level dependent on the
value-giving power of the believing communities and
destroys the final, supremely authoritative canonical form
of the text of Scripture.

The approach of Sanders is criticized and opposed by
Childs' "canonical approach," which places a unique autho-
rial role on the final canonical form of the biblical text. It
remains to be seen whether the canonical criticism of
Sanders will carry the day in critical scholarship or whether
the more historical emphasis of Childs will win out in critical biblical research.

19. Ibid., 193–94.
20. Ibid., 9–39.
21. See above, chap. 2.

These new understandings and the alleged small amounts of genuine Amos sayings have raised radical, and for some people, even shocking questions. Is Israelite prophecy fact or fiction?[22] The historical prophets as persons seem to be in eclipse.

Much research focuses on redactional, compositional, or community action. The individual author or writer is replaced by the communities that reinterpret, refashion, and reshape the text to fit new needs based on sociocultural interests. The latter is seen as the shaping force of Old Testament prophecy. Is this aspect of the sociological study of ancient Israel and the Old Testament entirely faithful to the text as it stands? Or is this type of research more oriented to go behind, above, or beneath the text as it stands? And if the latter is true, as it seems to be, what larger hermeneutical implications are involved?

Beyond these issues in recent historical-critical research relating to the "original" authors of the biblical books, there are other matters of debate and study that call for our attention. J. Alberto Soggin notes correctly that the "profession exercised by Amos before being called to the prophetic ministry is also a matter of controversy."[23] The classical view until about three decades ago was that Amos came from humble origins. He was a simple shepherd and dresser of sycamore trees. He came from either poorly paid and exploited segments of Judah[24] or he was a simple gatherer of sycamore fruit,[25] or both.

This more traditional understanding of Amos before he was called to prophetic ministry has seen a complete reversal in much modern scholarship since the 1950s. This issue is seen differently by those who suggest that Amos 7:10–17

22. Ringgren, "Israelite Prophecy," 204–10.

23. J. Alberto Soggin, *The Prophet Amos: A Translation and Commentary* (London: SCM, 1987), 9.

24. So most of the older commentaries. See, for example, George Adam Smith, *The Book of the Twelve Prophets*, 2 vols. (London: Hodder and Stoughton, 1929), 1:72–74.

25. G. Rinaldi, *I Profeti Minori*, 3 vols. (Turin, 1952–68), as cited by Soggin, *Amos*, 10.

is secondary rhetorical fiction[26] or that "it is unlikely that it derives from Amos himself or any near contemporary."[27]

Today there is a strong consensus in various scholarly circles that Amos was a member of some type of upper class or at least professional middle class in Judah (or Israel[28]). He belonged to the "haves." He is perceived either as a large-scale sheep breeder (based on the term *noqed*[29] in 1:1),[30] "a dealer in large quantities of livestock,"[31] or he "probably owned or managed large herds of sheep and engaged in the marketing of their products."[32]

The Hebrew term *noqed* is only used in Amos 1:1 and 2 Kings 3:4[33] (in the latter text as a title for Mesha, the king of Moab). The biblical evidence for its meaning is fairly limited. Therefore, Ugaritic, Moabite, Babylonian, and Arabic materials of rather diverse times have been drawn on to interpret the term.

Based on materials from the Neo-Babylonian period and provenance, it has been suggested that the Akkadian term *naqidu*[34] ("shepherd"), a *nomen professionis* (a noun used for a profession), is employed for a second-level official associ-

26. Hermann Schult, "Amos 7,15a und die Legitimation des Aussenseiters," in *Probleme biblischer Theologie. Gerhard von Rad zum 70. Geburtstag*, ed. H. W. Wolff (Munich: Chr. Kaiser, 1971), 462–89.

27. So A. G. Auld, *Amos* (Sheffield: JSOT, 1986), 40.

28. Wilson, *Prophecy and Society in Ancient Israel*, 266–70; Rosenbaum, *Amos of Israel*, 26–69.

29. The root *nqd* was used in Akkadian, Arabic, and Syriac for both sheep and shepherd. See A. S. Kapelrud, *Central Ideas in Amos* (Oslo: Aschehoug, 1956), 5–7; S. Segert, "Zur Bedeutung des Wortes *noqed*," in *Hebräische Wortforschung. Festschrift zum 80. Geburtstag von Walter Baumgartner*, eds. B. Hartmann et al. (Leiden: E. J. Brill, 1967), 279–83.

30. See especially Peter C. Craigie, "Amos the *noqed* in the Light of Ugaritic," *SR* 11 (1982): 29–32, whose incisive critique of M. Bič, "Der Prophet Amos—Ein Haepatoskopos," *VT* 1 (1951): 293–96, supported those of A. Murtonen, "The Prophet Amos—A Hepatoscoper?" *VT* 2 (1952): 170–71; and T. J. Wright, "Did Amos Inspect Livers?" *ABR* 23 (1975): 3–11.

32. Douglas Stuart, *Hosea–Jonah* (Waco: Word, 1987), 290.

32. Peter C. Craigie, *Ugarit and the Old Testament* (Grand Rapids: Eerdmans, 1983), 73.

33. Words used only twice in the Hebrew Bible are called *dis legomena*.

34. Wolfram von Soden, *Akkadisches Handwörterbuch* (Wiesbaden: O. Harrassowitz, 1965), 744a; A. Leo Oppenheim et al., *Chicago Assyrian Dictionary* (Chicago: Oriental Institute, 1978), vol. N., 1:333–35.

ated with the temple.[35] This is the alleged background of
Amos. Based on this connection of the terms it is said that
Amos was a second-level official in the Jerusalem temple in
charge of the flocks in the Tekoa area.[36] Yet is there any
evidence that the Jerusalem temple or any Israelite shrine
ever had such temple flocks and shepherds? A. E.
Murtonen and others have shown that this was not the
case.[37] Shalom M. Paul insists that "there is no reason that
such an individual was a cultic functionary (who practiced
augury) or belonged to the temple personnel."[38]

From a different angle it has been argued that once the
Moabite term *nqdy* is restored in line 30 of the Mesha Stone
to mean "my *noqed*"[39] ("sheep breeder") it could be related
directly to some Ugaritic evidence.[40] We can then understand Amos as a cultic functionary in some way related to
the temple or palace.[41] Various recent commentators are
reluctant to endorse such reconstructed cultic connections.

There is widespread consensus, however, that Amos was
a well-to-do Judahite. He was not a simple farmer or peasant from a relatively unknown town in the hills south of
Jerusalem. As Peter C. Craigie sums it up, "Amos was not a
simple shepherd. He was in the sheep business, a manager of
herds, contributing both wool and meat to the economy."[42]
Following Craigie's connection of the term *noqed*, which in
Hebrew is a term for "the holder of an office or profession,"[43] with the Ugaritic term *nqdm*, "sheep managers" who

35. M. San Nicolo, "Materialien zur Viehwirtschaft in den neubabylonischen
Tempeln. I," *Or* 17 (1948): 273–93.
36. Ibid. Cf. von Soden, *Akkadisches Handwörterbuch*, 744a.
37. Murtonen, "Prophet Amos," 170–71; Andersen and Freedman, *Amos*, 188.
38. Paul, *Amos*, 34.
39. So J. G. L. Gibson, *Textbook of Syrian Semitic Inscriptions: Hebrew and Moabite
Inscriptions* (Oxford: Clarendon, 1971), 75.
40. Cyrus H. Gordon, *Ugaritic Textbook* (Rome: Pontifical Biblical Institute Press,
1965), #62.55; 300.12; 308.12.
41. See the discussion by Hayes, *Amos*, 44, who allows for only a possibility of
this connection.
42. Craigie, "Amos the *noqed*," 33.
43. B. Kedar-Kopfstein, "Semantic Aspects of the Pattern *Qôtêl*," *HAR* 1 (1977):
161; adopted by Bruce K. Waltke and M. O'Connor, *An Introduction to Biblical
Hebrew Syntax* (Winona Lake, Ind.: Eisenbrauns, 1990), 85.

are "responsible for large herds . . . the servants of a king . . .
liable to the king for service and taxation,"[44] Rosenbaum
claims that Amos had "a middle-level position in his government's service" that "would have given Amos the visibility
and status requisite to commanding an audience."[45]

Andersen and Freedman are among the more recent commentators who are more circumspect in assessing the evidence. They note that "the distance in time, space, and culture between Ugarit and Tekoa is even greater than that
between Mesha and Amos."[46] On the latter relationship they
note that Amos 7:14–15 gives a "different impression. Apart
from possible seasonal employment as a (hired?) worker in
the sycamore fig industry, itself a lowly task, he [Amos]
describes himself as 'following the flock' (7:15), a phrase not
applicable to the king of Moab, and with no hint of owner-
ship of numerous flocks."[47] Thus they argue that: (1) Amos
was unlike the king of Moab; (2) Amos lived in a different
country; (3) terms for social rank are unstable and tend to
slide down the scale; (4) Amos lived in a different century;
and (5) the Old Testament provides no evidence that Israelite
shrines had their own flocks and shepherds. They conclude
that "Amos' social and economic status cannot be reconstructed from this meager evidence."[48] Regardless of the
scholarly consensus, these two commentators remain unconvinced by the comparative arguments regarding the relatively
high social and economic status of Amos.

Helga Weippert concludes that Amos did not belong to
the well-to-do strata of Judaic society. She bases her conclusions on the pictures, images, and metaphors that Amos
employs in his message. He functioned as a "peasant"
(*Bauer*) or "farmer" (*Landwirt*).[49] This occupation is in no

44. Craigie, "Amos the *noqed*," 33.
45. Rosenbaum, *Amos of Israel*, 46.
46. Andersen and Freedman, *Amos*, 188.
47. Ibid.
48. Ibid.
49. Helga Weippert, "Amos: Seine Bilder und ihr Milieu," in *Beiträge zur prophetischen Bildsprache in Israel und Assyrien*, eds. Helga Weippert, Klaus Seybold, and Manfred Weippert (Göttingen: Vandenhoeck und Ruprecht, 1985), 1–5.

sense derogatory or demeaning. Shalom M. Paul's recent large-scale commentary does not give more vocational clout to Amos than careful research warrants. Amos was a man "who owns cattle and, as such, . . . also tends sheep and goats."[50] There is no biblical evidence that the farming and shepherding vocation was lower than any other. Modern prejudices must not be read into ancient settings.

Stanley N. Rosenbaum disagrees with all of this.[51] He argues that Amos was from Israel, not from Judah, and that he held a middle-level position in the government of Israel. Rosenbaum, along with a number of other recent scholars, maintains that most of the Book of Amos derives from the historical Amos himself. The Amos of which Rosenbaum speaks, however, comes from the northern kingdom of Israel. Amos "himself was an Israelite [not Judean] official and he spoke in their own rich Northern tones."[52] This gives him the standing and the status to address the people and the establishment of the northern kingdom. Rosenbaum follows the Ugaritic connection of terms and also the one from Neo-Babylonian usage.[53] He argues against Jehuda Ziv's[54] interpretation of the expression "dresser of sycamores" to be a figure of speech only, connoting a modest station in life.

Rosenbaum moves in another direction to explain the Hebrew expression *bôles shiqmîm* of 7:14, traditionally rendered "dresser of sycamores," by claiming that the Ephraimite Hebrew, that is, the Hebrew of the northern kingdom, lacked the Hebrew consonant *shin*.[55] He thus emends the Hebrew *bôles* to an unattested *belas*, which he wishes to connect with a *balas* or *bôles* in Targumic Aramaic, which in turn can be connected with *balshî* ("searching tax

50. Paul, *Amos*, 248.

51. Rosenbaum was not aware of Weippert's study. He did not have access to the works of Andersen/Freedman and Paul. I suspect, however, that even if he had consulted these scholars, this would not have changed his line of argument.

52. Rosenbaum, *Amos of Israel*, 100.

53. Ibid., 44–47.

54. Jehuda Ziv, "Bôper Ubôlesh Shikmîm—b'Teqoa," *Beth Miqra* 92 (1982–83): 49–53.

55. Rosenbaum, *Amos of Israel*, 48.

commissioner")[56] in postbiblical Aramaic. Rosenbaum suggests on this basis that Amos was a "government official." He, however, recognizes that this is a radical emendation with significant weaknesses: "Admittedly, there is no compelling reason to accept linguistic speculations of this sort on their own."[57] Is there any reason to accept them on grounds other than linguistic ones?

Sycamore figs grow in the Shephelah (1 Chron. 27:28), or low hill country, to which also the Targum testify.[58] The Shephelah area around Timnah is also famous for the pasturing of sheep. Besides this there is the later report that "sycamores grow in lower Galilee."[59] The sycamore fig also grows in Ein Gedi near the Dead Sea. Finally, there is no compelling reason to suggest that because of the sycamore fig activity that Amos was involved in he must be moved to the north and be a citizen of the northern kingdom. There is no evidence that restricts sycamores to the northern kingdom.[60]

Conclusions regarding the high- or middle-level social and economic status of Amos before his call, that is, his role as some sort of cultic or government official, are built on reconstructed circumstantial evidences that are truly distant both in provenance and time. The question is whether a reasonable level of certainty can be had beyond that provided in the Book of Amos itself for such reconstruction. Will circumstantial reconstructions and "linguistic speculations" from questionable emendations based on materials from other times, cultures, and languages provide a secure basis for identifying the profession or vocation of Amos or any prophet before his call and commissioning to prophetic ministry? Can they provide enough solid information to determine his cultural-intellectual background? Should such reconstructions be employed in determining the meaning or meanings of the message and theology of Amos?

56. Ibid., 48–49.

57. Ibid., 49.

58. Thomas J. Finley, *Joel, Amos, Obadiah* (Chicago: Moody, 1990), 295.

59. Tosef. Shev. 7:11 (Pes. 53a).

60. See on the whole T. J. Wright, "Amos and the Sycamore Fig," *VT* 26 (1976): 49–53.

3

AMOS' NATURE
AS PROPHET

M any people use the expression "I am no prophet nor the son of a prophet" for certain claims about themselves. Few today are aware that this quotation comes from Amos 7:14, probably the most widely written about text in the entire Book of Amos—and one of the most disputed. The major debate about the prophetic nature of Amos centers on this text and the report of Amos' conflict with the (high)priest Amaziah in 7:10–17—a report written in the third person.

Various modern interpreters consider Amos 7:10–17 to come from a hand other than that of Amos.[1] There are

1. This is also true of the recent commentaries by Hayes (1988) and Andersen/Freedman (1989), who note that this episode is biographical, reading like a fragment that an early editor placed in the final edition of the book. While Hayes places it at the end of his commentary, keeping it totally unrelated to the setting in which it is presently placed (similarly Soggin, *The Prophet Amos* [London: SCM, 1987], 125–33), Andersen and Freedman consider it as being placed properly in its present context and so linked to this context in a number of ways. (So also independently Stuart, *Hosea–Jonah* [Waco: Word, 1987], 369–70; and Hubbard, *Joel and Amos: An Introduction and Commentary* [Leicester: Inter-Varsity,

other scholars who hold it to be from Amos himself, who wrote in the third person.[2]

Indeed the best-known *crux interpretum* of the book is found in this third-person report. Amos 7:14 has been rendered by Klaus Koch in his well-known book on the prophets in Israel as follows:

> I no *nabi*, / I no prophet's disciple,
> but I, a herdsman, / also a cultivator of mulberry trees,
> away from the herd did Yahweh tear me, / he told me, Yahweh,
> Go, prophecy / to my people Israel![3]

This translation, whatever its merits, seeks to reflect the fact that the verbal forms must be supplied in English, because the Hebrew text has only nouns and the personal pronoun "I."

The debate relates in a significant part to the matter of whether the Hebrew sentences are to be understood in the past or present tense.[4] Various English translations differ, reflecting the translator's understanding of the "tense" and/or the complexity of the issues involved.

1989], 211. Hubbard considers it from the hand of the "editor of Amos.") See also H. Utzschneider, "Die Amazjaerzählung (Am 7,10–17) zwischen Literatur und Historie," *BN* 41 (1988): 76–101.

2. Robert Gordis, "The Composition and Structure of Amos," *HTR* 33 (1940): 239–51; idem, "Studies in the Book of Amos," *Proceedings of the American Academy for Jewish Research* 46/47 (1979–80): 249–53; J. D. W. Watts, *Vision and Prophecy in Amos* (Grand Rapids: Eerdmans, 1958), 31–35; Gerhard Pfeifer, "Die Ausweisung eines lästigen Ausländers. Amos 7,10–17," *ZAW* 96 (1984): 112–18; T. J. Finley, *Joel, Amos, Obadiah* (Chicago: Moody, 1990), 290; G. V. Smith, *Amos: A Commentary* (Grand Rapids: Zondervan, 1989), 228–29; Stanley N. Rosenbaum, *Amos of Israel: A New Interpretation* (Macon, Ga.: Mercer University Press, 1990), 80–83.

3. Klaus Koch, *The Prophets: The Assyrian Period* (Philadelphia: Fortress, 1983), 37.

4. Among those who favor the past are H. H. Rowley, "Was Amos a Nabi?" *Fetschschrift für Otto Eissfeldt zum 60. Geburtstag*, ed. J. Fück (Halle: Niemeyer, 1947), 191–98; I. Engnell, "Profetismens Ursprung och Uppkomst," *RoB* 8 (1949): 191–98; E. Würthwein, "Amos-Studien," *ZAW* 62 (1950): 16–17; G. Quell, *Wahre und falsche Propheten* (Gütersloh: Gütersloher Verlagshaus, 1952), 139–40; J. MacCormack, "Amos VII 14a," *ExpTim* 67 (1955/56): 318–19; A. S. Kapelrud, *Central Ideas in Amos* (Oslo: Aschehoug, 1956), 7; H. Junker, *CBQ* 29 (1957): 377; Henning Graf Reventlow, *Das Amt des Propheten bei Amos* (Göttingen: Vandenhoeck und Ruprecht, 1962), 20; G. M. Tucker, "Prophetic Authenticity: A Form-Critical Study of Amos 7:10–17," *Int* 27 (1973): 423–34; R. Bach, "Erwägungen zu Amos

Among the various suggestions that have been made over the years, we will briefly refer to only five.

First, the past tense translation is used by JB, NAB, NIV, and NKJV. We can then take the sentence to mean, "I was no prophet and neither was I the son of a prophet." The implication would be that Amos was not a prophet to begin with, but on the basis of his call to prophetic activity he *became* a prophet. This position harmonizes neatly with verse 15.

Second, if the present tense translation is used (as in RSV, NRSV, NEB, JPSV, and NASB[5]) then it may be rendered, "I am no prophet and neither am I the son of a prophet." Accordingly Amos never claimed to be a *nabi'* ("prophet"). This raises the issue of what *nabi'* means. Supporters of this view have often taken it to refer to a professional/cultic prophet. The expression "son of a prophet" is correspondingly understood to mean a member of a prophetic guild or school. Arvid S. Kapelrud, for example, suggested that a cult prophet had a recognized position or function in the worship practice of the community.[6] Milos Bič came to the conclusion that Amos was an *Opferbeschauer,* an "inspector of sacrifices."[7] But there are scholars who object.[8] Henning Graf Reventlow maintains that there was an "office" of a prophet, but that it

---

7, 14," in *Die Botschaft und die Boten. Festschrift für Hans Walter Wolff zum 70* (Neukirchen-Vluyn: Neukirchener Verlag, 1981), 203–16; Soggin, *Amos,* 128; Andersen and Freedman, *Amos,* 762; and Rosenbaum, *Amos of Israel,* 44, among others. For additional advocates of the past tense, see below, n. 5. There are many others who prefer the present translation with Wolff (*Amos and Joel,* 311–14). For a detailed discussion of this hypothesis, see Meir Weiss, *The Bible from Within: The Method of Total Interpretation* (Jerusalem: Magnes, 1984), 102–6, 417–20.

5. In addition to the scholars cited in n. 4, see A. H. J. Gunneweg, "Erwägungen zu Amos 7,14," *ZTK* 57 (1960): 1–16; R. Hentschke, *Die Stellunge der vorexilischen Propheten zum Kultus* (Berlin: W. de Gruyter, 1957), 150–51; J. Philip Hyatt, "Amos," in *Peake's Commentary on the Bible* (London: SCM, 1962), 624; R. E. Clements, *Prophecy and Covenant* (Napierville, Ill.: Allenson, 1965), 36–37; J. M. Ward, *Amos and Isaiah: Prophets of God's Word* (Nashville: Abingdon, 1969), 33–35; James L. Mays, *Amos: A Commentary* (Philadelphia: Westminster, 1969), 137–38.

6. Arvid S. Kapelrud, *Central Ideas in Amos,* 2d ed. (Oslo: Oslo University Press, 1961), 11.

7. Milos Bič, *Das Buch Amos* (Berlin: Evangelische Verlagsanstalt, 1969), 20.

8. Such as Tucker, "Prophetic Authenticity," 423–34.

was not cultic in nature.[9] This "office" was fixed and Amos stepped, as it were, into the function of this fixed office to gain access to the rulers and the people. But there is little evidence for such an "office" in the Old Testament.[10]

Third, there is the suggestion of taking the Hebrew negative particle *lo'* ("not") as an interrogative particle that is the equivalent of *halo'*. In this case Amos would affirm the prophetic vocation by means of "exclamatory negation."[11] This hypothesis yields the translation, "Am I not a prophet and am I not a prophet's son?" This rhetorical question demands a positive answer. Soggin objects that this explanation is inadequate since it contradicts verse 15.

Fourth, a very recent hypothesis takes the first particle *lo'* as an emphatic negative. Ziony Zevit translates, "No! I am a *nabi'*, I am not even a *ben nabi'*," meaning "No! I am not a prophet enjoying royal patronage (i.e., a *hozeh*); I am an independent prophet—my own man; nor am I the disciple of a prophet, working under his aegis and doing his bidding."[13] This view is similar to earlier suggestions that understand 7:14 as saying "I am surely a *nabi'* but not a member of the prophetic guild."[14] Zevit is followed recently by Stuart, who translates, "No! I am a prophet, though I am not a professional prophet."[15] This hypothesis assigns two

9. Henning Graf Reventlow, *Das Amt des Propheten bei Amos* (Göttingen: Vandenhoeck und Ruprecht, 1962), 14–24.

10. See James Muilenburg, "The 'Office' of the Prophet in Ancient Israel," in *The Bible and Modern Scholarship*, ed. J. Philip Hyatt (Nashville: Abingdon, 1965), 74–97.

11. So G. R. Driver, "Affirmation by Exclamatory Negation," *JANESCU* 5 (1973): 107–14; idem, "Amos VII 14a," *ExpTim* 67 (1955–56): 91–92; and P. R. Ackroyd, "Amos VII 14a," *ExpTim* 68 (1956–57): 94–95.

12. Soggin, *Amos*, 128.

13. Z. Zevit, "A Misunderstanding at Bethel—Amos VII 12–17," *VT* 25 (1975): 789–90.

14. So H. Neil Richardson, "A Critical Note on Amos 7:14," *JBL* 85 (1966): 89, who is in part dependent on S. Cohen, "Amos Was a Navi," *HUCA* 32 (1961): 175–78. Rosenbaum (*Amos of Israel*, 42) favors Cohen's suggestion.

15. Zevit, "Misunderstanding," and his defense in "Expressing Denial in Biblical Hebrew and Mishnaic Hebrew, and in Amos," *VT* 29 (1979): 505–9, against the criticism of Y. Hoffmann, "Did Amos Regard Himself as a *nabi*'?" *VT* 27 (1977): 209–12; Stuart, *Hosea–Jonah*, 374.

different meanings to the particle *lo'* in syntactically identical sentences! The first *lo'* is taken as an emphatic *lamed*, something like *lu'*, while the second one is taken as a negative. Why should this be the case in otherwise identical nominal clauses?

Fifth, the extensive study of the roles of the Israelite prophets by David L. Petersen, based on modern role theories, argues that the term *hozeh* ("seer") was a role label for a regular prophet from Judah in the south and that the term *nabi'* ("prophet") functioned as a designation for a prophet in the northern kingdom.[16] In this hypothesis there is no distinction between the terms *hozeh* and *nabi'*; both are designations for a prophet. Thus "both Amaziah and Amos are described as viewing the title *hozeh* as appropriate for Amos."[17] In Amos' denial that he is not a *nabi*, he makes clear that he does not belong to the northern prophets, because he is a prophet from the southern kingdom.

This suggestion has recently been adopted by David A. Hubbard.[18] If this neat geopolitical distinction holds, admittedly applying only to nouns and not to verbal forms (which in our view is a strange phenomenon), then a rather simple solution to a most vexing problem would finally be available. Neither term, in this hypothesis, has anything to do with cult prophecy. This position will be debated for some time, because it will hardly be acceptable to those who see Amos as a cult prophet or who link the term *nabi'* to cult prophetism.

In short, the most notorious *crux interpretum* of the Book of Amos remains largely unsolved, despite extensive efforts to find a fully satisfying solution. No complete scholarly consensus has emerged. Thus it is not surprising that Soggin, Andersen and Freedman, and Paul[19] again support the past tense interpretation, an interpretation that has

16. David L. Petersen, *The Roles of Israel's Prophets*, JSOT Supplement series, 17 (Sheffield: JSOT, 1981), 51–69.

17. Ibid., 57.

18. Hubbard, *Joel and Amos*, 213–14.

19. See Paul, *Amos*, 243–47.

fewer problems than any of the others. This view, however, implies that Amos was once no "son of a prophet." If "son" is understood in the sense of descendant, then Amos could now claim that he stands in the tradition of those who were previously designated "prophet," such as Abraham, Moses, and other figures. In this case, the final major problem to the past tense translation is solved.

The following methodological considerations may guide in a proper understanding of this challenging text:[20]

1. We would do well to detach the problem of the relationship of the great prophets from the cultic *nebi'im* ("prophets").[21]
2. The terms "prophet" and "son of the prophet" are best viewed as parallel terms. The term "son" may be taken to mean descendant. To take the term "prophet" as a term of opposition is unnatural.[22]
3. The same tense should be assumed for both of the verbless clauses in verse 14.
4. Appeal to extrabiblical linguistic considerations (namely, Ugaritic texts and Akkadian terms and offices) is to be held in suspension as long as the Hebrew itself provides a satisfactory meaning.
5. The interpretation of verse 14a should be consistent with what is said of both prophets and prophesying in the other parts of the Book of Amos and the eighth-century prophetic writings.

We can affirm that Amos was a "prophet" indeed, even if we were to leave out of consideration the autobiographical statement of 7:14. In verse 16 the verb "to prophesy" (Heb. root *nb'*) appears as a function of Amos. He functioned as a

20. Adapted from Hayes, *Amos*, 236. His suggestions are very helpful and we are indebted to them, despite the fact that he thinks they support the present tense rendering.

21. Soggin, *Amos*, 128.

22. This point is made by Hayes, *Amos*, 236, and can apply for either the present or past tense view.

prophet in the eyes and the hearing of Amaziah. And Amos functioned as a prophet also in his own view. He makes this clear by his question, "When God speaks, who will not prophesy?" (3:8). Aside from the affirmation that "God does nothing without revealing His secret to his servants the prophets" (3:7), Amos engages in the activities of a prophet. He receives "visions," he has messages of doom and salvation, he intercedes for the people, he is challenged about his prophetic function, he reports what he is told, he calls to repentance. And if we do not totally misunderstand what he is attempting to say, Amos uses for himself, at least by implication, the designation "prophet," while emphasizing that at one time, before his call, he followed other professions.

4

AMOS' ORIGIN—FROM
JUDAH OR ISRAEL?

Traditionally Amos has been said to come from Tekoa in Judah, the only town or village known by that name in the Bible.

Tekoa is located about five miles (eight kilometers) south of Bethlehem in the Judean hills. It is identified today with the ruins of Khirbet Tequ'a, but has not yet been excavated by archaeologists. In the Bible Tekoa is included among the cities of Judah (Josh. 15:59). It is mentioned several times in the historical books (2 Sam. 14:9; 23:26; 1 Chron. 11:28). After the division of the kingdom in 931 B.C.,[1] Rehoboam is reported to have fortified Tekoa along with other cities in Judah (2 Chron. 11:5–6).

At an elevation of 2,800 feet (850 meters) the town of Tekoa has a higher elevation than either Bethlehem or Jerusalem. The "wilderness of Tekoa" (2 Chron. 20:20) lies east of Tekoa and is part of the wilderness of Judah. Tekoa

1. We follow the chronology of Edwin R. Thiele, *The Mysterious Numbers of the Hebrew Kings*, 3d ed. (Grand Rapids: Zondervan, 1983).

lies on the "border of the cultivated land to the west and the wilderness to the east."[2]

Modern scholars have given considerable attention to the location of Tekoa. In 1971 S. Wagner devoted a carefully argued essay to the subject of the relationship of Amos to the kingdom of Judah,[3] acknowledging (while nonetheless maintaining) the limited information in the book about this linkage. In this connection Wagner refers to a Judean Tekoa.

Klaus Koch takes issue with the nearly universal consensus that Amos comes from Judean Tekoa. He argues that Amos comes from "a Galilean Tekoa, which is attested in postbiblical times."[4] This Galilean Tekoa is identified with the Israeli town of Ḥovat Shema' or the ancient ruins of Khirbet Shema'.[5] This place is not referred to in the Old Testament but is mentioned in postbiblical (Talmudic) times.[6]

Koch's hypothesis is not new. Cyril of Alexandria (5th cent. A.D.) considered Amos a northern Israelite.[7] In the late nineteenth century, Henricus Oort revived this theory.[8] The Judean Tekoa, so it is argued, would not provide the proper environment for the cultivation of sycamore or mulberry (wild fig) trees.[9] Koch supports his contention further by

2. Shalom M. Paul, *Amos: A Commentary on the Book of Amos* (Minneapolis: Fortress, 1991), 35.

3. Siegfried Wagner, "Überlegungen zur Frage nach den Beziehungen des Propheten Amos zum Südreich," *TLZ* 96 (1971): 653–70.

4. Klaus Koch, *The Prophets: The Assyrian Period* (Philadelphia: Fortress, 1983), 70.

5. This is the identification of G. Dalman, *Lit. Zentralblatt* 37 (1912): 1188, as cited by S. Klein, "Drei Ortsnamen in Galiläa," in *Monatsschrift für Geschichte und Wissenschaft des Judentums* 67 (1922): 273 n. 4.

6. Klein, "Drei Ortsnamen in Galiläa," 270–73, supported by G. Dalman, *Orte und Wege Jesu*, 3d ed. (Gütersloh: Bertelsmann, 1924), 209.

7. See *Works*, ed. H. Pusey (Oxford, 1868), 1:368. See also Pseudepiphanius, "De Vitis Prophetarum," *Patrologia graeca*, ed. J. P. Migne, 43:393ff. Rabbi David Kimchi (ca. A.D. 1160–1235) speaks of a Tekoa in northern Israel (*Miqra'ot G'dolot* ad loc. Am 1:1).

8. Henricus Oort, "De Profeet Amos," *Theologische Tijdschrift* 14 (1880): 121–33; idem, "Het Vaterland van Amos," *Theologische Tijdschrift* 25 (1891): 121–26.

9. Koch, *Prophets*, 70. What Koch is apparently unaware of is that the Upper Galilean Tekoa is not known in pre-Christian texts and the history of occupation goes no farther back than the pre-Roman times (H. Weippert, "Amos: Seine Bilder und ihr Milieu," in *Beiträge zur prophetischen Bildsprache in Israel und Assyrien*, eds.

suggesting that Amos' proclamation of total disaster is better understood coming from an insider than an outsider.[10]

Stanley N. Rosenbaum argues that the evidence that Amos came from Tekoa in Judah is hardly compelling, based as it is on a single text (Amos 1:1) that fails to identify where Tekoa is located.[11] Rosenbaum has presented additional arguments favoring the view that Amos was a native of the northern kingdom who was plotting the overthrow of the government.[12]

Rosenbaum maintains that the evidence linking Amos to the southern kingdom "consists mainly of three verses (Amos 1:1; 1:2; and 6:1), the authenticity of which are generally questioned, and an uninformed reading of Amos 7:10–17."[13] The major arguments of Rosenbaum are as follows:

1. Sycamore trees do not grow at such high elevations as that of Judean Tekoa.
2. Linguistic arguments such as the command to Amos in the conflict with Amaziah to "flee" (barah), which

---

Helga Weippert, Klaus Seybold, and Manfred Weippert [Göttingen: Vandenhoeck und Ruprecht, 1985], 3). Helga Weippert points out, however, that according to Jewish tradition, sycamore figs did not grow in Upper Galilee. Weippert refers to Tosephta Shev. 7:11 (Pes. 53a): "Wherever sycamores do not grow is upper Galilee; wherever sycamores do grow is lower Galilee." This is contra Gustav Dalman (Orte und Wege Jesu, 209), who argues for this Upper Galilee location.

10. Koch, Prophets, 70.

11. Rosenbaum's position is based upon that of Hans Schmidt, Der Prophet Amos (Tübingen: J. C. B. Mohr, 1917), 5 n. 1; and especially in idem, "Die Herkunft des Propheten Amos," in Karl Budde zum 70. Geburtstag, ed. Karl Marti (Giessen: Töpelmann, 1920), 158–71. Schmidt was also followed—albeit cautiously—by S. Speier, "Bemerkungen zu Amos," VT 3 (1953): 305–10; and M. Haran, "Amos," in Encyclopedia Judaica (Jerusalem: Macmillan, 1971), 2:879, who also mentions Graetz and Oort as supporters of this view. K. Budde, "Die Überschrift des Buches Amos und des Propheten Heimat," Semitic Studies in Memory of Rev. Dr. Alexander Kohut (Jerusalem/Tel Aviv: Maqir, 1972), 1:106–10, argues against some emendations of Oort that he used to support his suggestion. For Rosenbaum's argument, see Stanley N. Rosenbaum, "Northern Amos Revisited: Two Philological Suggestions," HS 18 (1977): 132–48.

12. Stanley N. Rosenbaum, Amos of Israel: A New Interpretation (Macon, Ga.: Mercer University Press, 1990).

13. Ibid., 30.

"almost always means to cross a border or boundary in order to escape the jurisdiction to which one is normally subject,"[14] and the usage of the term *gesher* with the meaning of "treason" (Amos 7:10), imply that Amos must have been a northern-born citizen.[15]

3. Amos was a "Northern civil servant" and an "Israelite official" who belonged to the "haves."[16]

4. Amos "wrote or was recorded in a dialect of Hebrew peculiar to the Northern Kingdom."[17]

Does it matter whether Amos comes from the southern kingdom of Judah or from the northern kingdom of Israel? In 7:10–17 the (high)priest Amaziah is challenging the right of Amos to threaten the king and his realm. Is Amaziah charging or commanding the prophet simply to go home or is he saying, "Leave our kingdom because you are a foreign interloper and you have no business involving yourself in the religious, social, and state affairs of our kingdom where we worship according to the cult practices germane to our national heritage"?

Part of the argument for a northern Tekoa in Upper Galilee is based on the assumption that sycamore trees (Heb. *shiqmîm*) are not found at such a high elevation as southern Tekoa. From all evidence presently available it is certainly correct that the biblical sycamore—which is unrelated to the North American sycamore or plane tree or the English maple tree—does not grow in the highlands. It grows only at lower elevations. As Philip J. King points out, "the biblical sycamore grows only in the lowlands and coastal plains, protected from the frost."[18] If this view is correct, then the northern Tekoa in Upper Galilee hardly qualifies better than the Judean Tekoa. The Tekoa

14. Ibid., 35.

15. Ibid., 37–40.

16. Ibid., 50, 100. The occupations of Amos are reconstructed on pp. 41–50.

17. Ibid., 5; cf. 85–95.

18. Philip J. King, *Amos, Hosea, Micah: An Archaeological Commentary* (Philadelphia: Westminster, 1988), 116.

of Galilee is located at an elevation of 760 meters above sea level, only 90 meters lower than the Judean Tekoa, if it is to be identified with Shema' Khirbet.[19] Furthermore, according to ancient Jewish tradition the Upper Galilean Tekoa was not an area in which sycamore trees were able to grow.[20] Gustav Dalman notes that only Lower Galilee entertained sycamore cultivation.[21] This contention is supported by ancient Jewish tradition.

There is no compelling reason to reject the Judean Tekoa position. King notes that "at the end of the summer the shepherds moved their goats and sheep to the Jordan Plain in the Jericho Valley, an area flourishing with forage during the summer months. This was the season when unripe sycamore fruit covered the tips of branchlets. The fruit had to be pierced and then wiped with oil if it was to ripen. . . . In exchange for grazing rights for their flocks, the shepherds dressed the sycamore trees."[22] The northern Tekoa hypothesis faces problems similar to the southern or Judean Tekoa hypothesis as regards the elevation for growing sycamore trees. Neither is located in areas and elevations suitable for the cultivation of sycamores.[23] In either case Amos would have to move to lower elevations where sycamores grew.

This does not answer fully how an Amos of the south became so knowledgeable about matters pertaining to the north. It has been suggested that Amos may have met shepherds from Bethel or other places in the northern kingdom in the Jericho Valley where he took his sheep

19. S. Klein, *The Land of Galilee* (Jerusalem, 1946), 130 (in Hebrew); Y. Aharoni and M. Avi-Yonah, *The Macmillan Bible Atlas* (New York: Macmillan, 1968), 141, map 223.

20. J. Feliks, *Nature and Man in the Bible* (London/Jerusalem/New York, 1981), 59 with reference to Tosephta Sheb. 10.9.

21. Dalman, *Orte und Wege Jesu*, 209.

22. King, *Amos, Hosea, Micah*, 117, citing the keeper of the Biblical Landscape Reserve.

23. It is not clear why Rosenbaum refrains from identifying the northern Tekoa more precisely. Is he aware of the elevation problem for the growth of sycamores?

and learned there of the plight and injustices of the northern kingdom.[24]

Rosenbaum's linguistic arguments pertaining to the words "flee" and "treason," as he himself admits, "cannot be conclusive. For one thing, we do not know whether Amaziah was using Hebrew with academic precision, or whether we even have his exact words."[25] In addition, we can have no assurance that the words discussed demand that the person addressed has to be a citizen of the northern kingdom, or whether there is sufficient evidence for the type of citizenship that is demanded by Rosenbaum's arguments.

The matter of Amos being steeped in a northern Hebrew dialect calls for some attention. Rosenbaum argues that "if the text betrays a northern origin, the most likely reason is that its author/speaker was a Northerner."[26] Yet is it required for a person of one linguistic subgroup to have such fixed dialectical/linguistic perspective that this person cannot adapt to differing dialectical usages? Few would agree. There is too much modern and ancient evidence that persons can acquire, consciously or subconsciously, varying dialectical idiosyncracies. Of course, Rosenbaum is ready to admit that "by themselves, linguistic arguments of the sort presented here [in the chapter on languages and dialect in Amos] cannot be conclusive."[27] Few would disagree with this.

If Amos should be a native of the northern kingdom, a view which as we have seen does not seem as attractive geographically as is made out, then many of the Amos studies of the past and present would be in need of some or much revision. A rather different picture of Amos and the origin of classical prophecy might emerge than the one

24. Ibid. King cites the study and report of N. Hareuveni, *Tree and Shrub in Our Biblical Heritage* (Kiryat Ono: Kedumim, 1984), 90–92.

25. Rosenbaum, *Amos of Israel*, 39–40.

26. Ibid., 95.

27. Ibid., 94.

favored by the majority point of view. The possibility of Amos coming from the northern kingdom is a newly revived position that seems to fail to solve the main problem of the presence of the sycamore fig. The northern Tekoa hypothesis is based on a substantial acceptance of the text of Amos as it stands. The southern Tekoa interpretation can also be supported on the acceptance of the Hebrew text. It appears that the northern Tekoa hypothesis calls for complex linguistic exercises that go beyond the readings of the Hebrew text. Furthermore, in other professional linkages the distances of time, space, and cultures do not receive adequate consideration. Regardless of the northern or southern Tekoa hypotheses the near nihilism regarding our knowledge of the man Amos that exists in some segments of modern scholarship is not the final word.

5

AMOS' ORACLES
AGAINST
THE NATIONS

The first major unit of the Book of Amos (1:3–2:16) is made up of "oracles against the nations."[1] These prophecies are the first oracles of this type in the Old Testament. No other book among the Old Testament writing prophets begins with OAN, although later prophetic writings (Isa. 13–23; Jer. 46–51; Zeph. 2; Obad. 1–6; Nah. 2:14–3:4; Hab. 2:6–17; 3:7–15) do have such oracles.

The "biggest question is the unity of 1.3–2.16."[2] An equally big question is the authenticity and assignment of this passage to the prophet Amos. Aside from these important issues, there is the challenge of determining why the Book of Amos begins with these prophecies against the nations surrounding Israel and Judah. Is there a communication here for the first time in biblical religion that the nations as well as the elect people of Yahweh are under

1. Hereafter, OAN.
2. A. G. Auld, *Amos* (Sheffield: JSOT, 1986), 41.

the judgment of the covenant God? On what basis are these nations held responsible for their activities? Is God stepping in when atrocities are committed by other nations? Is the prophet Amos showing his anger in the name of Yahweh when other nations overstep the boundaries of acceptable moral behavior? Is the accountability of these nations in some sense proportionate to the knowledge they have of the true God? Are they judged because they were once under the hegemony of the Davidic empire? Are these judgment oracles based on a cause-effect relationship that is universally understood? Do these prophecies function as rhetorical devices? Is Amos reflecting a universal international law, or is he building his argument on "natural law"?

The post-World War II period has produced a significant number of studies on the OAN with rather diverse conclusions.[3] Until recently there was a consensus in modern

3. Aside from the commentaries, the following studies on the OAN need to mentioned: Meir Weiss, "The Pattern of Numerical Sequence in Amos 1–2: A Re-Examination," *JBL* 86 (1967): 416–23; Menahem Haran, "Observations on the Historical Background of Amos 1:2–2:6," *IEJ* 18 (1968): 201–12; John H. Hayes, "The Usage of the Oracles Against the Foreign Nations in Ancient Israel," *JBL* 87 (1968): 81–92; E. Beauchamp, "Amos 1–2: Le peshà d'Israel et des nations," *ScEs* 21 (1969): 435–41; Meir Weiss, "The Pattern of the 'Execration Texts' in the Prophetic Literature," *IEJ* 191 (1969): 150–57; Shalom M. Paul, "Amos 1:3–2:3: A Concatenous Literary Pattern," *JBL* 90 (1971): 397–403; Wilhelm Rudolph, "Die angefochtenen Völkersprüche in Amos 1–2," in *Schalom. Studien zu Glaube und Geschichte Israels: Festschrift für A. Jepsen*, ed. K.-H. Bernhardt (Stuttgart: Calwer Verlag, 1971), 45–59; Menahem Haran, "The Graded Numerical Sequence and the Phenomenon of 'Automatism' in Biblical Poetry," *VTS* 22 (1972): 238–67; Duane L. Christensen, "The Prosodic Structure of Amos 1–2," *HTR* 67 (1974): 427–36; Keith N. Schoville, "A Note on the Oracles of Amos Against Gaza, Tyre, and Edom," *VTS* 26 (1974): 55–63; Duane L. Christensen, *Transformations of the War Oracle in Old Testament Prophecy* (Missoula: Scholars, 1975), 17–97; T. H. McAlpine, "The Word Against the Nations," *Studia Biblica et Theologica* 5/1 (1975): 3–14; David L. Petersen, "The Oracles Against the Nations: A Form-Critical Analysis," *SBLSP* (1975), 1:39–61; G. Pfeifer, "Denkformenanalyse als exegetische Methode, erläutert an Amos 1:2–2:16," *ZAW* 88 (1976): 56–71; Rolf Knierim, "'I Will Not Cause It to Return' in Amos 1 and 2," in *Canon and Authority: Essays in Old Testament Religion and Theology*, eds. G. W. Coats and B. O. Long (Philadelphia: Fortress, 1977), 163–75; J. Vermeylen, *Du prophète Isaïe à l'apocalyptique. Isaie, I-XXXV, miroir d'un demi-millenaire d'experience religieuse en Israel* (Paris: Gabalda,

critical scholarship that the original sequence of the OAN consisted in its most minimal form of four oracles: those against Aram (1:3–5), Philistia (1:6–8), Ammon (1:13–15), and Moab (2:1–3). This consensus followed the outlines of the form-critical suggestion made by H. Gunkel and subsequently by Hugo Gressmann.[4] Gressmann suggested that the OAN of Amos were taken over from a period before Amos and were representative of Israelite eschatology from an early period. The OAN are *Heidenorakel* (oracles about pagans) through which doom was prophesied to the nations. A. Bentzen suggested that the OAN of Amos were modeled after Egyptian execration texts.[5] This cultic connection spawned some following.[6] F. C. Fensham turned to ancient Near Eastern treaty texts, claiming that the OAN

1978), 2:529–42; Robert Gordis, "Amos, Edom and Israel—An Unrecognized Source for Edomite History," in *Essays on the Occasion of the Seventieth Anniversary of the Dropsie University*, eds. A. Katsh and L. Nemoy (Philadelphia: Dropsie University, 1979), 109–32; J.-L. Vesco, "Amos de Teqoa, défenseur de l'homme," *RB* 87 (1980): 481–513; John Barton, *Amos's Oracles Against the Nations* (Cambridge: Cambridge University Press, 1980); Hartmut Gese, "Komposition bei Amos,"*VTS* 32 (1981): 74–95; Shalom M. Paul, "A Literary Reinvestigation of the Authenticity of the Oracles Against the Nations in Amos," in *De la Tôrah au Messie. Melanges Henri Cazelles*, eds. M. Carrez et al. (Paris: Desclee, 1981), 189–204; B. Z. Luria, "The Prophecies unto the Nations in the Book of Amos from the Point of View of History," *Beth Miqra* 54 (1983): 287–300; Jarl Henning Ulrichsen, "Oraklene i Amos 1:3ff.," *NorTT* 85 (1984): 39–54; John B. Geyer, "Mythology and Culture in the Oracles Against the Nations," *VT* 36 (1986): 129–45; Volkmar Fritz, "Die Fremdvölkersprüche des Amos," *VT* 37 (1987): 26–38; Gerhard Pfeifer, "'Rettung' als Beweis der Vernichtung (Amos 3.12)," *ZAW* 100 (1988): 269–77; Bernhard Gosse, "Le recueil d'oracles contre les nations du livre d'Amos et l'histoire deutéronomiqué,'" *VT* 38 (1988): 22–40; Jörg Jeremias, "Völkersprüche und Visionsberichte im Amosbuch," in *Prophet und Prophetenbuch. Festschrift für Otto Kaiser zum 65. Geburtstag*, eds. Volkmar Fritz, Karl-Friedrich Pohlmann, and Hans-Christoph Schmitt (Berlin/New York: W. de Gruyter, 1989), 82–97.

4. This is outlined in an article by Hermann Gunkel in the first edition of the encyclopedia *Religion in Geschichte und Gegenwart* at the beginning of this century under the title, "The Earliest Israelite Prophecy from the Time of Amos," reprinted in *Twentieth Century Theology in the Making. I. Themes of Biblical Theology*, ed. J. Pelikan (New York: Harper & Row, 1969), 48–65. See also Hugo Gressmann, *Der Ursprung der israelitisch-judäischen Eschatologie* (Göttingen: Vandenhoeck und Ruprecht, 1905); idem, *Der Messias* (Göttingen: Vandenhoeck und Ruprecht, 1929).

5. A. Bentzen, "The Ritual Background of Amos 1:2–2:16," *OTS* 8 (1950): 85–99.

6. H. Graf Reventlow, *Das Amt des Propheten bei Amos* (Göttingen: Vandenhoeck und Ruprecht, 1962), 62–75; G. Fohrer, "Prophetie und Magie," *ZAW* 78 (1966): 40–44.

reflect the curse clauses in such texts and thus the background for the OAN is to be sought in treaties.[7]

Other scholars sought the origin of the OAN in preclassical biblical prophecy.[8] Here the connection with the war oracles has been widely investigated. John H. Hayes claims that "warfare is the original *Sitz im Leben* for the Israelite oracles against the foreign nations."[9] D. L. Christensen refines this hypothesis of molding older literary traditions by arguing that "Yahweh's holy war is now directed not only against Israel's foes, but against Israel as well."[10] For Y. Hoffmann the war oracle is precisely the "oracle-before-battle" that Amos reshaped and transformed into his own genre with new content.[11] This conspectus of ideas reveals that currently there is a trend that links the OAN of Amos with earlier Israelite traditions.

The authenticity of the OAN has evoked much discussion. Bernhard Gosse makes a strong case to add the oracle against Israel (2:6–13) to this genuine core of the basic oracles of Aram, Philistia, Ammon, and Moab, based on his study of the Deuteronomistic history.[12] Volkmar Fritz argues that none of the OAN come from Amos. They are *vaticinia ex eventu* (prophecies written after the event) that reflect the fall of Samaria and the end of the northern kingdom in 722 B.C.[13] He has received a spirited response

7. F. C. Fensham, "Common Trends in Curses of the Near Eastern Treaties and *Kudurru*-Inscriptions Compared with Maledictions of Amos and Isaiah," *ZAW* 75 (1963): 155–75.

8. For example, M. Haran, "An Archaic Remnant in Prophetic Literature" (in Hebrew), *Bulletin of the Israel Exploration Society* 13 (1946–47): 7–16; I. A. Seligman, "On the History and Nature of Prophecy in Israel" (in Hebrew), ErIsr 3 (1954): 125–32; N. Gottwald, *All the Kingdoms of the Earth: Israelite Prophecy and International Relations in the Ancient Near East* (New York: Harper & Row, 1964), 47–49.

9. John H. Hayes, "The Usage of Oracles Against the Foreign Nations in Ancient Israel," *JBL* 87 (1968): 84.

10. Christensen, *Transformations*, 70.

11. Y. Hoffmann, *The Prophecies Against Foreign Nations in the Bible* (Tel Aviv: Kibbutz Hameuhad, 1977); idem, "From Oracle to Prophecy: The Growth, Crystallization and Disintegration of a Biblical Gattung," *JNES* 10 (1982): 75–81.

12. Gosse, "Le recueil d'oracles contre les nations," 37–40.

13. Fritz, "Die Fremdvölkersprüche des Amos,"38.

from Gerhard Pfeifer, who shows that the arguments used by Fritz inadequately support his radical conclusions.[14] Fritz's suggestion that the OAN do not derive from "prophetic revelation" but from prophetic circles that attempt an interpretation of history is likewise unsupported by the independent recent study of Gosse.

The disputed OAN against Tyre (1:9–10) and Edom (1:11–12) have been considered genuine by Christensen based on "prosodic-textual analysis"[15] and a variety of connections with Israelite traditions, not least of all the war oracle that is "transformed into a judgment speech against Israel."[16] John Barton concludes that the "Judah oracle is certainly, the Edom oracle almost certainly, and the Tyre oracle very probably, not by Amos."[17] This conclusion, as cautious as it seems and as widely as it is quoted, appears to be reached without seriously considering the arguments of W. Rudolph, M. Haran, M. Weiss, D. Christensen, S. M. Paul, E. Hammershaimb, and K. N. Schoville (whom he does not cite), scholars who have devoted careful study to these oracles and who have concluded that they are genuine. Hartmut Gese supports the genuineness of the oracle against Israel on other grounds than Gosse.[18] This survey of but a few of the major views reveals that there is no scholarly consensus on the genuineness of these oracles. It may be surprising, therefore, that this picture is totally different in commentaries published since 1987.[19] While these scholars belong to differing schools of interpretation, they

14. Gerhard Pfeifer, "Die Fremdvölkersprüche des Amos—spätere *vaticinia ex eventu?*" *VT* 38 (1988):230–33.

15. Christensen, *Transformations*, 68; idem, "Prosodic Structure," 427–36. Christensen's textual reconstructions are highly speculative.

15. Christensen, *Transformations*, 71.

16. Barton, *Amos's Oracles*, 24.

18. Gese ("Komposition," 88–95) argues that Amos joined to the two pairs of OAN a fifth oracle against Israel.

19. D. K. Stuart, *Hosea–Jonah* (Waco: Word, 1987), 308–9; John H. Hayes, *Amos, His Time and His Preaching: The Eighth Century Prophet* (Nashville: Abingdon, 1988), 50–61; D. A. Hubbard, *Joel and Amos: An Introduction and Commentary* (Leicester: Inter-Varsity, 1989), 127–30; Gary V. Smith, *Amos: A Commentary* (Grand Rapids: Zondervan, 1989), 29–64; Francis I. Andersen and David Noel

agree independently of each other in their assessment that the OAN derive from Amos himself.

Hayes understands the OAN to be a single "speech."[20] Andersen and Freedman consider the eight oracles as one eightfold oracle by virtue of its rhetorical structure.[21] Paul shows that there is a concatenation of similar catchwords, phrases, or ideas in the OAN that manifests "an internal literary order [that] can be discerned that weaves the various units into a coherent whole."[22] These new trends indicate that the earlier atomistic approach of form criticism as applied to the OAN in Amos is being replaced with an approach that sees larger units functioning as literary wholes. It is to be noted that Hayes, Andersen and Freedman, and Paul among others are critical of the form-critical and traditio-historical methods as appropriate approaches for the study of Amos (and, by implication, of other Old Testament materials). Hayes insists that "to treat the book [of Amos] as a collection of several dozen small units (as in the commentaries by Wolff and Mays) is to involve form-critical concerns in the same fallacies that beset the old etymologizing word study approach to Scripture."[23] He goes on to compare the mistakes of the "root" meaning method in word studies, which superimposes itself upon the meaning of a given term in its own contextual setting, with "much modern form-critical work [that] divides the material into its smallest sense unit or genre, and then postulates an original intention and meaning for each genre, that is everywhere retained."[24] Those who are well enough acquainted with the scholarly work

---

Freedman, *Amos: A New Translation with Introduction and Commentary* (New York: Doubleday, 1989), 30–32, 206–22; T. J. Finley, *Joel, Amos, Obadiah* (Chicago: Moody, 1990), 133–60; Shalom M. Paul, *Amos: A Commentary on the Book of Amos* (Minneapolis: Fortress, 1991), 7–30.

20. Hayes, *Amos*, 48.
21. Andersen and Freedman, *Amos*, 211.
22. Paul, *Amos*, 13.
23. Hayes, *Amos*, 39.
24. Ibid.

of Hayes need not be reminded that he is neither a funda-
mentalist nor suspicious conservative.

At this point it may be helpful to summarize the structural features of the OAN. We will follow here the presentation of Hayes:

> (1) A common framing pattern is characteristic of all the
> sub-units. (2) Within the structuring framework, two
> sub-categories can be detected: one group contains an
> expanded description of the coming disaster, thus high-
> lighting the punishment, and the other an expanded
> description of the wrongdoing, thus highlighting the
> crimes. (3) The units alternate between the two types.
> Two of the former (Damascus and Gaza) are followed
> by two of the latter (Tyre and Edom) and the pattern is
> then repeated (Ammon-Moab and Judah). (4) Variation
> in terminology and mode of expression occurs within
> both categories. (5) The Israel section (2:6–16) contains
> an elaboration of both the description of the wrong-
> doings and of the coming disasters.[25]

Three major criteria are used for determining the genuineness or authenticity of the OAN: linguistic-stylistic,
historical, and structural issues.[26] Syntax and style have
been used to declare the OAN of Tyre (1:9–10), Edom
(1:11–12), and Judah (2:4–5) to be inauthentic. This is
achieved by taking the oracles against Damascus (1:3–5),
Gaza (1:6–8), Ammon (1:13–15), and Moab (2:1–3) as the
norm against which the others are measured.[27] It remains
an open question whether this standard of measurement
can indeed be justified.

The historical arguments involve the OAN of Tyre,
Judah, and Edom (and also Gaza). The Tyre oracle contains
a reference to slave trade (1:9), which is mentioned in later

---

25. Hayes, *Amos,* 6.
26. Hayes provides a ready overview (*Amos,* 51).
27. See Hans W. Wolff, *Joel and Amos: A Commentary on the Books of the Prophets
Joel and Amos* (Philadelphia: Fortress, 1977), 135–41, for the application of this
procedure.

texts such as Ezekiel 27:13 and Joel 3:4–8. The oracles against Tyre in the Old Testament are thus dated or redated to Babylonian times.[28] The phrase "to remember a covenant" is redated to other texts of allegedly late origin such as Genesis 9:6–15; Exodus 2:24; 6:5; and Leviticus 26:42, 45. This issue of an early or late "covenant" in ancient Israel is a hotly debated one. The literature on this issue is vast and summarized by E. W. Nicholson.[29] The shift from an early covenant in the Old Testament to a late covenant is witnessed in such studies as those by G. Fohrer (1963), L. Perlitt (1969), and E. Kutsch (1973) against whom particularly D. McCarthy and others argued. Perlitt suggests that the covenant became known only in the seventh century B.C. while Nicholson pushes it back to the eighth century. But it has been shown by Kenneth Kitchen that Nicholson's discussion and conclusions are very one-sided, even though he pushes the covenant back by one hundred years.[30] A recent detailed investigation involving Hosea, Amos' contemporary, and the covenant argues that the covenant idea was an early Israelite phenomenon fully functioning by the time of the eighth century.[31] This removes one aspect of the historical argument. Furthermore, to deny to an earlier writer a reference to an idea or thought just because there are more frequent references in a later period makes no sense. Furthermore, some texts dated late are actually early (even earlier than Amos).

The argument about the structural elements of the OAN as a basis for determining authenticity is a tricky business. We do not know which structures are absolute for Amos. Is the fivefold structure proposed by Hartmut Gese (2 + 2 + 1) typical for Amos?[32] Or is James Limburg more

28. Ibid., 158.

29. E. W. Nicholson, *God and His People: Covenant and Theology in the Old Testament* (Oxford: Oxford University Press, 1986).

30. Kenneth A. Kitchen, "The Fall and Rise of Covenant, Law and Treaty," *Tyndale Bulletin* 40 (1989): 118–35.

31. Heinz-Dieter Neef, *Die Heilstraditionen Israels in der Verkündigung des Propheten Hosea* (Berlin/New York: W. de Gruyter, 1987), 120–74.

32. Gese, "Komposition."

correct in maintaining the structure of seven?[33] If one takes the latter stance, then all OAN in Amos are genuine. But this way of looking at it does not solve the more basic question, namely, which structural considerations can be used for determining authenticity. Are these not constructs of modern scholarship that are open to scrutiny, criticism, and reflection?

The recently published Anchor Bible commentary on Amos clearly breaks with the dominant approaches of form criticism and tradition criticism used in such major critical commentaries as the ones produced by Hans Walter Wolff and James Mays, both published first in 1969. The well-known commentary by Italian Old Testament scholar J. Alberto Soggin was recently translated into English (1987). It is deeply steeped in tradition criticism. Andersen and Freedman, the commentators of the Anchor commentary on Amos, do not hesitate to state that "the major discipline of form criticism now seems to have reached its limits without solving its problems, and it has become so preoccupied with the parts that it misses—or even denies the existence of—the whole."[34] Andersen and Freedman "do not wish to deny the validity and value of the results of modern criticism, but," as they state, "we can no longer display those results with the confidence and finality that are found in many old handbooks; for example, we cannot assert that the book is mainly the work of postexilic editors, a theory that is often repeated but seldom defended in detail."[35] Thus those scholars who attempt to find the true message of a reconstructed historical Amos in the proclamation of doom only, but not in the parts of the book that clearly express a message of repentance and return and point to the genuine possibility of survivors and a positive remnant are charged with manipulating the text of the

33. James Limburg, "Sevenfold Structures in the Book of Amos," *JBL* 106 (1987): 217–22.
34. Andersen and Freedman, *Amos*, 4.
35. Ibid.

Book of Amos as it stands. "The text has to suffer considerable surgery to reach this result."[36] Today such freedom to
manipulate the text either by literary criticism as done by
an earlier generation of historical-critical scholars or
through the atomizing approach of form criticism and sub-
sequent tradition criticism and redaction criticism, which
puts each small unit or genre into a reconstructed and
newly devised *Sitz im Leben,* are challenged by a new and
great respect for the text as it stands.

Gene M. Tucker concludes his survey of prophecy and
prophetic literature with the statement that "one may
expect more attention to be concentrated [in the future]
on the final form of the prophetic books."[37] This seems to
be exactly what is happening in these new commentaries,
including the one by Shalom Paul that replaces that of
Wolff in the Hermeneia series. There is the distinct attempt
to find meaning in the book as a whole and to refrain
from the atomizing of modern critical interpretation.
There seems to be the beginning of a paradigm change
toward literary approaches and the appreciation of the
biblical books as works of literary art.

John H. Hayes of Emory University wrote a very influential dissertation on the Old Testament OAN in 1964, in
which he pointed to variegated *Sitz im Leben* of the OAN.[38]
In his 1988 commentary on Amos he considers the full
number of OAN to derive from Amos. It would take us too
far afield to outline the full range of arguments used to limit
the number of oracles against the nations to the minimal
number on various critical grounds.[39] Hayes notes that "the
individual 'oracles on the nations' in this material are devel-

36. Ibid., 7.

37. Gene M. Tucker, "Prophecy and Prophetic Literature," in *The Hebrew Bible and Its Modern Interpreters,* eds. Douglas A. Knight and Gene M. Tucker (Philadelphia: Fortress; Chico, Calif.: Scholars, 1985), 356.

38. John H. Hayes, *The Oracles Against the Nations in the Old Testament: Their Usage and Theological Importance* (Th.D. diss., Princeton Theological Seminary, 1964).

39. This is done effectively and precisely by Hayes, *Amos,* 49–61; Barton, *Amos's Oracles,* 16–35; and others.

oped with repetitive regularity."[40] He concludes his study of the structural features by noting that: (1) there is a "common framing pattern" characteristic of each unit; (2) two "subcategories" are present in the general pattern, one of which has an "expanded description of the coming disaster" and the other that has "an expanded description of the wrongdoing" whereby the crimes are highlighted; (3) the oracles alternate between the two in sets of two descriptions with the Israel oracle containing elaborations of both descriptions; and (4) both types of descriptions or both subcategories contain "variations in terminology and mode of expression."[41]

In determining the authenticity of the OAN scholars have frequently and customarily taken the patterns of the oracles against Damascus (1:3–5), Gaza (1:6–8), Ammon (1:13–15), and Moab (2:1–3), as noted above, as norms for judging whether the other oracles are genuine. Five common elements are detected in these four oracles and are used to determine which of the remaining ones are original.[42] In addition to these structural criteria certain historical arguments have been used against the authenticity of the oracles against Tyre, Edom, Judah, Gaza, and Philistia.[43] Finally there are scholars who argue that certain other structural considerations should be used to determine which oracles are genuine.[44]

Not all scholars are convinced by the arguments used and a fair number have pointed out that the criteria for inauthenticity are inadequate or arbitrary. Among them are Wilhelm Rudolph, Shalom M. Paul, and Robert Gordis.[45] John H. Hayes

40. Hayes, *Amos*, 49.
41. Ibid., 51.
42. See Wolff, *Joel and Amos*, 135–39.
43. For a summary, see Hayes, *Amos*, 51–52.
44. For instance, Gese, "Komposition," 86–93.
45. Rudolph, "Die angefochtenen Völkersprüche in Amos 1–2," 45–49; Paul, "Amos 1:3–2:3," 397–403; idem, "Literary Reinvestigation," 189–204; R. Gordis, *Poets, Prophets and Sages: Essays in Biblical Interpretation* (Bloomington, Ind.: Indiana University Press, 1971), 95–103.

affirms that "there are no compelling reasons for dating the oracles later than the time of Amos."[46] Andersen and Freedman note that "it has been a common opinion among modern critics to doubt the originality of one or more of the eight oracles in the cycle; but we consider the list of nations to be complete as it stands."[47] They consider it to derive from Amos and state that "Amos' list comprehends the entire region from Egypt to the Euphrates, an expanse of territory of enormous importance in Israel's history and memory."[48]

Having surveyed some general trends, we need to turn now to some issues. First, can form-critical and traditio-historical investigations be integrated or related to rhetorical and/or literary analysis? Or, to state the question differently, is it possible to join the diachronic approach of traditional historical-critical scholarship with the synchronic approach of more recent scholarship? In the particular instance of the OAN scholars have been unable to achieve such an integration.

Second, if the OAN manifest themselves for the first time in the Book of Amos in Hebrew prophetic literature, and few would doubt this (V. Fritz, however, thinks that all are from a later period), are they but a reflection, adaptation, or transformation of pre-Amos OAN and/or other ancient traditions, both Hebrew and non-Hebrew, such as covenant, holy war, election, wailing, or execration/curse and the like? Each of these points raised here in question form has been made by one or more scholars of the past. Each needs careful independent analysis.

Third, to what extent is Amos, the *hozeh*, respectively *nabi'*, himself an originator/creator of such a literary composition? As the text stands in the Book of Amos this book is the oldest prophetic evidence for such type of literature among the "writing prophets." If Amos is not the originator, which unknown prophet or editor of genius would

46. Hayes, *Amos*, 55.
47. Andersen and Freedman, *Amos*, 206.
48. Ibid.

have such an honor? Would such a person remain incognito? Is it likely that the real "prophets" were the unknown editors or redactors of whatever "school" for which there is no explicit evidence?

Fourth, if Amos, the first "classical prophet" in the Old Testament, is in some way dependent on Israelite traditions, an earlier religious heritage of the Yahweh faith, would the OAN be dependent on a single Israelite tradition or on a variety of traditions?

Fifth, what about the reconstructions of the OAN by means of "prosodic-textual analysis," which seems to alter significantly the present poetic form, or other forms of reconstruction? What controls are available in these endeavors?

Sixth, is the principle of the consistency of structure and form a surefire norm for determining origin and development?

Seventh, on a theological level, are the OAN in Amos *vaticinia ex eventu* (so V. Fritz but opposed by G. Pfeifer) or are they true, genuine prophecy? What implication does this have regarding the nature of eighth-century Israelite prophecy?

Finally, what is the ground upon which Amos can attack foreign nations? Is it "natural law" (as suggested by James Barr), or a universal covenant (as held by R. E. Clements), or nationalism (as affirmed by M. Haran and others), or universal morality (as supported by P. Humbert and others), or universal law (as suggested by K. Cramer and others), or international law (as defended by J. Barton among others), or common ethos? Answers to these and related questions determine, to a large extent, the very nature of Amos as prophet and Israelite prophecy in the eighth century and beyond.

6

AMOS' USE
OF ISRAELITE
TRADITIONS

Toward the end of the nineteenth century men like
Heinrich Ewald (1803–1875)[1] and Julius Wellhausen
(1844–1918), and their followers such as Bernhard
Duhm and others in the first half of the twentieth
century,[2] considered the classical prophets as innovative
proponents of "ethical monotheism,"[3] providing the foundation for a new phase of religion in ancient Israel. On the
basis of form-critical and traditio-historical research—
developed by Hermann Gunkel (1862–1932), Martin Noth

1. On Ewald's influence on prophetic interpretation, see H.-J. Kraus, *Geschichte der historisch-kritischen Erforschung des Alten Testaments*, 2d ed. (Neukirchen-Vluyn: Neukirchener Verlag, 1969), 205–9.

2. Ibid., 275–83. For a survey of research on the prophets, see Roland E. Clements, *One Hundred Years of Old Testament Interpretation* (Philadelphia: Westminster, 1976), 51–75.

3. This view is still held by E. Balla, *Die Botschaft der Propheten* (Tübingen: J. C. B. Mohr, 1958), 92: "With him [Amos] starts truly a new epoch of the history of religion, the *epoch of ethical monotheism.*"

71

(1902–1968), and Gerhard von Rad (1901–1971), and used in full-fledged form from the 1930s onward—this view is radically changed and mostly rejected today.[4] James M. Ward writes: "Recent research tends to confirm the opinion that the forms and substance of Amos' message were deeply rooted in the religious traditions of Yahwism and were not merely the unprecedented innovations of a creative mind."[5] While this assessment still holds in modern scholarly circles today, the issue of exactly which Israelite traditions Amos uses and fills with new meaning and power is hotly debated.

Does Amos use covenant traditions? John H. Hayes states categorically that "there is no evidence in the book that the relationship between Yahweh and Israel was understood in terms of covenant theology at the time."[6] This denial of the use of covenant traditions by Amos is particularly interesting inasmuch as Hayes accepts the entire book as genuine, except for 1:1 and 7:10–17. Other scholars are often tempted to declare passages that reveal covenantal ideas as secondary, assigning them to the period when the Deuteronomist functioned or later.[7] The whole covenant notion is denied to the Old Testament by a new trend in scholarship, except from the seventh century onward. This view has received some stiff opposition, however.[8]

R. Martin-Achard does not go quite so far but downplays

4. See above, chap. 1.

5. J. M. Ward, "Amos," *IDB(Sup)* (Nashville: Abingdon, 1976), 23.

6. John H. Hayes, *Amos, His Time and His Preaching: The Eighth Century Prophet* (Nashville: Abingdon, 1988), 38.

7. See Ernst Kutsch, *Verheissung und Gesetz* (Berlin/New York: W. de Gruyter, 1973); Lothar Perlitt, *Bundestheologie im Alten Testament* (Neukirchen-Vluyn: Neukirchener Verlag, 1969); W. Thiel, "Die Rede vom 'Bund' in den Prophetenbüchern," *Theologische Versuche* 9 (1977): 11–36.

8. For example, Dennis J. McCarthy, *Treaty and Covenant* (Rome: Pontifical Biblical Institute Press, 1968); idem, *Covenant in the Old Testament: A Survey of Current Opinions* (Oxford, 1972); and now particularly by Heinz-Dietrich Neef, *Die Heilstraditionen Israels in der Verkündigung des Propheten Hosea* (Berlin/New York: W. de Gruyter, 1987), 120–74; Kenneth A. Kitchen, "The Fall and Rise of Covenant, Law and Treaty," *Tyndale Bulletin* 40 (1989): 118–35.

the covenant usage by Amos.[9] This is reflective of a trend among scholars who speak of a relationship between Yahweh and Israel in Amos without ever linking it to the covenant or covenant traditions.[10] This seems to be due to the view of a group of scholars such as Lothar Perlitt, Ernst Kutsch, W. Thiel, and those who follow them, that the covenant is not known and used by the eighth-century prophets Amos, Hosea, Micah, and Isaiah.[11] This view will not command the support of the majority of scholars today.[12]

Douglas Stuart, on the other hand, maintains that "the covenantal perspective governs the content [of Amos] to a substantial degree."[13] David A. Hubbard is even more emphatic in stating that "covenant-theology is fundamental to Amos (and Hosea), even where technical terms may not be present."[14] Andersen and Freedman also presuppose the covenant for the message of Amos. His judgment message is based on covenant violations.[15] These scholars are joined by many others who are convinced that the correct way to understand the message of Amos is against a covenant background and that his message is shaped by covenantal thought.[16]

The problems that confront the researcher, if the cov-

9. Robert Martin-Achard, *Amos—L'homme, le message, l'influence* (Geneva: Labor et Fides, 1984), 75–77.

10. For example, J. Vollmer, *Geschichtliche Rückblicke und Motive in der Prophetie des Amos, Hosea und Jesaja* (Berlin/New York: W. de Gruyter, 1971), among many others.

11. Perlitt, *Bundestheologie im Alten Testament*; E. Kutsch, *Verheissung und Gesetz* (Berlin/New York: W. de Gruyter, 1973); Thiel, "Die Rede vom 'Bund,'" 11–36.

12. See n. 8 above.

13. D. K. Stuart, *Hosea–Jonah* (Waco: Word, 1987), 288.

14. D. A. Hubbard, *Joel and Amos: An Introduction and Commentary* (Leicester: Inter-Varsity, 1989), 112 n. 1.

15. Francis I. Andersen and David Noel Freedman, *Amos: A New Translation with Introduction and Commentary* (New York: Doubleday, 1989), 81, 91–93, 236, and in many other places.

16. Peter C. Craigie, *Twelve Prophets* (Philadelphia: Westminster, 1984), 1:122–23; W. Brueggemann, "Amos 6:4–13 and Israel's Covenant Worship," *VT* 15 (1965): 1–15; H. Graf Reventlow, *Das Amt des Propheten bei Amos* (Göttingen: Vandenhoeck und Ruprecht, 1962); Leslie C. Allen, "Amos, Prophet of Solidarity," *Vox Evangelica* 6 (1969): 42–53, esp. 47–51; Michael Fishbane, "The Treaty

enant should be as late as is suggested by some, would be how to account for the language that seems to have covenantal connections. It has been argued that the references to the covenant must be the result of later Deuteronomic editing. This means on the one hand that the covenantal language is acknowledged to be present by those who do not allow for the covenant traditions to function as early as the eighth century B.C. On the other hand it means that only a radical tour de force can expunge from the true words of Amos the covenant usage by a radical redating. If the redating position is not accepted as persuasive, then it could be suggested that there existed pre-Deuteronomic covenant traditions, or alternatively, it could be argued even more convincingly that the covenant is not as late in origin as is claimed by these critical scholars. The recent dissertation by Heinz-Dieter Neef on the salvation traditions in Hosea seems to demonstrate clearly that Hosea is heavily indebted to the covenant tradition (against Perlitt, Kutsch, et al.).[17] If this is true of Hosea, could it be true of Amos as

Background of Amos 1:11 and Related Matters," *JBL* 89 (1970): 313–18; idem, "Additional Remarks on *rhmym* (Amos 1:11)," *JBL* 91 (1972): 391–93; Marjorie O'Rourke Boyle, "The Covenant Lawsuit of the Prophet Amos: III 1–IV 13," *VT* 21 (1971): 338–62; R. B. Coote, "Amos 1:11: *rhmym*," *JBL* 90 (1971): 208; Frank N. Seilhamer, "The Role of Covenant in the Mission and Message of Amos," in *A Light unto My Path: Old Testament Studies in Honor of Jacob M. Myers*, eds. H. N. Bream et al. (Philadelphia: Temple University Press, 1974), 435–51; Paul-E. Dion, "Le message moral du prophete Amos s'inspirait-il du 'droit de l'alliance'"? *ScEs* 27 (1975): 5–34; J. Bright, *Covenant and Promise* (Philadelphia: Westminster, 1976), 83–87; Patrick Miller, Jr., *Sin and Judgment in the Prophets: A Stylistic and Theological Analysis* (Chico, Calif.: Scholars, 1982), 21–25; George Snyder, "Law and Covenant in Amos," *ResQ* 25 (1982):158–66; Michael de Roche, " Yahweh's *rîb* Against Israel: A Reassessment of the So-called 'Prophetic Lawsuit' in the Preexilic Prophets," *JBL* 102 (1983): 565–74; A. S. van der Woude, "Three Classical Prophets: Amos, Hosea, and Micah," in *Israel's Prophetic Tradition: Essays in Honor of Peter Ackroyd*, eds. R. Coggin et al. (Cambridge: Cambridge University Press, 1984), 218–19; Michael James Hauan, "The Background and Meaning of Amos 5:17B," *HTR* 79 (1986): 337–48; and others.

17. Neef, *Die Heilstraditionen Israels in der Verkündigung des Propheten Hosea*, 120–74. See also E. W. Nicholson, *God and His People: Covenant and Theology in the Old Testament* (New York: Oxford University Press, 1986), 206–10. This monograph was not available to Neef, but independently supports his conclusions (although from a different angle).

well, because both are contemporaries and both minister (primarily) in the northern kingdom? These issues will continue to vex scholars for some time. But it seems clear that the covenant cannot be dismissed as glibly as is done by some scholars.

Amos cannot be linked singularly to cultic, wisdom, or other traditions.[18] The thought and connections of Amos are too rich to restrict him to one or another major tradition. His connections are multiple and varied. Amos is indebted to the rich faith of ancient Israel and is well versed in the popular beliefs of his time, which he frequently attacks or turns upside down. It has to be admitted time and again that the evaluation of what Amos is said to have used or is indebted to depends to the largest degree on what reconstructions each investigator accepts about the development of Israelite religion, how the various Old Testament texts are dated, and what parts of the Old Testament are acknowledged to be reflective of one or another concept, motif, or tradition. Has Amos not used the faith of Israel of the past and expounded that faith on the basis of new divine revelations in his prophetic message?

18. See chap. 7, below.

7

AMOS'
INTELLECTUAL
BACKGROUND

B eginning in the 1950s there developed a trend in modern scholarship, particularly on the Continent, that placed Amos in the framework of Israelite cultic traditions. This is the view of such eminent scholars as Ernst Würthwein, Henning Graf Reventlow, and others.[1] Graf Reventlow argued forcefully that Amos was a cultic functionary who presented his message at a covenant renewal festival.

This placing of Amos into the framework of the Israelite cult came as a reaction against the Wellhausen–Duhm hypothesis, which made the classical prophets masters of creativity and innovation. Historical-critical scholars around

---

1. E. Würthwein, "Amos-Studien," *ZAW* 62 (1950): 10–52; idem, "Kultpolemik oder Kultbescheid?" *Wort und Existenz. Studien zum Alten Testament* (Göttingen: Vandenhoeck und Ruprecht, 1970), 143–60; Henning Graf Reventlow, *Das Amt des Propheten bei Amos* (Göttingen: Vandenhoeck und Ruprecht, 1962); H. Gottlieb, "Amos und Jerusalem," *VT* 17 (1967): 430–63; G. Farr, "The Language of Amos, Popular or Cultic?" *VT* 16 (1966): 312–24.

the turn of the century, and their followers into the 1930s, saw the prophets of the eighth century (Amos, Hosea, Micah, and Isaiah of Jerusalem) as innovators of a new and advanced phase of Israelite religion. The old "classical prophets," such as Elijah, Elisha, Samuel, Micaiah ben Imlah, and Nathan, who functioned as prophets before Amos, did not write anything. It was debated whether they originated out of the larger religious world of the Canaanites or whether they were a "distinctively Israelite phenomenon."[2]

The more recent view is that the earliest "writing prophets" are the "classical prophets."[3] Their "words were addressed to the nation as a whole, because the mission of these prophets was to set the life of the people of God in the light of the future God was preparing for them."[4] This idea was fully dependent upon the result of Pentateuchal criticism and the redating of the materials in the Pentateuch. The so-called five Books of Moses were no longer regarded as deriving from Moses but were understood as consisting of a mosaic of ancient sources to which such sigla as J, E, D, and P were attached. The earliest source was held to derive from not earlier than 850 B.C., and the final product of the Pentateuch as we have it now could not be dated to a time earlier than the postexilic period. This laid the groundwork for seeing the prophets of the eighth century as innovators. Based on these revisions and conclusions of the most advanced historical-critical hypotheses,[5] which many assumed to be assured results of scientific research on the

2. See Hans Schmidt, "The Earliest Israelite Prophecy before Amos," in *Twentieth Century Theology in the Making*, vol. 1, *Themes of Biblical Theology*, ed. J. Pelikan (New York: Harper & Row, 1971), 47. Note that Schmidt wrote in 1915.

3. For a discussion of the designation "classical prophecy" in terms of literary, chronological, and content criteria, see Hans Walter Wolff, "Prophecy from the Eighth Through the Fifth Century," in *Interpreting the Prophets*, eds. James Luther Mays and Paul J. Achtemeier (Philadelphia: Fortress, 1987), 14–16.

4. Ibid., 14.

5. See Gerhard F. Hasel, *Biblical Interpretation Today: An Analysis of Modern Methods of Biblical Interpretation* (Washington, D.C.: Biblical Research Institute, 1985), 7–99.

Old Testament, there was believed to be sufficient justifica-
tion for the reassessment of the prophets during this first
phase of historical-critical scholarship.[6]

The cultic interpretation of Amos that began originally
in the 1930s and was continued into the 1950s was dependent on the new methods of modern critical research,
namely, form criticism and tradition criticism. It was soon
challenged by historical-critical scholars who suggested
that Amos' "intellectual home" (*geistige Heimat*) is to be
sought in noncultic, tribal wisdom circles. In 1962 Samuel
Terrien presented evidence from the language of Amos
that showed that "peculiar affinities existed between Amos
and the wise."[7]

Hans Walter Wolff of Heidelberg University published a
monograph on Amos' *geistige Heimat* in which he presented detailed arguments based on form-critical and traditio-historical methods that Amos is not rooted in the cult
at all but in tribal wisdom.[8] He did so by referring to various stylistic devices and the usage of certain terms that he
felt linked Amos clearly with tribal wisdom circles.

The alternative of seeing Amos uniquely rooted in either
the cult or in wisdom did not remain unchallenged. James
Crenshaw, H. J. Hermisson, H. H. Schmid, and others
reacted to Wolff.[9] Crenshaw proposed a theophanic tradi-

6. Ibid., 44–60.
7. Samuel Terrien, "Amos and Wisdom," in *Israel's Prophetic Heritage*, eds. B. W.
Anderson and W. Harrelson (New York: Harper & Row, 1962), 108–15.
8. An English translation of Wolff's *Amos' geistige Heimat* (Neukirchen-Vluyn:
Neukirchener Verlag, 1962) appeared under the title *Amos the Prophet: The Man
and His Background* (Philadelphia: Fortress, 1973).
9. James L. Crenshaw, "The Influence of Wisdom upon Amos," *ZAW* 79
(1967): 42–52; H. J. Hermisson, *Studien zur israelitischen Spruchweisheit* (Neukir-
chen-Vluyn: Neukirchener Verlag, 1968), 88–96; Hans H. Schmid, "Amos. Die
Frage nach der 'geistigen Heimat' des Propheten," *WD* 10 (1969): 85–103; R. N.
Whybray, "Prophecy and Wisdom," in *Israel's Prophetic Traditions*, eds. J. Collins et
al. (Cambridge: Cambridge University Press, 1982), 181–99; Georges Farr, "The
Language of Amos, Popular or Cultic?" *VT* 16 (1966): 324 n. 2; H. J. Stoebe,
"Überlegungen zu den geistlichen Voraussetzungen der Prophetie des Amos,"
*Wort-Gebot-Glaube: Beiträge zur Theologie des Alten Testament. W. Eichrodt zum 80.
Geburtstag*, ed. H. J. Stoebe (Zürich: Ev. Verlag, 1970), 209–25.

tion as the background to Amos.[10] This was independently
the subject of a doctoral dissertation by Manfred Kuntz at
Tübingen, who indicated a connection between theophany
and covenant traditions.[11]

We may speak of a third phase of Amos studies that seeks
to overcome the prior single (cult or wisdom) or double
(theophany and covenant) tradition rootage of Amos. The
much-respected German commentator Wilhelm Rudolph
noted in 1971 that Amos was a wise and knowledgeable
farmer with various connections.[12] This means that the
thought of Amos is hardly sufficiently explained by pointing to a single tradition or rootage, whether cult, wisdom,
theophany, or even a double rootage such as theophany
and covenant. A. S. van der Woude's assessment of the
matter under review is as follows: "Form-critical and traditio-historical studies exhibit a tendency to cast a prophet
almost exclusively in one mold or another. Like all other
men, prophets must have been exposed to many, even
opposing, influences, though nobody would deny that they
could have relied more on one than another."[13]

John Hayes seems to support the multiple connection
notion, saying that "his [Amos'] language and thought are
probably more reflective of the culture at large than of a
particular segment such as the cult or the wisdom circles."[14]

10. James L. Crenshaw, "Amos and the Theophanic Tradition," *ZAW* 80
(1968): 203–15.

11. Manfred Kuntz, *Ein Element der alten Theophanieüberlieferung und seine Rolle
in der Prophetie des Amos* (diss., University of Tübingen, 1968). The connection of
theophany and covenant goes far beyond the study on theophany by Jörg
Jeremias, *Theophany. Die Geschichte einer alttestamentlichen Gattung* (Neukirchen-
Vluyn: Neukirchener Verlag, 1965).

12. W. Rudolph, *Joel-Amos-Obadja-Jona* (Gütersloh: Gerd Mohn/Gütersloher
Verlagshaus, 1971), 99, followed by A. S. van der Woude, "Three Classical
Prophets: Amos, Hosea, and Micah,"in *Israel's Prophetic Tradition: Essays in Honor of
Peter Ackroyd*, eds. R. Coggins et al. (Cambridge: Cambridge University Press,
1982), 38; and D. A. Hubbard, *Joel and Amos: An Introduction and Commentary*
(Leicester: Inter-Varsity, 1989), 96.

13. Van der Woude, "Three Classical Prophets," 38.

14. John H. Hayes, *Amos, His Time and His Preaching: The Eighth Century Prophet*
(Nashville: Abingdon, 1988), 39.

Shalom M. Paul shows that Amos was well acquainted with covenant laws, psalms, and wisdom genres of literature, concluding that "Amos was heir to many variegated literary influences and poetic conventions and formulae, which he employed with creative sophistication to propound and expound his divinely given message."[15] The current trend is to steer away from unilinear backgrounds and connections and to see Amos as drawing on a rich reservoir of Israelite thought that he creatively adapts and transforms to his proclamation.[16] This trend is directly related to the direction of recent research, which holds that most (if not all) of the Book of Amos derives from the historical Amos.

Can Amos be "imprisoned" in ancient traditions? Can he be forced into a "straitjacket" of a singular connection? Is Amos, the prophet of Yahweh, limited to what has gone before? Can he merely adapt, transform, and reinterpret? Should he be allowed also to create something new, using the revelatory "word" that came to him from Yahweh in his prophetic ministry? This is not only a possibility but very likely indeed, if a "close reading" of the text is allowed. It should not be denied that Amos is deeply dependent on the religious heritage of God's people and spokespersons that have gone before him. Amos is rooted in the common stock of his religious heritage. He became the first of a new kind of "writing" prophet, called by God to proclaim fearlessly the divine message to a failing people, in order to arouse them to positive behavior and upright moral action and lifestyle.

15. Shalom M. Paul, *Amos: A Commentary on the Book of Amos* (Minneapolis: Fortress, 1991), 4.
16. So already Arvid S. Kapelrud, "New Ideas in Amos," *VTS* 15 (1965): 193–206, esp. 205–6.

AMOS'
HYMNIC
DOXOLOGIES

In 4:13 we encounter for the first time in the Book of Amos what is called a doxology, hymn, or hymn-fragment. Two other doxologies are encountered (5:8–9; 9:5–6). These three doxologies have been the focus of many studies in this century. The issues regarding them relate to their origin, unity, present position in the book, and *Sitz im Leben*. The debate continues and no consensus has yet been achieved.

Two major monographs were published in the 1970s on these doxological hymns.[1] These two studies provide some insight into the complexity of the debate about these

---

1. Werner Berg, *Die sogenannten Hymnenfragmente im Amosbuch* (Bern/Frankfurt: Peter Lang, 1974); James L. Crenshaw, *Hymnic Affirmation of Divine Justice*, Society of Biblical Literature Dissertation series, 24 (Missoula: Scholars, 1975). Crenshaw published his 1964 dissertation unchanged with the exception of adding an appendix in which he surveys the literature published from 1964 to 1974 without having had access to Berg's study.

alleged hymns aside from another full-fledged investigation of the history of research of these passages in Amos.[2]

There is a general agreement that these three passages
are related. Otherwise opinions are quite divided. Whether
these passages are hymns, hymn-fragments, or hymnic
elements remains a matter of discussion to the present. So
is the matter of dating these texts.

What criteria have been used to ascribe all three passages,
or one of them, to a later editor? Among the major points
are the following (for 4:13): it "(1) does not smoothly flow
from its context; (2) has an elevated theology of God as creator; and (3) uses participles in the title, 'Yahweh, God of
hosts, is his name' which gained popularity after the time of
Amos."[3] Each of these points are argued by scholars. They
suggest that the picture of God in this hymn is different
from that in the rest of the Book of Amos.[4]

Crenshaw is typically cautious as regards the date of the
hymns. He suggests a date in the exilic or early postexilic
period,[5] but admits that the evidence is not decisive. These
doxologies (of judgment) may even antedate Amos.[6] The
latter position is taken by Andersen and Freedman as well.
The latter note that "numerous attempts have been made to
retrieve and reconstruct the original piece. Whether there
was one original source of the quotations in Amos, and
whether it can be recovered with a measure of certainty
that would make the exercise worthwhile, are debatable
questions."[7] Berg concludes that these three hymn-frag-

2. Siegfried Bergler's Th.D. dissertation explores the history of research on the hymn passages with a view to determine the focal point or center of the message of Amos. See *Die hymnischen Passagen und die Mitte des Amosbuches: Ein Forschungsbericht* (Th.D. diss., University of Tübingen, 1979).

3. Gary V. Smith, *Amos: A Commentary* (Grand Rapids: Zondervan, 1989), 140. Smith, it should be noted, supports the authenticity of this hymn.

4. For example, A. S. Kapelrud, *Central Ideas in Amos*, 2d ed. (Oslo: Oslo University Press, 1961), 39.

5. Crenshaw, *Hymnic Affirmations*, 143.

6. Ibid., 143–44 n. 6. Also W. Brueggemann, W. Rudolph, M. O. Boyle, E. Hammershaimb, C. Story, E. V. Smith, and others.

7. Francis I. Andersen and David Noel Freedman, *Amos: A New Translation with Introduction and Commentary* (New York: Doubleday, 1989), 5.

ments can hardly come from the time of Amos or an even earlier time based on the vocabulary employed.[8] Evidently differing criteria are employed for the dating process.

An early dating and Amos' authorship were proposed quite some time ago by J. D. W. Watts.[9] These hypotheses have found more recent support from James L. Mays, although he feels that this hymnic material was inserted by the earliest tradents of the Amos material.[10] Wilhelm Rudolph, Erling Hammershaimb, John H. Hayes, Douglas Stuart, J. Alberto Soggin, and Andersen and Freedman, among others, argue that the hymnic material was used by Amos himself and may derive from an earlier hymn or may be the reworking of earlier hymnic elements.[11]

Thomas E. McComiskey has devoted a careful study to the form-critical methodology employed in the analysis of the hymnic doxologies in the Book of Amos. He notes that the first hymn is explicative in function while the third hymnic doxology is "not conceptually or structurally intrusive and forms an appropriate conclusion to the preceding oracle."[12] The same holds for the second hymnic doxology. McComiskey also discusses the creation theology found in

8. Berg, *Die sogenannten Hymnenfragmente*, 319, states that 5:9 cannot be dated.

9. J. D. W. Watts, "An Old Hymn Preserved in the Book of Amos," *JNES* 15 (1956): 33–39; idem, *Vision and Prophecy in Amos: 1955 Faculty Lectures, Baptist Theological Seminary, Rüschlikon/Zürich, Switzerland* (Leiden: E. J. Brill, 1958), 51–68.

10. J. L. Mays, *Amos: A Commentary* (Philadelphia: Westminster, 1969), 84.

11. W. Rudolph, *Joel-Amos-Obadja-Jona* (Gütersloh: Gerd Mohn/Gütersloher Verlagshaus, 1971), 1181–83; E. Hammershaimb, *The Book of Amos: A Commentary*, trans. J. Sturdy (Oxford: Basil Blackwell, 1970), 133; John H. Hayes, *Amos, His Time and His Preaching: The Eighth Century Prophet* (Nashville: Abingdon, 1988), 150; D. K. Stuart, *Hosea–Jonah* (Waco: Word, 1987), 286; Soggin (*The Prophet Amos* [London: SCM, 1987]) supports 4:13 with "controversial authenticity" (p. 80). "As after 4.12 and 5.7 Amos also adds a doxology at this point, or repeats a traditional one which serves as a proof text for [what, *sic*] he had been arguing" (p. 123); Andersen and Freedman, *Amos*, 42–43, 51–52, 72, 455–57, 486–90, 844–54; Thomas E. McComiskey, "The Hymnic Elements of the Prophecy of Amos: A Study of Form-Critical Methodology," *JETS* 30 (1987): 139–57. This essay was reprinted from *A Tribute to Gleason Archer*, eds. Walter C. Kaiser, Jr., and Ronald F. Youngblood (Chicago: Moody, 1986), 105–28.

12. McComiskey, "Hymnic Elements," 113.

the hymns and suggests that the "idea that Yahweh is the Creator of the universe is consonant with Amos's theology."[13] McComiskey suggests that "the doxologies are poetic representations of theological truth written by Amos himself to give awesome validation to the content of the oracle that precedes each doxology. According to this view, the setting would thus be a literary one."[14]

Thomas J. Finley also emphasizes the literary relationship of the hymns in the Book of Amos. He holds that there is a "tight relationship of these pieces, both poetically and semantically."[15] The first hymn is the "climax to the first 'word' that Amos called the people to hear";[16] the second one comes at the center of the book (here he follows Jan de Waard and William A. Smalley[17]) and "can be viewed as the center of the entire book";[18] the last hymn "climaxes the startling vision of the Lord's judgment against the religious activities of Israel."[19] McComiskey and Finley exemplify those who use an integrative contextual approach based on literary sensitivities and a "close reading" of the text of Amos.

Some scholars have felt that one or another of these hymns or hymn-fragments are misplaced. For example, Andersen and Freedman believe that 5:8–9 fits better at the end of chapter 6.[20] Shalom M. Paul seems to support the hypothesis of a misplacement of the second hymn of 5:8–9 so widely favored by certain commentators. Paul does not suggest where it had its original place in the book.[21] The level of certainty on these issues is tenuous and remains a matter of continuing debate.

13. Ibid., 114.

14. Ibid., 120.

15. Thomas J. Finley, *Joel, Amos, and Obadiah* (Chicago: Moody, 1990), 332.

16. Ibid., 333.

17. Jan de Waard and William A. Smalley, *A Translator's Handbook on the Book of Amos* (New York: United Bible Societies, 1979), 192.

18. Finley, *Joel, Amos, and Obadiah*, 333.

19. Ibid.

20. Andersen and Freedman, *Amos*, 89.

21. Shalom M. Paul, *Amos: A Commentary on the Book of Amos* (Minneapolis: Fortress, 1991), 167.

Another line of research based on the literary structure of 5:1–17 runs counter to the misplacement hypothesis. Jan de Waard has produced an influential study of the chiastic structure of 5:1–17. Amos 5:8–9 is the middle part and thus the hinge, the center as it were, that combines the two panels of 5:1–7 and 5:10–17, each of which is divided into three corresponding sections.[22] De Waard's chiastic literary structure of 5:1–17 is as follows:[23]

A Lament for Israel, 5:1–3
  B Seek God and Live, 5:4–5
    C Warning to Sinners, 5:7
      D The Power of God to Create, 5:8a [hymn]
       E The Lord is his Name, 5:8b [hymn]
      D' The Power of God to Punish, 5:9 [hymn]
    C' Warning to Sinners and Righteous, 5:10–13
  B' Seek Good and Live, 5:14–15
A' Lament for Israel, 5:16–17

De Waard suggests that this chiasm is original to Amos. Furthermore, he argues that the hymn at the center of 5:1–17 is indeed the center of the Book of Amos.

Other scholars who use form-critical and redaction-critical methodologies demur. Soggin states that "while the symmetry and coherence of structures of this kind are always impressive, there is no need for them to go back to the author himself or even to the earliest phase of the redaction."[24] In a similar vein Jörg Jeremias remains unconvinced and suggests that "a new ordering of Amos's speeches has taken place also in chapter 5 is not so certain but still quite probable . . . and 5:1–17 thus shows that the exilic edition of the book of Amos did not merely add explanatory notes to a previous text but, at the very least,

22. J. de Waard, "The Chiastic Structure of Amos V 1–17," *VT* 27 (1977): 170–77. Similar conclusions were reached independently by N. J. Tromp in his stylistic and rhetorical analysis of the same chapter. See his "Amos V 1–17: Toward a Stylistic and Rhetorical Analysis," *OTS* 33 (1984): 56–84.

23. Taken from de Waard and Smalley, *Translator's Handbook*, 192.

24. Soggin, *Amos*, 81.

rearranged a few passages in order to show an unrepentant Israel that praise of the judging and punishing God is its principal task (cf. 1 Kings 8:33ff.)."[25] Jeremias thus holds tenaciously to the traditio-historical and redactional theory that the hymn(-fragment) is a later insertion by a redactor who skillfully wove it into a previous chiasm.

The decisions regarding authenticity diverge among scholars of different schools of thought. Should we assume that an exilic editor was the master literary craftsman who put this hymn where it is located and finally put the book in the shape it is today?[26] Form critics, tradition critics, and redaction critics believe that this is the case and support this hypothesis. Others raise the question of whether it could have been the prophet himself who placed these pieces where they are. The latter scholars provide evidence from internal criteria for their position. James Crenshaw states in his epilogue to his carefully argued form-critical dissertation on the Amos doxologies that "in a sense we find ourselves trapped in a vicious circle. We date texts on the basis of our understanding of the development of Israel's language, literature and thought, and we arrive at that understanding by means of the very texts we seek to date."[27] This forthright admission of circular reasoning involved in the dating process of prophetic materials reveals that there is a distinct need to develop more objective criteria for making important decisions on both dating and the production of the final form of the text.

The study of literary form, rhetorical design, stylistic purpose, structural shape, and other forms of literary study are at the cutting edge of Amos studies today. These

25. Jörg Jeremias, "Amos 3–6: From the Oral Word to the Text," in *Canon, Theology, and Old Testament Interpretation: Essays in Honor of Brevard S. Childs*, eds. G. M. Tucker, D. L. Peterson, and R. R. Wilson (Philadelphia: Fortress, 1988), 220–21; idem, "Amos 3–6. Beobachtungen zur Entstehungsgeschichte eines Prophetenbuches," *ZAWSuppl* 100 (1988): 105. The former is a translation of the latter with small changes of content.

26. Jeremias, "Amos 3–6," 217–29.

27. Crenshaw, *Hymnic Affirmations*, 154.

will be of continuing interest and significance in the future. They have called into question a number of results of earlier phases of literary criticism of the diachronic methods that once seemed rather assured. A "close reading" of the biblical text seems to keep the individual text within the larger internal context and allows it to function as a control for other reconstructed contexts, whether sociological or other.

How do these passages function in the Book of Amos? What contribution do they make to the message of the book as a whole? The theological contribution these doxologies of Amos make is immense. They affirm that Yahweh is the all-powerful Creator who is above any might or power from any source, human or other. Yahweh is the only and unique Protector.

9

AMOS' COMPOSITION
AND
LITERARY APPROACHES

In recent times the matter of the composition of the Book of Amos has received increased attention. The most recent trend in the study of Amos attempts to investigate the internal structures of the book's composition. In addition there are a variety of literary approaches that are applied to the book in the form in which it is preserved in the Hebrew Bible. These new approaches are in radical contrast to the former literary-critical investigations of the Book of Amos. It seems most helpful for us to describe the stage of research before the newest composition and literary studies have commenced in order to depict adequately and fairly the two divergent approaches.[1]

In 1969 Hans Walter Wolff published his magisterial

---

1. Here major emphasis is to be given to the studies of Klaus Koch, *Amos. Untersucht mit den Methoden einer strukturalen Formgeschichte*, 3 vols. (Neukirchen-Vluyn/Kevalaer: Neukirchener Verlag/Butzon & Bercker, 1976); C. Coulot, "Propositions pour une structuration du livre d'Amos au niveau rédactionnel," *RSR* 51 (1977): 169–86; A. van der Wal, "The Structure of Amos," *JSOT* 26 (1983): 107–13.

commentary on Amos in the Biblischer Kommentar Altes Testament series. It was a masterpiece of form-critical and traditio-historical study. It was translated into English in 1977. Wolff does not see the composition of the Book of Amos as a gradual enlargement of a collection of Amos-words in a supplementation process, but "more as the over-laying of one stage of redaction upon another."[2]

Wolff sees six levels in the formation of the Book of Amos.[3] The first level is designated "The words of Amos of Tekoa" and is largely found in chapters 3 to 6. The second one is called "The literary fixation of the cycles" and is derived from Amos in the groups of the vision reports of 7:1–8; 8:1–2; 9:1–4; and the oracles against the nations (1:3–2:16, excluding the Tyre, Edom, and Judah oracles). The third level consists of "The old school of Amos" which functioned for two or three decades after the prophet's death. This redactional and compositional activity includes 7:10–17; 8:4–14; 9:7–10; 5:13–15; 6:2; and 7:13 and incorporates some genuine Amos sayings. The old school of Amos is responsible for combining both of the earlier collections respectively before and after chapters 3 to 6. It added a phrase to the superscription ("which he saw two years before the earth-quake"), reworked some of the older tradition, and reapplied the original words of Amos. The fourth level is "The Bethel-exposition of the Josianic age" (a pre-Deuteronomistic redac-tion occasioned by Josiah's destruction of the temple in Bethel); it included the hymn-fragments of 4:13; 5:8–9; and 9:5–6, and inserted 3:14ba and 5:6. Amos 4:6–12, 13 is a reinterpretation. This redaction made a few other changes. Then comes the fifth level, "The Deuteronomistic redaction" (Wolff here reflects the influence of Werner H. Schmidt[4]),

2. W. Eugene March, "Redaction Criticism and the Formation of Prophetic Books," in *Society of Biblical Literature 1977 Seminar Papers*, ed. Paul J. Achtemeier (Missoula: Scholars, 1977), 91.

3. H. W. Wolff, *Joel and Amos: A Commentary on the Books of the Prophets Joel and Amos* (Philadelphia: Fortress, 1977), 106–13.

4. Werner H. Schmidt, "Die deuteronomistische Redaktion des Amosbuches. Zu den theologischen Unterschieden zwischen dem Prophetenwort und seinem Sammler," *ZAW* 77 (1965): 168–93.

which inserted the oracles of Tyre, Edom, and Judah. Amos 2:10–12 is reworked and words are added. Amos 5:25; 3:1b; and 8:11–12 are added. The words "who was among the shepherds" in 1:1 is added along with the names of the kings. The final level consists of "The postexilic eschatology of salvation," a redactional activity that adds, finally, 9:11–15 and the expression "like David" in 6:5.

J. Alberto Soggin and J. Vermeylen more or less follow Wolff.[5] Robert Coote, writing on the composition and theology of Amos, attempts to schematize and simplify Wolff's six-stage composition into three stages. Coote's stage A is made up of words of Amos himself; stage B, entitled "Justice and the Scribe," reactualizes the words of Amos in the seventh century; and stage C is said to include materials from the exile and beyond. Coote is recently followed by William J. Doorly.[7]

Wolff's approach has been evaluated from various quarters. Wilhelm Rudolph takes exception to Wolff's traditio-historical method and its conclusions.[8] Roy F. Melugin critiques Wolff's hypothesis by showing how difficult it is to engage in the reconstruction of the six layers: "Indeed, anyone who studies the formation of the Book of Amos must ask to what extent such a reconstruction is even possible."[9] Then he raises an issue that anticipates more recent developments:

5. J. A. Soggin, *The Prophet Amos* (London: SCM, 1987), 17–18; J. Vermeylen, *Du prophète Isaïe à l'apocalyptique* (Paris: Gabalda, 1978), 2:519–69.

6. Robert B. Coote, *Amos among the Prophets: Composition and Theology* (Philadelphia: Fortress, 1981).

7. William J. Doorly, *Prophet of Justice: Understanding the Book of Amos* (New York/Mahwah, N.J.: Paulist, 1989).

8. W. Rudolph, *Joel-Amos-Obadja-Jona* (Gütersloh: Gerd Mohn/Gütersloher Verlagshaus, 1971), 100–103.

9. Roy F. Melugin, "The Formation of Amos: An Analysis of Exegetical Method," *Society of Biblical Literature 1978 Seminar Papers*, ed. Paul J. Achtemeier (Missoula: Scholars, 1978), 1:375. John Bright ("A New View of Amos," *Int* 25 [1971]: 357) raises similar questions: "But do the tools at our disposal allow us anything like the precision in describing this process that we find here? In so small a book as Amos do we have a broad enough field of evidence to entitle us to say that this stylistic trait, this line of thought, this formal characteristic, could not have been employed by the prophet, but must be assigned to some later stratum of the tradition?"

"Another important limitation of Wolff's study in the formation of the Book of Amos is his lack of attention to the structure and meaning of the book in the final form."[10]

Klaus Koch and his team at the University of Hamburg completed a study in 1976 based on what the team designated a "structural-form-critical" approach, which they published in three volumes. Koch and his team members believe that a synchronic analysis has precedence over a diachronic one and are thus more sensitive to the matter of the composition of the book.[11] Koch proposes four stages or sections: 1–2; 3–4; 5:1–9:6; and 9:7–15. Koch's work is vulnerable to literary studies that show larger connections than are allowed in his methodology.[12]

H. Gese maintains that in the Book of Amos there is a five-part structure that shows a three-tiered level. This type of composition is used in gradation form, where the last level or step reaches the climax and goal of the whole.[13]

Redaction-critical studies of the Book of Amos as surveyed above have shown rather divergent results. Scholars have argued for three, four, five, six, and eight stages[14] or levels of composition/redaction. Should one assume with redaction-critics that the Book of Amos grew "like a snowball rolling downhill" in the words of Stanley Rosenbaum?[15] Contrary to these studies more recent literary studies reveal larger connections than redaction-critical studies allow.[16]

More recently James Limburg has detected in the Book of Amos a recurring structure of seven-plus-one. This sequence is present in 1:3–2:16; 3:3–8; 4:4–5; 4:6–12; 5:21–14; 6:4–6;

10. Ibid.

11. Koch, *Amos*, 1:9. While we cannot present the details of their approach here, Melugin ("Formation of Amos," 375–85) has provided an excellent survey and summary.

12. See the studies by J. de Waard referred to by Tromp and noted by A. G. Auld, *Amos* (Sheffield: JSOT, 1986), 57.

13. H. Gese, "Komposition bei Amos," *VTS* 32 (1981): 75–95.

14. Susamu Jozaki, "The Secondary Passages of the Book of Amos," *Kwansei Gakuin University Annual Studies* 4 (1956): 25–100.

15. Stanley N. Rosenbaum, *Amos of Israel: A New Interpretation* (Macon, Ga.: Mercer University Press, 1990), 72.

16. See below, nn. 25–29, 38–39.

and 9:1–4. In addition there are groupings of seven, such as in 2:6–8; 2:14–16; 5:8–9; and possibly, 8:4–6. These intentional groupings have been arranged for stylistic reasons. In addition there are forty-nine (7 x 7) divine speech formulas in Amos. "These formulas occur in such a way that there are seven or, in one case, fourteen of them in each major section of the book."[17] Limburg notes that these structures explain why no speech formulas are added to the oracles against Tyre, Edom, and Judah. This could mean that the whole sequence comes from Amos himself, who in his genuine sayings manifests this sevenfold structure.

Evidently the compositional picture of Amos in current scholarship is anything but unified. "This is the more remarkable since the book of Amos cannot be considered to be one of the most difficult writings of the minor prophets, from a literary point of view."[18] John H. Hayes affirms that "it is easier to assume either that Amos wrote his own words, whether before or after delivering them or, more likely, that they were written down by someone in the audience, than it is to believe in the existence of a circle of disciples or an old school of Amos, for which there is no evidence whatever."[19]

Andersen and Freedman argue for "the cumulative demonstration of the *literary coherence* of all the diverse ingredients in the whole assemblage [of the Book of Amos], which is more than an assemblage; it is a highly structured unity."[20] Accordingly they see the structure of the entire book in four parts: The Book of Doom (1:1–4:13); The Book of Woes (5:1–6:14); The Book of Visions (7:1–9:6); and the Epilogue (9:7–15).[21]

17. James Limburg, "Sevenfold Structures in the Book of Amos," *JBL* 106 (1987): 217–22; citation is from p. 221.

18. A. S. van der Woude, "Three Classical Prophets: Amos, Hosea, and Micah," in *Israel's Prophetic Tradition: Essays in Honor of Peter Ackroyd*, eds. R. Coggins et al. (Cambridge: Cambridge University Press, 1982), 42.

19. John H. Hayes, *Amos, His Time and His Preaching: The Eighth Century Prophet* (Nashville: Abingdon, 1988), 38.

20. Francis I. Andersen and David Noel Freedman, *Amos: A New Translation with Introduction and Commentary* (New York: Doubleday, 1989), 144.

21. Ibid., 23–72.

Douglas Stuart sees a threefold structure, if one considers 1:1 as the barest sort of introduction: first group of oracles (1:2–6:14); visions, with related narrative (7:1–8:3); and final group of oracles (8:4–9:15).[22] A similar threefold structure is presented by Gary V. Smith: judgments on the nations (1:1–2:14); the verification of God's warnings of punishment on Samaria (3:1–6:14); and visions and exhortations of the end (7:1–9:15).[23] David A. Hubbard has proposed essentially the same structure as Smith with the exception that he divides the introduction of 1:1–2 and the salvation promise of 9:11–15 into separate sections.[24] Adrian van der Wal divides Amos into two major sections, 1–6 and 7–9.[25]

It is evident that complex compositional processes stretching over several centuries are called into question by a number of recent literary studies. "Almost all of the arguments for later interpolations and redactions, including a Deuteronomistic one, are shown to be based on fragile foundations and inconclusive evidence. When each case is examined and analyzed on its own, without preconceived conjectures and unsupported hypotheses, the book in its entirety (with one or two minor exceptions) can be reclaimed for its rightful author, the prophet Amos," concludes Shalom M. Paul.[26] In the previous chapter we referred to the literary studies by J. de Waard, J. Lust, and N. J. Tromp. To these have to be added those of W. A. Smalley, J. de Waard/W. A. Smalley, R. Gordis, Y. Gitay, and A. van der Wal,[27] to men-

22. D. K. Stuart, *Hosea–Jonah* (Waco: Word, 1987), 287.

23. G. V. Smith, *Amos: A Commentary* (Grand Rapids: Zondervan, 1989), 7–9.

24. D. A. Hubbard, *Joel and Amos: An Introduction and Commentary* (Leicester: Inter-Varsity, 1989), 118–19.

25. A. van der Wal, "The Structure of Amos," *JSOT* 26 (1983): 107–13.

26. Shalom M. Paul, *Amos: A Commentary on the Book of Amos* (Minneapolis: Fortress, 1991), 6.

27. W. A. Smalley, "Recursion Patterns and the Sectioning of Amos," *BT* 30 (1979): 118–27; Jan de Waard and William A. Smalley, *A Translator's Handbook on the Book of Amos* (New York: United Bible Society, 1980), 189–214, contains detailed discussions on the structures of 5:1–17 and shows three balanced parts for the entire book of Amos (1:1–5:3; 5:4–15; 5:16–9:15); R. Gordis, "The Composition and Structure of Amos," in *Prophets and Sages: Essays in Biblical Interpretation* (Bloomington: Indiana University Press, 1971), 217–29; Y. Gitay, "A Study of Amos's Art Speech: A Rhetorical Analysis of Amos 3:1–15," *CBQ* 42 (1980): 239–409; van der Wal, "Structure of Amos," 107–13.

tion only a few of the studies using discourse analysis or various literary approaches.[28] The various investigations by Gerhard Pfeifer, who uses the method of "thought form analysis," are also to be reckoned with.[29]

In short, these recent literary studies based on various systems of literary approaches reveal a new trend in Amos studies. It cannot be concluded that they have settled the complex question of the literary structure of the Book of Amos in all its details to the satisfaction of everyone, but they have opened up totally new vistas with significant implications for the compositional activity of Amos himself. John H. Hayes calls his approach to the Book of Amos "a close reading of the text in light of the historical events as reconstructed from all available sources."[30]

The Andersen and Freedman approach may also be considered to belong to these new literary approaches to the biblical text. The authors themselves do not use a designation such as "close reading" or the like, but state, "we now concentrate on the text itself. By this we mean the traditional Masoretic text, not a revised form of the text produced by modern scholars, which is more commonly used in contemporary translations. . . . We are interested in look-

---

28. Among other studies in the area of the literary structure or literary study of Amos are C. Coulot, "Propositions pour une structuration du livre d'Amos au niveau rédactionnel," *RSR* 51 (1977): 169–86; A. Spreafico, "Amos: structura formale e spunti per una interpretazione," *RivB* 29/2 (1981): 147–76; Z. Weisman, "Stylistic Parallels in Amos and Jeremiah: Their Implications for the Composition of Amos," *Shnaton* 1 (1975): 129–49; Shalom M. Paul, "Amos 3:3–8: The Irresistible Sequence of Cause and Effect," *HAR* 7 (1983): 203–20; C. Westermann, "Amos 5,4–6.14.15: Ihr Werdet Leben!" in *Erträge der Forschung. Gesammelte Studien III*, ed. R. Albertz (München: Kaiser, 1984), 107–18; Duane A. Garrett, "The Structure of Amos as a Testimony to Its Integrity," *JETS* 27 (1984): 275–76.

29. G. Pfeifer, "Denkformenanalyse als Aufgabe der Hermeneutik," in *Disciplina Domini. Thüringer kirchliche Studien* 1 (1963): 278–80; idem, "Denkformenanalyse als exegetische Methode, erläutert an Amos 1:2–2:16," *ZAW* 88 (1976): 51–76; idem, "Unausweichliche Konsequenzen: Denkformenanalyse von Amos III 3–8," *VT* 33 (1983): 341–47; idem, "Die Ausweisung eines lästigen Ausländers, Amos 7, 10–17," *ZAW* 96 (1984): 112–18; idem, "Die Denkform des Propheten Amos (III 9–11)," *VT* 34 (1984): 476–80; idem, "'Rettung' als Beweis der Vernichtung (Amos 3.12)," *ZAW* 100 (1988): 269–77.

30. Hayes, *Amos*, 38.

ing once more at the available text of the Book of Amos. We are more concerned with its literary form as a finished, though not necessarily perfect, product."[31] Quite contrary to the late dating of 5:14–15 as in the case of Werner H. Schmidt, Hans Walter Wolff, and others, Andersen and Freedman argue on the basis of the "structural unity of the completed book"[32] that these verses form "the center of the book."[33] The arrangement of the book as it stands "is literary, not chronological. It presents an artistic schema, not a chain of cause and effect."[34]

Stanley N. Rosenbaum works on the basis of "a guiding assumption" that holds "that there is nothing in the Book of Amos the original Amos could not have written." This does not mean, however, that "nothing in Amos differs from what the prophet himself first uttered."[35] He believes that the alleged Deuteronomistic redaction cannot be sustained, because "Amos's consistent use of many speech forms points . . . to the authenticity of precisely those pieces that look most intrusive."[36] Having considered the problems, he concludes that the "underlying structure based on clusters of seven (or five) things, the use and reuse of vocabulary, especially in 3:8 and 6:1–10, the extensive literary framework that connects chapter 9 with chapter 1, and the many wordplays that dot the text all point to a single author of considerable skill."[37]

Various recent literary studies of Amos claim explicitly that the literary approach has methodological priority "over historical investigation, the aesthetic wholeness of the text [has priority] over its hypothetical evolution."[38] The issue before us is the perpetual problem of our time, namely,

31. Andersen and Freedman, *Amos*, 3.
32. Ibid., 5.
33. Ibid., 6.
34. Ibid., 8–9.
35. Rosenbaum, *Amos of Israel*, 73.
36. Ibid., 75.
37. Ibid., 84.
38. Francis Landy, "Vision and Prophetic Speech in Amos," *HAR* 11 (1987): 223.

whether the diachronic approach of the past or the synchronic approach used more widely at present has priority. One recent author puts it this way: "There is, to be sure, an education to be had in the study and reading of historical-critical redactions of the book of Amos. . . . The modern reader must simply decide by whom it is that he or she wishes to be educated"[39]—the historical-critical or the literary-critical reading. Are the two approaches diametrically opposed to each other? These scholars seem to think so. Can there be an integration? Will scholars have to choose one approach and leave the other aside? These and related questions call for serious consideration and penetrating methodological clarification. So far there has been no successful integration. The commentaries of Hayes, Andersen and Freedman, and Paul, aside from others, and the investigations of Rosenbaum, Limburg, de Waard, Smalley, Gitay, and others, each in their own way, seem to make it clear that the synchronic approach has priority in modern scholarship. The diachronic approach will continue to attract some scholars, but it is no longer at the cutting edge of research.

39. Lyle Eslinger, "The Education of Amos," *HAR* 11 (1987): 55.

10

AMOS'
SOCIAL
CRITICISM

When we describe Amos as a prophet of social justice, we put our finger on the principal . . . theme of his arraignment," states Werner H. Schmidt.[1] There is a rich body of literature that concerns itself with the social criticism of Amos. The interest that sparks this concern in our time is, on the one hand, rooted in the thought of Ernst Bloch, the well-known Marxist philosopher of hope.[2] On the other hand, impetus has been given through the various theologies of liberation that have been developed over the last decades on various continents and their usage of biblical themes.[3]

1. Werner H. Schmidt, *Old Testament Introduction* (New York: Crossroad, 1984), 199.
2. S. Holm-Nielsen, "Die Sozialkritik der Propheten," *Denkender Glaube. Festschrift Carl Heinz Ratschow*, ed. Otto Kaiser (Berlin/New York: W. de Gruyter, 1976), 8 n. 1.
3. See the comprehensive overview by Arthur F. McGovern, *Liberation Theology and Its Critics: Toward an Assessment* (Maryknoll, N.Y.: Orbis, 1989); Norbert F. Lohfink, *Options for the Poor: The Basic Principles of Liberation Theology in the Light of*

101

Among the major passages in the Book of Amos that reappear in discussions of the prophet's social criticism are 2:6–8; 3:9–15; 4:1–3, 4–5; 5:4–6, 7, 10–13, 14–15, 21–27; 6:1–8, 11–12; and 8:4–7. Amos addresses exploitation and suppression, such as forfeiture (2:8a) and tribute gathering (2:8b), extracting levies and taxes (5:11), selling the righteous and the poor into feudal slavery (2:6), economic cheating and striving for unreasonable profit (8:5–6), immoral sexual behavior (2:7), corrupt court systems (5:7, 10), bribery (5:12), the amassing of wealth (3:10–12, 15; 6:4), and the enjoyment of a life of luxury (4:1; 6:4–7) at the expense of the exploited classes. This destruction of the structures of Israelite society breaks the šālôm with God and among men.

Is this social criticism a side-product of Amos' prophetic proclamation? This was the thrust of studies in the 1950s. Or is this social criticism the key to the message of Amos? The latter was the general direction of scholarship in the 1980s. It is suggested that Amos is a "revolutionary," a "preacher of social reform."[4] Amos is understood to condemn wealth in principle and support an egalitarian (Marxist) society.[5] Is Amos a forerunner of modern socialism?

James L. Mays concludes that "the wealth he [Amos] denounces was specifically the result of oppression of the poor and corruption of the court."[6] Herbert B. Huffmon notes, in a similar vein, that "an important aspect of the potential social role of Amos' message is that he does not condemn wealth in principle. Instead, the issues are how one acquires wealth and how one uses it."[7] In other words,

---

the Bible, ed. D. L. Christensen (Berkeley: Berkeley Institute of the Bible, Archaeology and Law, 1986); J. R. Donahue, "Biblical Perspective on Justice," in The Faith That Does Justice, ed. John C. Haughey (New York: Paulist, 1977).

4. J. G. Bailey, "Amos: Preacher of Social Reform," TBT 19 (1981): 306.

5. Holm-Nielsen, "Die Sozialkritik der Propheten," 8 n. 1 notes that Ernst Bloch speaks of an original communist memory that is present in the Israelite prophets down to John the Baptist.

6. J. L. Mays, Amos: A Commentary (Philadelphia: Westminster, 1969), 11.

7. H. B. Huffmon, "The Social Role of Amos' Message," in The Quest for the Kingdom of God: Studies in Honor of G. E. Mendenhall, eds. H. B. Huffmon et al. (Winona Lake, Ind.: Eisenbrauns, 1983), 114.

Amos is not condemning wealth in principle and does not lift up poverty as the ideal.

Although the poor are powerless and exploited by those in power, Amos does not proclaim salvation for them. They will not escape judgment. There is no future bliss for the exploited martyr. In fact, the guilt of the exploiter is increased because the exploited *saddîq* suffers the judgment along with the guilty.

What is the root of Amos' social message? Amos 3:2 has been seen as reflecting a "covenant-election tradition"[8] according to which Israel is under even greater obligation as God's special people. It is maintained that these accusations "correspond in most cases with stipulations of the so-called Covenant Code (Ex. 20:23–23:19) and therefore cohere in an ideal of a society willed by God to be just and righteous."[9] Svend Holm-Nielsen makes the terms *sedeq* and *mishpaṭ* the starting point of the social proclamation of the prophets.[10] Both terms are rooted in the covenant tradition.[11] Klaus Koch argues (contrary to much scholarly opinion) that the social criticism of Amos "is connected with a religious attitude to the land."[12] The gift of the land was celebrated in the cultic festivals at Gilgal and Bethel in memory of Yahweh's promise "to the patriarchs in the days of old, implementing his promise through the events of salvation history."[13] It should not entirely escape our attention that the land promise to the patriarchs is also connected to the covenant.

Reinhold Bohlen gives basic support to the thesis of Koch without buying fully into the cultic linkage. He says that the root of Amos' social criticism is provided in the land given to each Israelite family. Along with the land come certain ideals: *mishpaṭ* ("justice") and *sedeqah* ("righteous-

8. Ibid.

9. Joseph Blenkinsopp, *A History of Prophecy in Israel* (Philadelphia: Westminster, 1983), 96.

10. Holm-Nielsen, "Die Sozialkritik der Propheten," 13.

11. Ibid., 20–22.

12. Klaus Koch, *The Prophets*, 2 vols. (Philadelphia: Fortress, 1983–84), 1:50.

13. Ibid., 1:55–56.

ness"). The latter is "community faithfulness" (*Gemeinschaft-streue*) and *mishpat* is "institutional order" (*institutionelle Ordnung*). The possession of the land within a system of social order that corresponds to the will of God is to be based on *mishpat* within which one functions with community faithfulness.[14]

At present the roots of Amos' social criticism seem to include: (1) covenant-election traditions; (2) the land promise tradition; (3) the orders of *mishpat* and *sedeqah* in connection with the land promise traditions[15] and the cult; and (4) God's charismatic empowerment of the prophet.[16]

Along the last line Milton Schwantes suggests in his recent study of the poor in the Old Testament that they have Yahweh as their champion.[17] The picture that seems to emerge is that Amos was not a social revolutionary on humanitarian grounds. He cannot be aligned in a direct way with modern culturally oriented social criticism. Amos cannot be appropriated for a Marxist order of society. He lifts up "his voice not as champion of the oppressed, but as defender of the cause of Yahweh."[18] Amos thus speaks for those who are in need of liberation from oppression. He does so in the name of true Yahwism.

14. R. Bohlen, "Zur Sozialkritik des Propheten Amos," *TTZ* 95 (1986): 298; supported by G. Wanke, "Zu Grundlagen und Absicht prophetischer Sozialkritik," *KD* 18 (1972): 13.

15. See also James L. Mays, "Justice: Perspectives from the Prophetic Tradition," in *Prophecy in Israel: Search for and Identity*, ed. David L. Petersen (Philadelphia: Fortress; London: SPCK, 1986), 144–58.

16. Huffmon, "Social Role of Amos' Message," 114.

17. Milton Schwantes, *Das Recht der Armen* (Frankfurt am Main: Peter Lang, 1977), 87–98.

18. Bohlen, "Zur Sozialkritik der Propheten Amos," 297; in a similar vein, Holm-Nielsen, "Die Sozialkritik der Propheten," 22–23.

11

AMOS' FUTURE HOPE AND ESCHATOLOGY

Amos and the Alleged "Absolute No"

One of the most hotly contested issues, perhaps even the most difficult problem of the entire Book of Amos, is the assessment of Amos' message about the future. Does Amos have a message that contains a future for Israel—or even an entity of Israel? Do his words contain an eschatology, or one or more aspects of eschatology?

There are two foundational considerations that seem to be undeniable. The first relates to the fact that the Book of Amos in its canonical form contains messages that clearly hold out a future, if not for Israel as a whole, then at least for a "remnant of Joseph" (5:15). Whether this future hope is eschatological in nature depends to a large degree, but by no means entirely, upon the definition of eschatology. For our purpose it may suffice to say that we follow a broad definition of eschatology in the sense of an end of the present world order that can be either within the flow of history or in an absolute and final sense at the end of all history.[1]

The second foundational consideration involves a recognition that the Book of Amos contains the radical announcement, "The end has come for my people Israel" (8:2). This prophecy of doom is defined by Rudolf Smend as an "absolute No regarding the future existence of the nation."[2] Scholars who take this "No" as unconditional in nature, absolute in intention, and total in comprehensiveness have assigned passages that hold out a "perhaps" (e.g., 5:15), or a possibility of repentance, or a future of some sort, as the work of a later editor/redactor or later editors/redactors who seek to soften the absolute message of judgment with a sure end to the nation of Israel in its entirety.[3]

---

1. On the definition of eschatology, see W. Vollborn, *Innerzeitliche oder endzeitliche Gerichtserwartung: Ein Beitrag zu Amos und Jesaja* (Kiel, 1938); J. Lindblom, "Gibt es eine Eschatologie bei den alttestamentlichen Propheten?" *StTh* 6 (1952): 79–114; Th. C. Vriezen, "Prophecy and Eschatology," *VTS* 1 (1953): 199–219; E. Rohland, *Die Bedeutung der Erwählungstraditionen Israels für die Eschatologie der alttestamentlichen Propheten* (Th.D. diss., University of Heidelberg, 1956); H.-J. Grönbaek, "Zur Frage der Eschatologie in der Verkündigung der Gerichtspropheten," *SEÅ* 24 (1959): 5–21; S. Mowinckel, *He That Cometh* (New York/Nashville: Abingdon, 1959), 149–55; G. von Rad, *Old Testament Theology* (Edinburgh/London: Oliver & Boyd, 1965), 2:114–19; R. E. Clements, *Prophecy and Covenant* (Napierville, Ill.: Allenson, 1965), 103–12: "We may, therefore, adopt a broad definition of biblical eschatology which renders it suitable to describe the biblical ideas of God's purpose in history. Eschatology is the study of ideas and beliefs concerning the end of the present world order, and the introduction of the new order" (p. 105); H. D. Preuss, *Jahweglaube und Zukunftserwartung* (Stuttgart: Kohlhammer, 1968), 208–14; H.-P. Müller, *Ursprünge und Strukturen alttestamentlicher Eschatologie* (Berlin: W. de Gruyter, 1969), 1–11; J. M. P. van der Ploeg, "Eschatology in the Old Testament," *OTS* 17 (1972): 89–99; G. Habets, "Eschatologie–Eschatologisches," in *Bausteine biblischer Theologie. Festgabe für G. Johannes Botterweck zum 60. Geburtstag dargebracht von seinen Schülern*, ed. H.-J. Fabry (Köln/Bonn: Peter Hanstein, 1977), 351–69, and others. Among those who follow a broader definition of eschatology are Vollborn, Vriezen, Lindblom, von Rad, Rohland, Clements, Müller, and Preuss.

2. Rudolph Smend, "Das Nein des Amos," *EvTh* 23 (1963): 415.

3. For example, H. W. Wolff, *Joel and Amos* (Philadelphia: Fortress, 1977), 231–34; and A. Weiser, *Die Profetie des Amos* (Giessen: Töpelmann, 1929), 191–92. Similarly J. Lust, "Remarks on the Redaction of Amos V 4–6, 14–15," *OTS* 21 (1981): 141–56; and Robert C. Carroll, *When Prophecy Failed: Cognitive Dissonance in the Prophetic Traditions of the Old Testament* (New York: Seabury, 1979), 24–29.

As we shall see a number of scholars have followed Smend's conclusion: "Amos speaks the No of God, not the Yes of God, he announces wrath and not grace."[4] Smend argues that Amos says No to Israel's social relations, to her understanding of history, to her election and cultus. Consequently, Amos says No to the entire existence of Israel as a whole. In this view Amos is made out to be a consistent prophet of doom with no hope whatsoever.

It is important to consider the nature of "the day of the Lord" (5:18–20), the idea of the remnant, and the future hope preserved in the conclusion of the book (9:11–15) with a view to elucidate, if possible, Amos' No and Amos' future hope and eschatology. While there are numerous scholars who have denied any eschatological message for Amos of Tekoa and have thus maintained the No of Smend without leaving in the message of Amos "any ray of hope,"[5] there are recent voices who claim that "Amos never unequivocally proclaimed the total destruction and end of the people."[6] Klaus Koch puts it this way: "Amos certainly proclaims unconditional disaster, but he does not proclaim it wholesale."[7] Georg Fohrer maintains that Amos continued to hold out that repentance was possible and that it was part of Amos' proclamation to keep the door of salvation open.[8]

---

4. Smend, "Das Nein des Amos," 423.

5. Werner H. Schmidt, *Old Testament Introduction* (New York: Crossroad, 1984), 199. Carroll (*When Prophecy Failed*, 25) is forced to claim that "in Amos the remnant motif is purely a negative one," without preventing Amos from having some hope. But it is not really significant. Carroll can hold this view only because he understands that the prophets were not thinkers: "Of course the prophets were not thinkers so neither articulation nor consistency should be demanded of their oracles" (p. 25). Based on this understanding of the Israelite prophets Carroll's critical scalpel cuts through the prophetic texts with such precision that there is a consistency of doom when he is finished. Is this, however, not a consistency of Carroll's own making? The texts themselves in their canonical form lead in other directions.

6. John H. Hayes, *Amos, His Time and His Preaching: The Eighth Century Prophet* (Nashville: Abingdon, 1988), 39; Willem A. Van Gemeren, *Interpreting the Prophetic Word* (Grand Rapids: Zondervan, 1990), 127–37.

7. Klaus Koch, *The Prophets: The Assyrian Period* (Philadelphia: Fortress, 1983), 70.

8. Georg Fohrer, *Die Propheten des 8. Jahrhunderts* (Gütersloh: Gütersloher Verlagshaus, 1974), 50.

Is there an absolute No regarding the future of Israel? Scholars disagree on this point. Their disagreement is not based on the text in its canonical form but on the text as reconstructed in its various redactional stages. There is no doubt in the mind of modern investigators, regardless of the scholarly tradition or school of thought they belong to, that the Book of Amos in its present form contains both a message of doom and destruction for Israel and also a message of future hope and salvation. The major issue is whether this dual focus is part of the message of Amos of Tekoa or the invention of a so-called later school of Amos. The form-critical and redaction-critical methods as exemplified by Hans Walter Wolff and those who follow him[9] claim that the text is constantly updated, constantly reactualized in reaction to specific historical events.

The "canonical approach" of Brevard Childs, while opposed to the one exemplified by Wolff and followers, also understands the text of Amos as having undergone extensive expansions.[10] But the expansion and redaction are not the result of historical circumstances; they are rather the result of theological forces. "The editors arranged the material by the use of editorial commentary, hymnic doxologies, and eschatological expansions to confront the hearer with the eternal God, the Creator and Redeemer of Israel, who was a living and active force both in the past, present, and future."[11] Both Wolff's redaction-critical method and Childs' "canonical approach" agree on redactional activities in the Book of Amos but with different forces at work. Both agree that there is eschatological expansion. There is still no agreement as to when it took place, how much of it there was, and why only later editors/redactors needed to engage in such activities.

Did not the prophet Amos plead with those whom he

9. Among those who could be mentioned are Willi-Plein, Markert, Vermeylen, Coote, Gese, Soggin, and Fritz.

10. Brevard S. Childs, *Introduction to the Old Testament as Scripture* (Philadelphia: Fortress, 1979), 395–410.

11. Ibid., 410.

addressed to "seek" God that they might live (5:4, 14)? Was it not possible for Israel, or at least some of Israel, to repent? Could they not return to their God and avoid the announced disaster? It appears that repentance was not just a rhetorical device. It must have been a reality for those who heard and heeded what God said.

Amos and "the Day of the Lord"

A pivotal passage in the debate about the eschatological nature of the message of Amos is the first usage in the Bible of the expression *yôm YHWH*, "day of the Yahweh/Lord," in 5:18–20, an expression that "Amos may well have coined."[12] Hugo Gressmann argues that the beginning of eschatology is found in this very passage.[13] Sigmund Mowinckel, who sees the matrix of eschatology in the cult, understands "the day of Yahweh/Lord" in Amos also as eschatological.[14] For Gerhard von Rad, who argues that eschatology is rooted in the holy war tradition, the *yôm YHWH* is likewise eschatological.[15]

A slightly different view is expressed by Klaus Koch. He believes that "the day of Yahweh/Lord" is "an important expression of popular eschatology."[16] In a similar vein J. Alberto Soggin has recently noted that "this [Am 5:18–20] is probably the earliest datable discussion of an eschatological theme, a theme which . . . cannot have just emerged then."[17] Koch and Soggin refrain from concluding

12. Shalom M. Paul, *Amos: A Commentary on the Book of Amos* (Minneapolis: Fortress, 1991), 182 n. 3.

13. H. Gressmann, *Der Ursprung der israelitisch-jüdischen Eschatologie* (Göttingen: Vandenhoeck und Ruprecht, 1905), 143–58.

14. S. Mowinckel, *Psalmenstudien II: Das Thronbesteigungsfest Jahwäs und der Ursprung der Eschatologie* (Kristiana, 1922; repr. Amsterdam, 1961), 211–35; idem, "Jahves dag, " *NTT* 59 (1958): 1–56, 209–29.

15. Gerhard von Rad, *Der Heilige Krieg im alten Israel* (Zürich: Ev. Verlag, 1951); idem, "The Origin of the Concept of the Day of Yahweh," *JSS* 4 (1959): 97–108; idem, *Theology of the Old Testament*, 2:136–38.

16. Koch, *Prophets*, 63.

17. J. Alberto Soggin, *The Prophet Amos* (London: SCM, 1987), 95.

that Amos' own saying on "the day of Yahweh/Lord" is eschatological.

Scholars such as Meir Weiss and C. Carniti see the expression and concept of "the day of Yahweh/Lord" as an invention of Amos himself.[18] Accordingly, they will not allow for a reaction on the part of Amos against a popular concept of "the day of Yahweh/Lord."

There are other scholars, among them John H. Hayes, who assert that Amos has no eschatological message whatsoever.[19] Hayes was preceded by Wolff, who suggests that "the day of Yahweh/Lord" in Amos is derived by him from the thought patterns of clan wisdom and the wandering shepherds (!).[20] Werner H. Schmidt, J. G. Trapiello, A. J. Everson, and H. M. Barstad deny any eschatological connections in their discussions on "the day of Yahweh/Lord."[21] Andersen and Freedman refrain from explicitly linking "the day of Yahweh/Lord" in 5:18–20 to eschatology, while otherwise the authors maintain with fervor that the message of Amos in its fourth stage/phase is thoroughly eschatological.[22] There is also the sustained argument of Y. Hoffmann that "the day of Yahweh/Lord" in 5:18–20 is noneschatological in its meaning,[23] a view shared subsequently by Barstad, who believes

18. M. Weiss, "The Origin of the 'Day of the Lord'—Reconsidered," *HUCA* 37 (1966): 29–60; C. Carniti, "L'espressione 'il giorno di JHWH,'" *BeO* 12 (1970): 11–25; followed by Paul, *Amos*, 182 n. 3.

19. Hayes, *Amos*, 38.

20. Wolff, *Joel and Amos*, 253–57. He cautiously states that "the oracle [of Amos 5:18–20] can be called eschatological only in the precise sense that it testifies, in the face of renewed assurances of security, that the end of the state of Israel is totally inescapable" (p. 257). See also idem, *Amos' geistige Heimat* (Neukirchen-Vluyn: Neukirchener Verlag, 1964), 11, 23.

21. Werner H. Schmidt, *Alttestamentlicher Glaube und seine Umwelt* (Neukirchen-Vluyn: Neukirchener Verlag, 1968), 95–97; J. G. Trapiello, "La nocien del 'Dia de Yahve' en el Antiguo Testamanto," *CuBi* 26 (1969): 331–36; A. J. Everson, "The Days of Yahweh," *JBL* 93 (1974): 329–37; idem, "Day of the Lord," *IDB(Sup)* (Nashville: Abingdon, 1976): 209–10; Hans M. Barstad, *The Religious Polemics of Amos* (Leiden: E. J. Brill, 1984), 89–94.

22. Francis I. Andersen and David Noel Freedman, *Amos: A New Translation with Introduction and Commentary* (New York: Doubleday, 1989), 519–22.

23. Y. Hoffmann, "The Day of the Lord as a Concept and a Term in the Prophetic Literature," *ZAW* 93 (1981): 37–50.

as does Hoffmann that eschatology is a postexilic Israelite phenomenon.[24] It is important to understand that the concept of eschatology is differently perceived by these interpreters. Many who believe that the expression "the day of Yahweh/Lord" is noneschatological take eschatology in a narrow sense of referring only to the end of history.

This brief survey of perceptions and interpretations of "the day of Yahweh/Lord" in 5:18–20 indicates that there are at present three major views regarding the eschatological nature of this expression: (1) "the day of Yahweh/Lord" concept is noneschatological in Amos 5, a view held also by those who define eschatology narrowly and of late origin; (2) "the day of Yahweh/Lord" concept reflects popular eschatology, which precedes the time of Amos and which Amos puts to an end; and (3) Amos' own statement on "the day of Yahweh/Lord" is eschatological in the broader sense of an eschatology that takes a decisive event in history as expressing finality in addition to the finality expressed at the end of all history.

The idea that "the day of Yahweh/Lord" (5:18–20) was a part of popular theology of some Israelites may be sustained on the assumption that the "you" in 5:18c refers to the people of Israel.[25] It seems to indicate that it was considered by at least some Israelites as a day when Yahweh would intervene in behalf of his people. This "popular eschatology,"[26] which understands the *yôm YHWH* as a day of Yahweh's saving intervention, is reversed by Amos into a day of doom for Israel. Israel has become like one of the

24. Barstad, *Religious Polemics*, 106. C. van Leeuwen, "The Prophecy of the *yôm YHWH* in Amos V 18–20," in *Language and Meaning: Studies in Hebrew Language and Biblical Exegesis*, eds. J. Barr et al. (Leiden: E. J. Brill, 1974), 133–34, concludes that the *yôm YHWH* in 5:18–20 is "not an eschatological phrase," but based on a broad definition of eschatology that could be seen as part of an eschatology of doom.

25. Here we do not follow the suggestion made by K. A. D. Smelik ("The Meaning of Amos V 18–20," *VT* 36 [1986]: 247) that those who long for the day of the Lord are the false prophets.

26. H. D. Preuss, *Jahweglaube und Zukunftserwartung* (Stuttgart: Kohlhammer, 1968), 172.

other nations and thus is in no better position to avert the coming calamity.

The picture of the *yôm YHWH* in the Book of Amos makes it clear that it is a day of disaster for Israel. It is a day of darkness and not light. It will be as when a person escapes with his life from the death threat of a lion and from the death threat of a bear to reach his house for safety. Once inside, assuming to be safe, the escapee will in the end still be bitten by a deadly snake. In this sense one may speak of the end of the person's life in terms of personal eschatology. The picture of the person, however, is to be applied to the nation and not to a single individual or group within Israel. Is this thus not a picture of national eschatology where the absolute, irrevocable end of the nation is proclaimed by Amos?

This picture is not one of universal eschatology that brings about the end of the world in the form of some cataclysmic event. If eschatology is understood in the larger sense of something final within history and not just the absolute end of all history,[27] then the *yôm YHWH* message of 5:18–20 can surely be considered eschatological. Accordingly Amos may be seen as the first eschatological preacher among the "writing prophets" in the Old Testament.[28] Furthermore, as the oldest and first "classical prophet" Amos is an eschatological prophet in this broad sense.

Amos and the Remnant

Would there be or could there be hope, at least some genuine hope? This inquiry invites us to consider the remnant motif in Amos. Many scholars contend that the rem-

---

27. See Hans-Peter Müller, *Ursprünge und Strukturen alttestamentlicher Eschatologie* (Berlin: W de Gruyter, 1969), 1–11 for a brief discussion on the definitions of eschatology in modern research. In modern times the concept of eschatology as the end of history, the end of the world, has given way to eschatology as a decisive end within history.

28. This is supported, among others, by Ralph W. Klein, "The Day of the Lord," *CTM* 39 (1968): 517–25, esp. 523; R. E. Clements, *Prophecy and Covenant* (London:

nant motif in Amos is not cancelled out by the finality of the judgment message, including the coming reality of the "the day of Yahweh/Lord." The essential question is whether Amos' message demands an interpretation of a radical either/or. Since Amos announces the end of the nation as a nation, is it true that there cannot be any future whatsoever for any entity? Does Amos' message contain some genuine hope for the future?

Some scholars feel that to make Amos into a consistent prophet of doom is to put him into a straitjacket of our own making.[29] If we were to force Amos into a mold of modern Western rational consistency, we would press him into a Procrustean bed of our own making. If Amos had no future hope whatsoever, his message would stand totally unique among the prophets of the eighth century B.C. Why would Yahweh reveal himself through Amos in a totally negative way?

Since the 1970s a number of major studies have been produced on the remnant idea in the Old Testament. All of them treat the remnant motif in the Book of Amos. The remnant idea does not originate in the sociopolitical sphere (contra Werner E. Müller[30] and supporters) of warfare but is deeply rooted in Israel's history. It is known from ancient Near Eastern texts prior to the establishment of Israel in contexts of natural catastrophes, economic hardships, physical difficulties, and military-political strife.[31]

There is a twofold usage of the remnant in Amos. In a negative sense the remnant heightens the picture of judg-

---

SCM, 1965), 103, 114–16; W. Rudolph, *Joel-Amos-Obadja-Jona* (Gütersloh: Gerd Mohn/Gütersloher Verlagshaus, 1971), 204; van Leeuwen, "Prophecy," 133–34.

29. J. Philip Hyatt, *Prophetic Religion* (Nashville: Abingdon, 1947), 100; A. S. Kapelrud, "New Ideas in Amos," *VTS* 15 (1965): 196.

30. Müller's dissertation was originally published in 1939, but was republished and enlarged by H. D. Preuss in Werner E. Müller and Horst Dietrich Preuss, *Die Vorstellung vom Rest im Alten Testament* (Neukirchen-Vluyn: Neukirchener Verlag, 1973).

31. Gerhard F. Hasel, *The Remnant: A History and Theology of the Remnant Idea from Genesis to Isaiah* (Berrien Springs, Mich.: Andrews University Press, 1980), 50–134. H. D. Preuss writes in the appendix to Müller and Preuss, *Die Vorstellung vom Rest im Alten Testament*, 114: "In view of the amount and variety of (new) materials [from

ment (3:12; 4:1–3; 5:3; 6:9–10; 9:1–4), because of the meaninglessness of the remnant. The positive aspect of the remnant theme holds out hope for a faithful remnant from within the nation (5:3, 14–15; 9:11–12) and defines more closely the message of doom. The remnant is a remnant *from* Israel, sifted along ethical-religious lines.[32] Although "in Amos the remnant motif is used for the first time in an eschatological sense,"[33] the idea of the remnant is, of course, much older than Amos.[34]

F. Dreyfus essentially supports the twofold picture of the remnant in Amos, but points out how various commentators on critical (form-critical, traditio-historical, and redaction-critical) grounds redate some or all passages with a positive notion of the remnant.[35] Hans Wildberger defends the positive remnant idea in 5:15 (against Wolff).[36]

Omar Carena attempts to bolster the earlier idea of Müller that the Israelite remnant idea derives from the sphere of warfare borrowed and adapted from Assyrian political texts.[37] He seeks to support his argument with ninety-seven

---

the ancient Near East] which Hasel has brought together and interpreted the thesis of Müller of an original military-political filling of the remnant idea and the conclusions based on them will have to be anew and critically scrutinized." See also Gerhard F. Hasel, "Linguistic Considerations Regarding the Translation of Isaiah's 'Shear-jashub,'" *AUSS* 9 (1971): 36–46; idem, "Semantic Values of Derivatives of the Hebrew Root *s'r*,'" *AUSS* 11 (1973): 152–96; idem, "Remnant," *IDB(Sup)* (Nashville: Abingdon, 1976), 735–36; idem, "'Remnant' as a Meaning of *'acharith,'* in *The Archaeology of Jordan and Other Studies*, eds. L. T. Geraty and L. G. Herr (Berrien Springs, Mich.: Andrews University Press, 1986), 511–24; idem, "*palaṭ, malaṭ, paliṭ, paleṭ, peleṭah, peleṭah, miplaṭ*," *TWAT* 6 (1987): 589–606; idem, "Remnant," in *International Standard Bible Encyclopedia* (Grand Rapids: Eerdmans, 1988), 4:130–34.

32. Hasel, *Remnant*, 173–215.

33. Ibid., 393.

34. Hugo Gressmann, *Der Ursprung der israelitisch-jüdischen Eschatologie* (Göttingen: Vandenhoeck und Ruprecht, 1905), 229–38, and others.

35. F. Dreyfus, "Reste d'Israel," *DBS 10* (1981): 422–23.

36. Hans Wildberger, "*š'r* übrig sein," in *Theologisches Handwörterbuch zum Alten Testament*, eds. Ernst Jenni and Claus Westermann (München: Kaiser, 1976), 2:850. Preuss also objects to the claim of inauthenticity of 5:15 by Wolff in Müller and Preuss, *Die Vorstellung vom Rest im Alten Testament*, 119.

37. Omar Carena, *Il resto di Israele* (Bologna: Edizione Dehoniane, 1985), 21–55.

cases of the appearance of the "remnant" in Assyrian royal inscriptions from the ninth to the seventh centuries B.C.[38] He concludes that the term "remnant" in these texts stands most typically for a political entity.[39] This conclusion remains highly problematic in view of the fact of the presence of the remnant idea in older nonpolitical texts from the ancient Near East[40] and in non-Assyrian texts, all of which remain outside the purview of Carena's study. The "political" origin of the remnant motif cannot be sustained.

Carena supports the remnant idea in 5:14–15; 3:12; and 9:7–10.[41] This little remnant forms the nucleus of the new people of God. The event that Amos speaks about is the fall of Samaria in 722 B.C., which Amos himself witnessed. Carena holds that the "remnant" in Amos are those who survive the latter catastrophe.

Jutta Hausmann takes a radically different perspective. She allows for but a most minimalist idea of the remnant in preexilic prophetic writings. She dates most of the major texts to exilic times and later and uses them to describe the development of the rich remnant idea in postexilic Judaism. She dismisses from her discussion the negative idea of the remnant in Amos.[42] Only 5:14–15 is acknowledged to come from Amos. This passage has a positive remnant idea with a "conditional salvation promise." The remnant is not a national possibility, but a religious notion conditioned by the "perhaps," which expresses a vague hope in a direct manner. It is part of Amos' future expectation.[43]

We may summarize the discussion on the remnant in Amos as follows. First, there is no unanimity in recent

38. Ibid., 22–42.
39. Ibid., 50–53.
40. See Hasel, *Remnant,* 50–134; Müller and Preuss, *Die Vorstellung vom Rest im AT,* 113–14.
41. Carena, *Il resto di Israele,* 62–66. He follows slavishly the commentary of Soggin and gives no evidence of being in touch with the rich literature on the subject in Amos.
42. Jutta Hausmann, *Israels Rest. Studien zum Selbstverständnis der nachexilischen Gemeinde* (Stuttgart: W. Kohlhammer, 1987), 184 n. 227.
43. Ibid., 186, 187.

scholarship as to how many of the remnant passages in
Amos are authentic, but there are few scholars today who
would deny 5:14–15 to the prophet himself (*pace* Wolff and
followers). Second, there is a consensus that Amos has both
a negative and positive remnant idea. Third, there is
widespread agreement that Amos does have a future expectation expressed by means of the remnant idea. Fourth, the
roots of the remnant idea cannot be linked uniquely with
political-military-sociological spheres (against W. E. Müller
and Carena) or with the cult (so S. Mowinckel). In the
ancient Near East and long before Amos the remnant is
linked to the problem of life and death and the need to
secure the continuity of life. It is noted that covenant
notions (O. Schilling), election traditions (H. H. Rowley),
connections with "the day of the Lord" (K.-D. Schunck[44]),
and other relationships with the remnant play a role as
well.[45] Finally, a positive remnant idea is present in 5:14–15
(9:11–12, see below); it is an eschatological idea located
right at the center of the Book of Amos.[46]

Amos and Future Restoration

Ever since Julius Wellhausen declared in 1892 that
9:13–15 suddenly deals out "roses and lavender instead of
blood and iron"[47] and that Amos cannot so quickly change
his mind in 9:8–15 to let from "the wrath of Yahweh flow
milk and honey," there have been scores of scholars who
have denied this passage to Amos. This influential assessment, however, "puts Amos too hastily on the same level
as a Christian theologian, ruled by dogmatic principles."[48]

In discussions since the 1970s it has been suggested that

44. K.-D. Schunck, "Strukturlinien in der Entwicklung der Vorstellung vom
'Tag Jahwes,'" *VT* 14 (1964): 319–30, esp. 323.
45. Preuss, *Jahweglaube und Zukunftserwartung*, 181–82.
46. Andersen and Freedman (*Amos*, 53) note that "the center of the book is vv
14–15, almost to the word. Taken together the two verses are a capsule of the
book's essential message."
47. Julius Wellhausen, *Die Kleinen Propheten*, 4th ed. (Berlin: W. de Gruyter,
1963), 96.
48. Koch, *Prophets*, 69.

the ending of the Book of Amos is a "voice of Deuteronomistic salvation hope"[49] of a much later period than the historical Amos. But even a scholar of the stature of Wolff, who is a strong supporter of the Deuteronomistic edition of the Book of Amos (following W. H. Schmidt), does not see here any Deuteronomistic influence at all, but considers it from "the hand of a redactor not in evidence elsewhere in the book."[50] J. Alberto Soggin also refuses to follow the Deuteronomistic redaction line of thought.[51]

Peter Weimar seeks to place this concluding section of Amos into the framework of the redaction of the Book of Amos.[52] W. A. G. Nel suggests that 9:11–15 is an unconditional prophecy to the people of the kingdom of Judah from the time of the exile.[53] Brevard Childs, based on his interest in the final form of the text and agreeing with those who see Amos as a consistent prophet of doom, suggests that the later redactor of the final edition of Amos "engaged in a decisive canonical re-interpretation of the book in that he placed the words of Amos into a broad eschatological framework which goes beyond the original perspective of the prophet himself."[54] Rolf Rendtorff, insisting that none of the texts in the Book of Amos should be interpreted independently from the context in which they are placed in the book itself, insists that in 9:7–15 "the proclamation of doom is integrated into the eschatological proclamation of salvation as in all other prophetic books."[55]

49. Ulrich Kellermann, "Der Amosschluss als Stimme deuteronomistischer Heilshoffnung," *EvTh* 29 (1969): 169–83. The theory that 9:11–15 is of Deuteronomistic origin is not unique to Kellermann. It has been argued previously in a variety of ways by Herrmann, Robinson, and Weiser.

50. Wolff, *Joel and Amos*, 353.

51. Soggin, *Amos*, 149–50.

52. Peter Weimar, "Der Schluss des Amos-Buches. Ein Beitrag zur Redaktionsgeschichte des Amos-Buches," *BN* 16 (1981): 60–100.

53. W. A. G. Nel, "Amos 9:11–15—An Unconditional Prophecy of Salvation during the Period of the Exile," *OTE* 2 (1984): 81–97.

54. Brevard S. Childs, "Die theologische Bedeutung der Endform eines Textes," *TQ* 167 (1987): 251.

55. R. Rendtorff, *Das Alte Testament. Eine Einführung* (Neukirchen-Vluyn: Neukirchener Verlag, 1983), 234.

In one way or another the long list of scholars since 1892 who have denied the concluding part of Amos to the prophet himself feel that the statements about the future salvation contained in this prophetic word presuppose the fall of Jerusalem in 586 B.C., or events of the year 485 B.C. (so J. Morgenstern). They are agreed that the unique phrase "the booth of David" (9:11) refers to the southern kingdom and the reference to its fall must be the events connected with the end of Judah in the time of the Neo-Babylonian period or the events connected with 485 B.C. This accommodation to a new historical reality of a later period is also understood to soften the harsh message of Amos. In one way or another an exilic or postexilic dating is bolstered with various historical and philological-linguistic arguments.[56]

Already in 1902 Otto Procksch raised an issue that has haunted exegetes and scholars ever since: "Most of all one can hardly imagine that Amos should let Yahweh triumph over nothingness."[57] The debated issue is whether Yahweh's triumph is the complete and total end of Israel and every Israelite.

Did Yahweh have really only an end to proclaim through Amos without any kind of a future for anyone or any entity? Why would only later editors/redactors be able to have a message of hope? There is no compelling reason why the final section of Amos could not derive from the historical Amos himself.[58]

The genuineness of the concluding part of the Book of

56. In recent times see Wolff, *Joel and Amos*, 345–55; and I. Willi-Plein, *Vorformen der Schriftexegese innerhalb des Alten Testaments* (Berlin/New York: W. de Gruyter, 1971), 55–62.

57. Otto Procksch, *Geschichtsbetrachtung und geschichtiche Überlieferung bei den vorexilischen Propheten* (Leipzig: Hinrichsche Buchandlung, 1902), 13 n. 1.

58. Those exegetes supporting the authenticity of 9:11–15 before 1967 include Boehmer, Procksch, Eichrodt, Kraus, Driver, Cramer, Danell, Hempel, Zimmerli, Neher, Maag, Alt, Rohland, Botterweck, Hammershaimb, Watts, Kaufmann, Engnell, Heschel, Graf Reventlow, Harrelson, Kapelrud, Fey, Otzen, Scharbert, Eissfeldt, Clements, von Rad, Carlsen, and Preuss. Those since 1967 include Huidberg-Hansen, Müller, Rudolph, Seybold, Yeivin, Davies, Lang, Stuart, Hayes, Andersen/Freedman, Hubbard, Smith, Finley, Rosenbaum, and Paul.

Amos depends on the whole understanding of the message of Amos.[59] Is this prophecy dependent on the ideology of a Davidic empire? Does it reflect a pro-Judean tendency? Is it a criticism of the royal dynasty of Jeroboam II? Does it reflect a psychological/religious tension? Is it rooted in the covenant? Does this prophecy reflect a message of hope from an earlier period that was later abandoned? These issues remain at the center of the discussion.

The most basic question is whether Amos is a consistent prophet of doom or whether there is hope held out for God's people, even if it is but for only a remnant of Israel. Is there a development from one to the other? These matters will exercise exegetes and theologians for some time to come, because it is not just a matter of what Amos said or did not say. It is also a matter of the entire origin of future hope in the earliest phase of Old Testament "classical prophecy." Why should a crisis of the magnitude to be encountered by the northern kingdom, when faced with the wholesale threat of the Neo-Assyrian Empire, end in an absolute No as regards a future for any remnant from the ten-tribe kingdom? Has Yahweh not more to offer than that? We can hardly allow our modern theology or thinking, our standard of consistency, to determine the meaning of a biblical book or a prophet's message. Should we allow our notion of consistency to force a text into a particular mold that is in harmony with our own modern expectations?

We may bring together the various interrelated topics as follows. First, "the day of Yahweh/Lord" passage (5:18–20) is indeed eschatological in nature, proclaiming in a lamentation setting the end of the national existence of Israel. Second, this final, eschatological end of Israel, the northern kingdom, as a national entity is not an absolute end of everything relating to the north. There is a "perhaps" (5:15)

---

59. In any case it is clear from both supporters and detractors that the genuineness has nothing to do with the conservative/liberal position of the respective exegete.

of God's mercy and thus the real possibility for a remnant that will be left from the "house of Joseph" (5:14–15). This remnant is one of faith, preserved by grace, and as a surviving entity of a historical crisis of major proportions it is eschatological in nature, carrying on the salvation intentions of Yahweh. Third, the eschatological message of the restoration of the "fallen/falling booth of David" into which other entities are joined ("the remnant of Edom") looks forward to a successful future. This too is a deed of Yahweh in which the failures of the people of the past, the separation of the Davidic Israel of the Golden Age, are overcome by a glorious reunion. Amos is a "prophet of re-union"[60] and more. As a prophet of eschatological doom *and* eschatological hope, he is a prophet of Yahweh's potential for the remnant of the people of God. Amos' proclamation has both a No *and* a Yes! He is the first prophetic preacher of eschatology, but not of a "popular eschatology." His eschatology is Yahwistic eschatology determined by moral demands from a covenant in which divine-human relationships are at the center, transforming and shaping all interhuman relationships, and giving continuing direction to the life of God's people.

---

60. G. H. Davies, "Amos—The Prophet of Re-Union," *ExpTim* 92 (1980–81): 196–200.

SELECT BIBLIOGRAPHY

Special emphasis is given to items written since 1960, except for commentaries and major studies.

Abramski, S. "'I Am Not a Prophet Nor a Son of a Prophet.'" *Studies in the Bible Dedicated to the Memory of Umberto Cassuto on the 100th Anniversary of His Birth,* ed. S. E. Loewenstamm. Jerusalem: Magnes, 1987, 64–68. (Heb.)

Ackroyd, P. R. "The Meaning of Hebrew *dwd* Reconsidered." *JSS* 12 (1968): 3–10.

_____. "A Judgment Narrative Between Kings and Chronicles? An Approach to Amos 7:9–17." *Canon and Authority: Essays in Old Testament Religion and Theology,* eds. G. W. Coats and B. O. Long. Philadelphia: Fortress, 1977, 71–87.

_____. "Recent Foreign Old Testament Literature." *ExpTim* 94 (1983): 170–74.

_____. *Studies in the Religious Traditions of the Old Testament.* London: SCM, 1987, 196–208.

Aharoni, M., and A. F. Rainey. "On 'the Israelite Fortress of Arad.'" *BASOR* 258 (1985): 73–74.

Aharoni, Y. *The Land of the Bible. A Historical Geography.* Philadelphia: Westminster, 1979.

Ahlström, G. W. "King Josiah and the *dwd* of Amos 6.10." *JSS* 26 (1981): 7–9.

Airoldi, N. "La cosiddetta 'decima' israelitica antica." *Bib* 55 (1974): 179–210.

Albright, W. F. "The Ostraca of Samaria." *Ancient Near Eastern Texts Relating to the Old Testament,* ed. James B. Pritchard. 3d ed. with suppl. Princeton: Princeton University Press, 1969, 321.

Alger, B. "The Theology and Social Ethics of Amos." *Scripture* 17 (1965): 109–16, 318–28.

Allen, Leslie C. "Amos, Prophet of Solidarity." *Vox Evangelica* 6 (1969): 42–53.

Amsler, S. "Amos, prophète de la onzième heure." *TZ* 21 (1965): 318–28.

_____. *Amos.* Neuchâtel: Delachaux & Niestlé, 1982.

____. "Amos et les droits de l'homme (Étude d'Am 1 et 2)." *De la Tôrah au Messie,* eds. M. Carrez et al. Paris: Desclée, 1981, 181–86.

____. "La parole visionnaire des prophètes." *VT* 31 (1981): 359–62.

Andersen, Francis I. *The Verbless Clause in the Pentateuch.* Nashville/New York: Abingdon, 1970.

Andersen, Francis I., and David Noel Freedman. *Amos: A New Translation with Introduction and Commentary.* New York: Doubleday, 1989.

Andersen, Francis I., and A. D. Forbes. *A Synoptic Concordance to Hosea, Amos, Micah.* Wooster, Ohio: Biblical Research Associates, 1972.

Anderson, Bernhard W. *The Eighth Century Prophets: Amos, Hosea, Isaiah, Micah.* Philadelphia: Fortress, 1978.

Andersson, C. H. *Commentarius in Amos.* Gotha, 1854.

Andiñach, P. R. "Amos: Memoria y Profecia. Análisis estructural y hermenéutica." *RivB* (Buenos Aires) 45/12 (1983–84): 209–301.

Andre, G. *Determining the Destiny, pqd in the Old Testament.* Lund: CWK Gleerup, 1980.

Angerstorfer, A. *Der Schöpfergott des Alten Testaments. Herkunft und Bedeutungsentwicklung des hebräischen Terminus br' (bara'), 'schaffen.'* Frankfurt am M.: Peter Lang, 1979.

Arieti, J. A. *A Study in the Septuagint of the Book of Amos.* Unpubl. Ph.D. diss., Stanford University, 1972.

____. "The Vocabulary of Septuagint Amos." *JBL* 93 (1974): 338–47.

Arnaud, D. "Humbles et superbes à Emar (Syrie) à la fin de l'âge du Bronze récent." *Mélanges bibliques et orientaux en l'honneur de M. Henri Cazelles,* eds. A. Caquot and M. Delcor. Kevelaer: Butzon & Bercker; Neukirchen-Vluyn: Neukirchener Verlag, 1981, 1–14.

Arnold, P. M. *Gibeah in Israel's History and Tradition.* Unpubl. Ph.D. diss., Emory University, 1986.

Asen, B. A. *Amos' Faith: A Structural-Developmental Approach.* Unpubl. Ph.D. diss., St. Louis University, 1980.

Ashbel, D. "Notes on the Prophecy of Amos: 'Does a Lion Raise His Voice from His Lair unless He Has Caught Something'?" *Beth Miqra* 25/26 (1965): 106–7. (Heb.)

____. "Notes on the Prophecy of Amos: 'Does a Bird Fall into a Trap . . . ?" *Beth Miqra* 25/26 (1965): 103–4. (Heb.)

Atger J. F. "Le message d'Amos." *Christianisme Social* 74 (1966): 302–12.

Augé, R. *Profetes Menores.* Barcelona: Monestir de Montserrat, 1957.

Auld, A. G. *Amos.* Sheffield: JSOT, 1986.

Avigad, N., and J. C. Greenfield. "A Bronze Phiale with a Phoenician Dedicatory Inscription." *IEJ* 32 (1982): 118–28.

Avishur, Y. "Word Pairs Common to Phoenician and Biblical Hebrew." *UF* 7 (1975): 13–47.

Baab, Otto J. "Old Testament Theology: Its Possibility." *The Study of the Bible Today and Tomorrow,* ed. H. R. Willoughby. Chicago: Chicago University Press, 1947, 401–18.

Bach, D. "Rite de parole dans l'ancien Testament." *VT* 28 (1978): 10–19.

Bach, R. "Erwägungen zu Amos 7, 14." *Die Botschaft und die Boten. Festschrift für Hans Walter Wolff zum 70. Geburtstag,* eds. J. Jeremias and L. Perlitt. Neukirchen-Vluyn: Neukirchener Verlag, 1981, 203–16.

____. "Gottesrecht und weltliches Recht in der Verkündigung des Propheten Amos." *Festschrift für Günther Dehn,* ed. W. Schneemelcher. Neukirchen-Vluyn: Neukirchener Verlag, 1957, 23–34.

Bailey, J. G. "Amos: Preacher of Social Reform." *TBT* 19 (1981): 306–13.

Baker, D. W. "Further Examples of the *waw explicativum.*" *VT* 30 (1980): 129–36.

Balentine, S. E. "A Description of the Semantic Field of Hebrew Words for 'Hide.'" *VT* 30 (1980): 137–53.

Balla, E. *Die Droh- und Scheltworte des Amos.* Leipzig: Edelmann, 1926.

Bardtke, H. "Altisraelitische Erweckungsbewegungen." *Near Eastern Studies in Honor of William Foxwell Albright,* ed. H. Goedicke. Baltimore/London: Johns Hopkins University Press, 1971, 17–34.

____. "Die Latfundien in Juda während der zweiten Hälfte des achten Jahrhunderts v. Chr." *Hommages à Dupont-Sommer.* Paris, 1971, 235–54.

Barnett, R. D. "Urartu." *CAH* 3/1 (1982): 314–71.

Barré, M. L. "Amos 1:11 Reconsidered." *CBQ* 47 (1985): 420–27.

____. "The Meaning of *l' 'shybnw* in Amos 1:3–2:6." *JBL* 105 (1986): 611–31.

Barstad, H. M. *The Religious Polemics of Amos: Studies in the Preaching of Am 2, 7B–8; 4, 1–13; 5, 1–27; 6, 4–7; 8, 14.* Leiden: E. J. Brill, 1984.

____. "Die Basankühe in Amos IV 1." *VT* 25 (1975): 286–97.

____. "Profetene i det gamle testamente, fakta eller fiksjon." *NorTT* 91 (1990): 149–56.

Bartczek, G. *Prophetie und Vermittlung. Zur literarischen Analyse und theologischen Interpretation der Visionsberichte des Amos.* Frankfurt am M./Bern: Peter Lang, 1980.

Barth, C. "Theophanie, Bundschliessung und neuer Anfang am dritten Tage." *EvTh* 28 (1968): 521–33.

Bartina, S. *The Book of Amos.* Madrid: Paideia, 1968.

Bartlett, J. R. "The Brotherhood of Edom." *JSOT* 4 (1977): 2–27.

Barton, J. *Amos's Oracles Against the Nations: A Study of Amos 1:3–2:5.* Cambridge: Cambridge University Press, 1980.

Baumann, E. *Der Aufbau der Amosreden.* Giessen: Töpelmann, 1903.

Baumgartner, W. "Kennen Amos und Hosea eine Heilseschatologie?" *Schweizer Theologische Zeitschrift* 30 (1913): 30–42, 95–124, 152–70.

Baur, G. A. L. *Der Prophet Amos erklärt.* Giessen, 1847.

Beaucamp, E. "Amos 1–2: Le *pèshâ* d'Israël et des nations." *ScEs* 21 (1969): 435–41.

Beck, E. *Gottes Traum, eine menschliche Welt: Hosea, Amos, Micha.* Stuttgart: Katholisches Bibelwerk, 1972.

Becker, J. "Wurzel und Wurzelspross." *BZ* 20 (1976): 22–44.

Beek, M. A. *Amos. Een inleiding tot het verstaan der Profeten van het OT.* Lochem: de Tijdstroom, 1947.

____. "Ein Erdbeben wird zum prophetischen Erleben." *ArOr* 17 (1949): 31–40.

Beentjes, P. C. "Oracles Against the Nations, a Central Issue in the Latter Prophets." *Bijdragen* 50 (1989): 203–9.

Begg, C. T. "The Classical Prophets in the Chronistic History." *BZ* 32 (1988): 100–107.

Beit-arieh, I. "New Light on the Edomites." *BAR* 14/2 (1988): 28–41.

Bella, B. M. *Amos.* Athens: Aster, 1947. (Gk.)

Bennett, C.-M. "Excavations at Buseirah (Biblical Bozrah)." *Midian, Moab and Edom,* eds. J. F. A. Sawyer and D. J. A. Clines. Sheffield: JSOT, 1983, 9–17.

Benson, A. "From the Mouth of the Lion. The Messianism of Amos." *CBQ* 19 (1957): 199–212.

Bentzen, A. "The Ritual Background of Amos 1,2–2,16." *OTS* 8 (1950): 85–99.

Berg, W. *Die sogenannten Hymnenfragmente im Amosbuch.* Bern: Herbert Lang; Frankfurt am M.: Peter Lang, 1974.

Berger, von P.-R. "Ein unerklärtes Wort in dem Weinberglied Jesajas." *ZAW* 82 (1970): 116–21.

Bernard, M. "Exegetical Study of Amos 9:8–15." *Ministry* 9 (1969): 22–26.

Bernhardt, K.-H. "Prophetie und Geschichte." *VTS* 22 (1972): 20–46.

Berridge, J. "Jeremia und die Prophetie des Amos." *TZ* 35 (1979): 321–41.

____. "Zur Intention der Botschaft des Propheten Amos. Exegetische überlegungen zu Am 5." *TZ* 32 (1976): 321–40.

Bettenzoli, G. "La tradizione del sabba't." *Henoch* 4 (1982): 265–93.

Bewer, J. A. *The Book of the Twelve Prophets.* New York: Harper & Brothers, 1949.

Bič, M. *Das Buch Amos.* Berlin: Evangelische Verlagsanstalt, 1969.

Bjørndalen, A. J. "Zu den Zeitstufen der Zitatformel . . . *rma hk.*" *ZAW* 86 (1974): 393–403.

____. "Erwägungen zur Zukunft des Amazja und Israels nach der Überlieferung Amos 7,10–17." *Werden und Wirken des Alten Testaments. Festschrift für Claus Westermann zum 70. Geburtstag,* ed. R. Albertz. Göttingen: Vandenhoeck und Ruprecht, 1980, 236–51.

____. "Jahwe in den Zukunftsaussagen des Amos." *Die Botschaft und die Boten. Festschrift für Hans Walter Wolff zum 70. Geburtstag,* eds. J. Jeremias and L. Perlitt. Neukirchen-Vluyn: Neukirchener Verlag, 1981, 181–202.

____. *Untersuchungen zur allegorischen Rede der Propheten Amos und Jesaja.* Berlin/New York: W. de Gruyter, 1986.

Blank, S. H. "Irony by Way of Attribution." *Semitics* 1 (1970): 1–6.

Blaquart, J. L. "Parole de Dieu et prophètes d'Amos à Ezechiel." *L'Ancien Testament approches et lectures. Des procedures de travail à la théologie,* ed. A. Vanel. Paris, 1977, 15–30.

Blechmann, M. *Das Buch Amos in Talmud und Midrasch.* Unpubl. diss., University of Würzburg, 1937.

Bleeker, C. J. "Some Remarks on the Religious Significance of Light." *JANES* 5 (1973): 23–34.

Bleeker, L. H. K. *De Kleine Propheten, I, Hosea, Amos.* Kroningen: Wolters, 1932.

Blenkinsopp, J. "The Prophetic Reproach." *JBL* 90 (1971): 267–78.

_____. *A History of Prophecy in Israel.* Philadelphia: Westminster, 1984.

Bloch, E. *L'athéisme dans le christianism. La religion de l'éxode et du royaume.* Paris, 1978 (= *Atheismus im Christentum. Zur Religion des Exodus und des Reichs.* Frankfurt am M., 1968).

Boer, P. A. H. de. "*Yhwh* as Epithet Expressing the Superlative." *VT* 24 (1974): 233–35.

Bohlen, R. "Zur Sozialkritik des Propheten Amos." *TTZ* 95 (1986): 282–301.

Bonora, A. *Amos, Il profeta della giustizia.* Brescia: Paideia, 1979.

_____. "Amos difensore del diritto e della giustizia." *Testimonium Christi: Scritti in onore de Jacques Dupont.* Brescia: Paideia, 1985, 69–90.

Booij, P. J. "Vertaalproblemen in de Amos-Doxologieen." *Beginnen Bij de Letter Beth. Fs. A. G. van Daalen.* Kampen: Kok, 1985, 90–97.

Borger, R. "Amos 5, 26, Apostelgeschichte 7, 43 and Surpu II, 180." *ZAW* 100 (1988): 70–81.

Bosman, H. L. "Does Disaster Strike Only When the Lord Sends It? Prophetic Eschatology and the Origin of Evil in Amos 3:6." *Old Testament Essays* 1 (1988): 21–30.

Botterweck, G. J. "Zur Authentizität des Buches Amos." *BZ* 2 (1958): 176–98.

_____. "Die soziale Kritik des Propheten Amos." *Das Amt des Bischofs. Eine Festgabe für den Erzbischof von Köln—Joseph Kardinal Höffner.* Köln: Bachem, 1971, 39–58.

_____. "'Sie Verkaufen den Unschuldigen um Geld.' Zur sozialen Kritik des Propheten Amos." *BiL* 12 (1971): 215–31.

_____. "Gott und Mensch in den alttestamentlichen Löwenbildern." *Wort, Lied und Gottesspruch. Festschrift für J. Ziegler.* Würzburg: Echter, 1972, 117–28.

Bovon, F. *Luc le théologien. Vingt-cinq ans de recerches (1950–1975).* Neuchâtel-Paris, 1978.

Boyle, M. O. "The Covenant Lawsuit of the Prophet Amos: III 1–IV 13." *VT* 21 (1971): 338–62.

Bracke, J. M. "*šûb šebût*: A Reappraisal." *ZAW* 97 (1985): 233–44.

Braslavi, J. "The Lions of the Desert of Tekoa in the Book of Amos." *Beth Miqra* 32 (1967): 56–64. (Heb.)

_____. "Amos—*Noqed, Boker,* and *Boles Shikmim.*" *Beth Miqra* 32 (1967): 87–100. (Heb.)

_____. "Jeremiah 16:5 and Amos 6:7." *Beth Miqra* 48 (1971): 5–16. (Heb.)

Braun, M. A. "James' Use of Amos at the Jerusalem Council: Steps toward a Possible Solution of the Textual and Theological Problems." *JETS* 20 (1977): 113–21.

Briend, J. "Jéroboam II, sauveur d'Israel." *Mélanges bibliques et orientaux en l'honneur de M. Henri Cazelles,* eds. A. Caquot and M. Delcor. Kevelaer: Butzon & Bercker; Neukirchen-Vluyn: Neukirchener Verlag, 1981, 41–49.

Bright, J. "Amos." *Dictionary of the Bible,* eds. F. C. Grant and H. H. Rowley. Edinburgh: T. & T. Clark, 1963.

_____. " A New View of Amos." *Int* 25 (1971): 355–58.

_____. "The Apodictic Prohibition: Some Observations." *JBL* 92 (1973): 185–204.

_____. *Covenant and Promise.* London: SCM, 1977.

Brillet, G. *Amos et Osée.* Paris: Cerf, 1944.

Brimet, G. "La vision de l'étain, réinterpretation d'Amos VII 7–9." *VT* 16 (1966): 387–95.

Brin, G. *The Prophet in His Struggle. Studies in Four Biographical Narratives in the Prophetic Literature.* Tel Aviv, 1983.

_____. "The Visions in the Book of Amos (7:1–8:3): Studies in Structure and Ideas." *I. L. Seeligman Volume: Essays in the Bible and the Ancient World,* eds. A. Rofé and Y. Zakovitch. 3 vols. Jerusalem: E. Rubenstein, 1983, 2:275–90. (Heb.)

Brongers, H. A. "Some Remarks on the Biblical Particle *halo'*." *OTS* 21 (1981): 177–89.

Bronznick, N. M. "'Metathetic Parallelism'—An Unrecognized Subtype of Synonymous Parallelism." *HAR* 3 (1979): 25–39.

_____. "More on *hlk 'el*." *VT* 35 (1985): 97–98.

Brooke, G. J. "The Amos–Numbers Midrash (CD 7 13b–8 1a) and Messianic Expectation." *ZAW* 92 (1980): 397–404.

_____. *Exegesis at Qumran. 4QFlorilegium in Its Jewish Context.* Sheffield: JSOT, 1985.

Brown, H. C. *The Positive Elements in the Preaching of Amos.* Unpubl. diss., Southern Baptist Theological Seminary, 1954.

Bruce, F. F. "Prophetic Interpretation in the Septuagint." *BIOSCS* 12 (1979): 17–26.

_____. "Eschatology: Understanding the End of Days." *Bible Review* 5/6 (1989): 43–44.

Brueggemann, W. "Amos 4:4–13 and Israel's Covenant Worship." *VT* 15 (1965): 1–15.

_____. "Amos' Intercessory Formula." *VT* 19 (1969): 385–99.

_____. "A Cosmic Sigh of Relinquishment." *CurTM* 11 (1984): 5–20.

_____. "A New Creation—after the Sigh." *CurTM* 11 (1984): 83–100.

Bruno, A. *Das Buch der Zwölf. Eine rhytmische und textkritische Untersuchung* Stockholm: Almquist & Wiksell, 1957.

Bruzzone, G. B. "*bwqr* nell'antico testamento." *BeO* 23 (1981): 175–83.

Budde, K. "Zur Geschichte des Buches Amos." *Studien zur semitischen Philologie und Religionsgeschichte. Julius Wellhausen zum 70. Geburtstag,* ed. K. Marti. Giessen: Töpelmann, 1914, 65–77.

_____. "Zum Text und Auslegung des Buches Amos." *JBL* 43 (1924): 46–131; 44 (1925): 63–122.

Buis, P. "Les formulaires d'alliance." *VT* 16 (1966): 396–411.

_____. "La civilisation de samarie contestée par Amos. Amos 6, 1, 4–7." *AsSeign* [Bruges] 57 (1973): 68–73.

Burais, T. "Amos 5:14." *StTh* 19 (1967): 1–17.

Bushey, S. L. *The Theology of Amos.* Unpubl. Ph.D. diss., Bob Jones University, 1979.

Canney, M. A. *Amos. A Commentry on the Bible*, ed. A. S. Peake. New York: Nelson, 1920, 547–54.

Caquot, A. "Le messianisme qumrânien, Qumrân, sa piété, sa théologie et son milieu." *BETL* 96 (1978): 231–47.

Carena, O. *Il resto di Israele*. Bologna: Edizione Dehoniane, 1985.

Carlsen, A. "Profeten Amos och Davidsriket." *RoB* 25 (1966): 57–78.

Carlsen, B. "Amos in Judeo-Persian." *Acta Iranica* 23 (= Fs. J. Duchesne-Guillemin). Leiden: E. J. Brill, 1984, 73–112.

Carmichael, C. M. "A Ceremonial Crux: Removing a Man's Sandal as a Female Gesture of Contempt." *JBL* 96 (1977): 321–36.

Carniti, C. "L'espressione 'il giorne di JHWH': Origine ed evoluzione semantica." *BeO* 12 (1970): 11–25.

Carny, P. "Doxologies: A Scientific Myth." *HS* 18 (1977): 149–59.

Carroll, R. *When Prophecy Failed: Cognitive Dissonance in the Prophetic Tradition of the Old Testament*. New York: Seabury, 1979.

____. *From Chaos to Covenant. Uses of Prophecy in the Book of Jeremiah*. London: SCM, 1981, 42–44.

____. "Poets and Prophets: A Response to 'Prophets' Through the Looking Glass." *JSOT* 27 (1983): 25–31.

Casalis, G. "Du texte au sermon. Amos 8." *ETR* 46 (1971): 113–24.

Cazelles, H. "L'arrière plan historique d'Amos 1.9–10." *Proceedings of the Sixth World Congress of Jewish Studies*, vol. 1, ed. A. Shinan. Jerusalem: Magnes, 1977, 171–76.

____. *Le Messie de la Bible. Christologie de l'Ancien Testament*. Paris: Desclée, 1978, 110–23.

Cerny, L. *The Day of Yahweh and Some Related Problems*. Prague: University Karlovy, 1948.

Ceuppens, P. F. *De Kleine Profeten*. Bruges: de Brouwer, 1924.

Chajes, H. P. *Biblia Hebraica—Liber duodecim prophetarum*, ed. A. Kahana. 2d ed. Jerusalem: Mekor, 1969.

Childs, B. S. *Introduction to the Old Testament as Scripture*. Philadelphia: Fortress, 1979.

____. "Die theologische Bedeutung der Endform eines Textes." *TQ* 167 (1987): 242–51.

Chisholm, R. B., Jr. "'For Three Sins . . . Even for Four': The Numerical Sayings of Amos." *BS* 147 (1990): 188–97.

Christensen, D. L. "The Prosodic Structure of Amos 1–2." *HTR* 67 (1974): 427–36.

____. *Transformations of the War Oracle in Old Testament Prophecy: Studies in the Oracles Against the Nations*. Missoula: Scholars, 1975.

Cleary, F. X. *The Interpretation of Suffering According to Amos and Hosea: The Origins of Redemptive Suffering*. Unpubl. Th.D. diss., Gregorianae Pontifical University, 1978.

Clements, R. E. *Prophecy and Covenant*. London: SCM, 1965.

____. "The Form and Character of Prophetic Woe Oracles." *Semitics* 8 (1982): 17–29.

____. *Prophecy and Tradition.* Oxford: Clarendon, 1975.

Coffman, J. B. *Minor Prophets: Joel, Amos and Jonah.* Vol. 1. Abilene, Tex.: Abilene Christian University Press, 1984.

Cogan, M. "Tyre and Tiglath-Pileser III: Chronological Notes." *JCS* 25 (1973): 96–99.

____. *Imperialism and Religion: Assyria, Judah and Israel in the Eighth and Seventh Centuries B.C.E.* New Haven: Society of Biblical Literature and Scholars Press, 1974, 97–110.

____. "'Ripping Open Pregnant Women' in the Light of an Assyrian Analogue." *JAOS* 103 (1983): 755–57.

Coggins, R. J. "The Old Testament and the Poor." *ExpTim* 99 (1987): 11–14.

____. "Recent Continental Old Testament Literature." *ExpTim* 98 (1987): 362–65.

Cohen, G. *Amos.* Chicago: Moody, 1971.

Cohen, G., and H. R. Vandermey. *Hosea and Amos.* Chicago: Moody, 1981.

Cohen, H. R. *Biblical Hapaxlegomena in the Light of Akkadian and Ugaritic.* Missoula: Scholars, 1978.

Cohen, M. A. "The Prophets as Revolutionaries." *BAR* 5/3 (1979): 12–19.

Cohen, S. "The Political Background of the Words of Amos." *HUCA* 36 (1965): 153–60.

____. "Amos Was a Navi." *HUCA* 32 (1961): 175–78.

Collins, J. J. "History and Tradition in the Prophet Amos." *ITQ* 41 (1974): 120–33; repr. in *The Bible in Its Literary Milieu,* eds. V. L. Tollers and J. R. Maier. Grand Rapids: Eerdmans, 1979, 121–33.

Collins, T. *Line-Forms in Hebrew Poetry. A Grammatical Approach to the Stylistic Study of the Hebrew Prophets.* Rome: Pontifical Biblical Institute Press, 1978.

Contesse, R. P. "Notes on the Semantic Domains of Two Hebrew Words: *pr* and *swr*." *BT* 27 (1976): 119–21.

Cook, G. A. *The Book of Amos, with Notes by A. E. Edghill.* London: Methuen, 1914.

Cooper, A. "On Reading the Bible Critically and Otherwise." *The Future of Biblical Studies: The Hebrew Scriptures,* eds. R. E. Friedman and H. G. M. Williamson. Atlanta, Ga.: Scholars, 1987, 61–79.

____. "The Absurdity of Amos 6:12a." *JBL* 107 (1988): 725–27.

Coote, R. B. "Amos 1:11: *rhmyw*." *JBL* 90 (1971): 206–8.

____. "Ripe Words for Preaching Connotative Diction in Amos." *Pacific Theological Review* 8 (1976): 13–19.

____. *Amos among the Prophets: Composition and Theology.* Philadelphia: Fortress, 1981.

Copass, B. A. *Amos.* Nashville: Broadman, 1939.

Coppens, J. *Les Douze Petits Prophètes.* Louvain: Publications Universitaires, 1950.

Cornelius, I. "Paradise Motifs in the 'Eschatology' of the Minor Prophets and the Iconography of the Ancient Near East. The Concepts of Fertility, Water, Trees, and 'Tierfrieden' and Gen 2–3." *JNSL* 14 (1988): 41–83.

Coulot, C. "Propositions pour une structuration du livre d'Amos au niveau rédactionnel." *RSR* 51 (1977): 169–86.

Cox, D. "Inspired Radicals. The Prophets of the Eighth Century." *SBFLA* 25 (1975): 90–103.

Craghan, J. F. "The Prophet Amos in Recent Literature." *BTB* 2 (1972): 242–61.

____. "Traditions and Techniques in the Prophet Amos." *TBT* 60 (1972): 782–86.

Craigie, P. C. "Amos the *noqed* in the Light of Ugaritic." *SR* 11 (1982): 29–33.

____. "The Tablets from Ugarit and Their Importance for Biblical Studies." *BARev* 9 (1983): 62–73.

____. *Twelve Prophets*. Philadelphia: Westminster, 1984.

____. *Ugarit and the Old Testament*. Grand Rapids: Eerdmans, 1983.

Cramer, K. *Amos. Versuch einer theologischen Interpretation*. Stuttgart: Kohlhammer, 1930.

Crenshaw, J. L. "The Doxology of Amos" (diss., Vanderbilt University, 1964), published as *Hymnic Affirmation of Divine Justice: The Doxologies of Amos and Related Texts in the Old Testament*. Missoula: Scholars, 1975.

____. "He Who Stretches Out the Heavens." *CBQ* 34 (1972): 417–33.

____. "A Liturgy of Wasted Opportunity (Am 4,6–12; Isa. 9,7–10; 5,25–29)." *Semitics* 1 (1970): 27–37.

____. *Old Testament Wisdom: An Introduction*. Atlanta: John Knox, 1981, 40–41.

____. "Popular Questioning of the Justice of God in Ancient Israel." *ZAW* 82 (1970): 380–95.

____. *Prophetic Conflict*. Berlin: W. de Gruyter, 1971.

____. "*Wdorek 'al-bamotê 'ares.*" *CBQ* 34 (1972): 39–53.

____. "*YHWH Seba'ôt Semô*: A Form-Critical Analysis." *ZAW* 81 (1969): 156–75.

____. *Story and Faith: A Guide to the Old Testament*. New York: Macmillan, 1986.

Cripps, R. S. *A Critical and Exegetical Commentary on the Book of Amos*. London: SPCK, 1920, 2d ed. 1955.

Crocetti, G. "'Cercate Me e Vivrete.' La ricerca di Dio in Amos." *Quaerere Deum—Atti della XXV Settimana Biblica*. Brescia: Paideia Editrice, 1980, 89–105.

Crocker, P. "History and Archaeology in the Oracles of Amos." *Buried History: A Quarterly Newsletter of the Australian Institute of Archaeology* 23 (1987): 7–15.

Cross, F. M. "Epigraphic Notes on the Amman Citadel Inscription." *BASOR* 193 (1969): 13–19.

Crüsemann, F. *Der Widerstand gegen das Königtum*. Neukirchen-Vluyn: Neukirchener Verlag, 1978, 194–222.

____. "Kritik an Amos im deuteronomistischen Geschichtswerk." *Probleme biblischer Theologie. Gerhard von Rad zum 70. Geburstag*, ed. H. W. Wolff. München: Chr. Kaiser Verlag, 1971, 57–63.

____. *Studien zur Formgeschichte von Hymnus und Danklied in Israel*. Neukirchen-Vluyn: Neukirchener Verlag, 1969.

Curtis, J. B. "A Folk Etymology of *nabi'.*" *VT* 29 (1979): 491–93.

Dahl, J. C. W. *Amos neu übersetzt und erläutert*. Göttingen: Vandenhoeck und Ruprecht, 1975.

Dahmen, U. "Zur Text- und Literarkritik vom Am. 6,6a." *BN* 31 (1986): 7–10.

Dahood, M. J. "To Pawn One's Cloak." *Bib* 42 (1961): 359–66.

____. "Amos 6,8 mt'b." Bib 59 (1978): 265–66.

____. "Can One Plow Without Oxen? (Amos 6:12): A Study of ba- and 'al." The Bible World: Essays in Honor of Cyrus H. Gordon, eds. G. Rendsburg et al. New York: Ktav, 1980, 13–23.

____. "Eblaite and Biblical Hebrew." CBQ 44 (1982): 1–24.

____. "Hebrew-Ugarit Lexicography." Bib 48 (1967): 421–38; 52 (1971): 344–45.

Davies, G. H. "Amos—The Prophet of Re-Union." ExpTim 92 (1980–81): 196–200.

de Azcarrage Severt, M. J. Minhat Say de Y. S. de Norzi—Profetas Menores (traduccion y anotacion critica). Madrid: Instituto de Filologia, CSIC, Departemento de Filologia Biblica y de Oriente Antiquo, 1987.

de Ferriol, S. L. El Yahve de Amos. Buenos Aires: Universidad de Buenos Aires, 1987.

de Geus, J. K. "Die Gesellschaftskritik der Propheten und die Archäologie." ZDPV 98 (1982): 50–57.

de Roche, M. "Yahweh's rîb Against Israel: A Reassessment of the So-Called 'Prophetic Lawsuit' in the Preexilic Prophets." JBL 102 (1983): 563–74.

de Sivatte, R. "'No soporto vuestras fiestas.' Cuando la fe se desentiende de la justicia." Sal Terre 77 (1989): 683–93.

deVries, S. J. Yesterday, Today, Tomorrow. Grand Rapids: Eerdmans, 1974.

de Waard, J. "The Chiastic Structure of Amos V 1–17." VT 27 (1977): 170–77.

____. "A Greek Translation-Technical Treatment of Amos 1:15." On Language, Culture and Religion: In Honor of Eugene A. Nida, eds. M. Black and W. A. Smalley. The Hague/Paris: Mouton, 1974, 111–18.

____. "Translation Techniques Used by the Greek Translators of Amos." Bib 59 (1978): 339–50.

de Waard, J., and C. Dieterle. "Le Dieu créateur dans l'hymne du livre d'Amos." Foi Vie 83 (1984): 35–44.

de Waard, J., and W. A. Smalley. A Translator's Handbook on the Book of Amos, Helps for Translators. Stuttgart/New York: W. Bibelgesellschaft, 1979.

Dearman, J. A. "Hebrew Prophecy and Social Criticism: Some Observations for Perspective." Per Rel St 9 (1982): 131–43.

____. Property Rights in the Eighth-Century Prophets: The Conflict and Its Background. Atlanta: Scholars, 1988.

Deden, D. De Kleine Profeten mit de Grondtekst vertaald en uitgelegd. 2 vols. Roermond en Maaseik: Romen & Zonen, 1953.

Deissler, A. Dann wirst du Gott erkennen. Die Grundbotschaft der Propheten. Freiburg/Basel/Vienna: Herder, 1987.

____. Zwölf Propheten: Hosea, Joel, Amos. Würzburg: Echter Verlag, 1981.

Deist, F. "The Prophets: Are We Heading for a Paradigm Shift?" Prophet und Prophetenbuch. Festschrift für Otto Kaiser zum 65. Geburtstag, eds. V. Fritz et al. Berlin/New York: W. de Gruyter, 1989, 1–18.

Delcor, M. Les Petits Prophètes I: Amos. Paris: Letouzey & Ané, 1961.

____. "Les Kerethim et les Cretois." VT 28 (1978): 409–22.

Dentzer, J.-M. "Aux origines de l'iconographie de banquet couché." RArch 2 (1971):15–58.

Dietrich, M., and O. Loretz. "Die ugaritische Berufsgruppe der *NQDM* und das Amt des *RB NQDM.*" *UF* 9 (1977): 336–37.

di Marco, A. "Der Chiasmus in der Bibel. 1. Teil." *LB* 36 (1975): 21–97.

Dines J. "Reading the Book of Amos." *Scripture Bulletin* 16 (1986): 23–32.

Dion, P.-E. "Le message moral du prophète Amos s'inspirait-il du 'droit de l'alliance'?" *ScEs* 27 (1975): 5–34.

Donner, H. "Die soziale Botschaft der Propheten im Lichte der Gesellschaftsordnung in Israel." *OrAnt* 2 (1963): 229–45.

Doorly, W. J. *Prophet of Justice. Understanding the Book of Amos.* New York/Mahwah, N.J.: Paulist, 1989.

Doron, P. "Paranomasia in the Prophecies to the Nations." *HS* 10/11 (1979–80): 36–43.

Dreyfus, F. "Reste d'Israel." *DBS* 10 (1981): 414–37.

Driver, G. R. "Affirmation by Exclamatory Negation." *JANESCU* 5 (1973): 104–14.

Driver, S. R. *The Books of Joel and Amos.* Cambridge: Cambridge University Press, 1915; 2d ed. 1934.

Duhm, B. "Anmerkungen zu den Zwölf Propheten, 1. Buch Amos." *ZAW* 31 (1911): 1–18.

Ebach, J. "Sozialethische Erwägungen zum alttestamentlichen Bodenrecht." *BN* 1 (1976): 31–46.

Ebo, D. J. "Another Look at Amos' Visions." *Africa Theological Journal* 18 (1989): 17–27.

Edelman, D. "The Meaning of *qitter.*" *VT* 35 (1985): 395–404.

Edghill, E. A. *The Book of Amos.* 2d ed. London: Longmans, Green, 1926.

Eggebrecht, G. "Die früheste Bedeutung und der Ursprung der Konzeption vom 'Tage Jahwes'." *Theologische Versuche*, eds. J. Rogge and G. Schille. Berlin: Evang. Verlagsanstalt, 1984.

Ehrlich, A. B. *Randglossen zur hebräischen Bibel.* 7 vols. Leipzig: Hinrichs, 1912, 5:227–56.

Eichrodt, W. "Die Vollmacht des Amos. Zu einer schwierigen Stelle im Amosbuch 3, 3–8." *Beiträge zur alttestamentlichen Theologie. Festschrift für Walther Zimmerli zum 70. Geburtstag*, ed. H. Donner. Göttingen: Vandenhoeck und Ruprecht, 1977, 124–31.

Eisenbeis, W. *Die Wurzel šlm im Alten Testament.* Berlin/New York: W. de Gruyter, 1969.

Eissfeldt, O. "Marzeah und Marzeha. Kultmahlgenossenschaft im spätjüdischen Schrifttum." *Kleine Schriften zum Alten Testament.* Tübingen: J. C. B. Mohr, 1973, 136–42.

____. "Der Zugang zu Hamath." *OrAnt* 10 (1971): 269–76.

Elhorst, H. J. *De Profetie van Amos.* Leiden: E. J. Brill, 1902.

Ellenbogen, M. *Foreign Words in the Old Testament. Their Origin and Etymology.* London: Luzac, 1962, 31–32.

Elliger, K. *Das Buch der zwölf kleinen Propheten, II.* Göttingen: Vandenhoeck und Ruprecht, 1950.

Epsztein, L. *Social Justice in the Ancient Near East and the People of the Bible*. London: SCM, 1986.

Erlandsson, S. "Nagra exempel pa *waw explicativum*." *SEÅ* (1976–77): 69–76.

____. "Amos 5,25–27, et crux interpretum." *SEÅ* 33 (1968): 76–82.

Eslinger, L. "The Education of Amos." *HAR* 11 (1987): 35–57.

Eubanks, S. W. *Amos: Artist in Literary Composition*. Unpubl. diss., Southern Baptist Theological Seminary, 1943.

Everson, A. J. *The Day of Yahweh as Historical Event*. Unpubl. Ph.D. diss., Union Theological Seminary, Virginia, 1969.

____. "The Days of Yahweh." *JBL* 93 (1974): 329–37.

____. "Day of the Lord." *IDB(Sup)*. Nashville: Abingdon, 1976, 209–10.

Ewald, H. *Die Propheten des Alten Bundes. Band I*. 5 vols. Göttingen: Vandenhoeck und Ruprecht, 1867–69.

Eybers, I. H. "Some Examples of Hyperbole in Biblical Hebrew." *Semitics* 1 (1970): 38–49.

Fabian, N. *Protest gegen Ausbeutung: Amos' sozialkritische Ansätze in der alttestamentlichen Prophetie*. Münster i. W.: Pfeiffer, 1973.

Fang, C. "Universalism and the Prophet Amos." *Collectanea Theologica Universitatis Fujen* 5/20 (1974): 165–71.

Farr, G. "The Language of Amos, Popular or Cultic?" *VT* 16 (1966): 312–24.

Feliks, J. *Nature and Man in the Bible*. London/Jerusalem/New York, 1981.

____. *The Plant World of the Bible*. Ramat-Gan: Bar Ilan University, 1968. (Heb.)

Fendler, M. "Zur Sozialkritik des Amos. Versuch einer wirtschafts- und sozialgeschichtlichen Interpretation alttestamentlicher Texte." *EvTh* 33 (1973): 32–53.

Fensham, F. C. "Common Trends in Curses of the Near Eastern Treaties and *Kudurru*-Inscriptions Compared with Maledictions of Amos and Isaiah." *ZAW* 75 (1963): 155–75.

____. "A Possible Origin of the Day of the Lord." *Biblical Essays*. Potchefstroom: Rege-Pers Beperk, 1966, 90–97.

Fey, R. *Amos und Jesaja. Abhängigkeit und Eigenständigkeit des Jesaja*. Neukirchen-Vluyn: Neukirchener Verlag, 1963.

Finley, T. J. *Joel, Amos, Obadiah*. Chicago: Moody, 1990.

____ "An Evangelical Response to the Preaching of Amos." *JETS* 28 (1985): 411–20.

Fishbane, M. "The Treaty Background of Amos 1:11 and Related Matters." *JBL* 89 (1970): 313–18.

____. "Additional Remarks on *rhmyw* (Amos 1:11)." *JBL* 91 (1972): 391–93.

Fisher, E. J. "Cultic Prostitution in the Ancient Near East? A Reassessment." *BTB* 6 (1976): 225–36.

Flammer, B. "Prophet und Tempel." *Franziskanische Studien* 65 (1983): 35–42.

Fleischer, G. *Von Menschenverkäufern, Baschankühen und Rechtsverkehrern. Die Sozialkritik des Amosbuches in historisch- kritischer, sozialgeschichtlicher und archäologischer Perspektive*. Frankfurt am M.: Athenäum Verlag, 1989.

Fohrer, G. *Die Propheten des 8. Jahrhunderts*. Gütersloh: Gütersloher Verlagshaus, 1974, 22–55.

____. "Der Tag JHWHs." ErIsr 16 (Harry Orlinsky Volume, eds. B. A. Levine and A. Malamat). Jerusalem: Israel Exploration Society, 1982, 43*–50*.

Foresti, F. "Funzione Semantica dei Brani Particali di Amos 4,13, 5,8s, 9,5s." *Bib* 62 (1981): 169–84.

Fosbroke, H. E. W. "The Book of Amos: Introduction and Exegesis." *The Interpreter's Bible*. Nashville: Abingdon, 1956, 6:671–853.

Freedman, D. N. "Headings in the Books of the Eighth-Century Prophets." *AUSS* 25 (1987): 9–26.

Freedman, D. N., and F. I. Anderson. "*Harmon* in Amos 4:3." *BASOR* 198 (1970): 41.

Frey, H. *Das Buch des Ringens Gotttes um seine Kirche. Der Prophet Amos*. 2d ed. Stuttgart: Calwer Verlagshaus, 1965.

Fritz, V. "Die Fremdvölkersprüche des Amos." *VT* 37 (1987): 26–38.

____. "Amosbuch, Amos-Schule und historischer Amos." *Prophet und Prophetenbuch. Festschrift für Otto Kaiser zum 65. Geburtstag*, eds. Volkmar Fritz, Karl-Friedrich Pohlmann, and Hans-Christoph Schmitt. Berlin/New York: W. de Gruyter, 1989, 29–43.

Fuhs, H. F. "Amos 1:1. Erwägungen zur Tradition und Redaktion des Amosbuches." *Bausteine Biblischer Theologie. Festgabe für G. J. Botterweck*, ed. H. J. Fabry. Bonn: Hanstein, 1977, 271–90.

Galil, J. "An Ancient Technique of Ripening Sycamore Fruit in the East-Mediterranean Countries." *Economic Botany* 22 (1968): 178–90.

Galil, J., and D. Eisikowitch. "Flowery Cycles and Fruit Types of *Ficus sycamorus*." *New Phytologist* 67 (1968): 752–55.

Garbini, G. "Note semitiche II." *Ricerche linguistiche* 5 (1962): 179–81.

Garcia de la Fuente, O. "La búsque da de Dios según el profeta Amos." *Augustinianum Roma* 12 (1972): 257–76.

Garcia-Treto, F. O. "The Three Day Festival Pattern in Ancient Israel." *Trinity University Studies in Religion* 9 (1967–69): 19–30.

Garland, D. D. *Amos: Bible Study Commentary*. Grand Rapids: Zondervan, 1973.

Garrett, D. A. "The Structure of Amos as a Testimony to Its Integrity." *JETS* 27 (1984): 275–76.

Gaster, T. H. "An Ancient Hymn in the Prophecies of Amos." *Journal of the Manchester University Egyptian and Oriental Society* 19 (1935): 23–26.

Gerleman, G. "Rest und Überschuss. Eine terminologische Studie." *Travel in the World of the Old Testament. Fs. M. A. Beek*. Assen: Kampen, 1974, 71–74.

Gerstenberger, E. "Covenant and Commandment." *JBL* 84 (1965): 38–51.

Gese, H. "Komposition bei Amos." *VTS* 32 (1981): 74–95.

____. "Das Problem von Amos 9,7." *Texgemäss. Festschrift für E. Würthwein zum 70. Geburtstag*, eds. A. H. J. Gunneweg and O. Kaiser. Göttingen: Vandenhoeck und Ruprecht, 1979, 33–38.

____. "Amos 8:4–8: Der kosmische Frevel händlerischer Habgier." *Propet und Prophetenbuch. Festschrift für Otto Kaiser zum 65. Geburtstag*, eds. V. Fritz, K.-F.

Pohlmann, and H.-C. Schmitt. Berlin/New York: W. de Gruyter, 1989, 59–72.

____. "Kleine Beiträge zum Verständnis des Amosbuches." *VT* 12 (1962): 417–38.

Gevritz, S. "A New Look at an Old Crux: Amos 5:26." *JBL* 87 (1968): 267–76.

Geyer, J. B. "Mythology and Culture in the Oracles Against the Nations." *VT* 36 (1986): 129–45.

Giesen, G. *Die Wurzel sb' 'schwören.' Eine semasiologische Studie zum Eid im Alten Testament.* Bonn: Hanstein, 1981.

Gilead, H. "Amos—Among the Herdsmen in Tekoa." *Beth Miqra* 54 (1973): 375–81. (Heb. with Eng. summary)

Giles, T. "An Introductory Investigation of Amos by Means of the Model of the Voluntary Social Movement." *PEGLBS* 8 (1988): 135–53.

Ginat, L. "Toward the Sequence of Amos's Prophecies Against the Nations." *Beth Miqra* 34 (1988–89): 250–54. (Heb.)

Ginsberg, H. L. "'Roots Below and Fruit Above' and Related Matters." *Hebrew and Semitic Studies Presented to G. R. Driver*, eds. D. W. Thomas and W. D. McHardy. Oxford: Clarendon, 1963, 72–76.

Gitay, Y. "A Study of Amos's Art of Speech: A Rhetorical Analysis of Amos 3:1–15." *CBQ* 42 (1980): 293–309.

Givati, M. "The Sabbat of the Words of the Prophet Amos." *Beth Miqra* 69 (1977): 194–98, 278–79. (Heb.)

Glanzman, G. S. "Two Notes: Amos 3:15 and Hosea 11:8–9." *CBQ* 23 (1961): 227–33.

Glück, J. J. "*'ryh* and *lby'* (labi')—An Etymological Study." *ZAW* 81 (1969): 232–35.

____. "Three Notes on the Book of Amos." *Studies in the Books of Hosea and Amos. Die Ou Testamentiese Werkgemeeskap in Suid Afrika, 7th and 8th Congresses.* Potchefstroom: Rege-Pers Beperk, 1964–65, 115–21.

Good, R. M. "The Just War in Ancient Israel." *JBL* 104 (1985): 385–400.

Gordis, R. *Poets, Prophets and Sages: Essays in Biblical Interpretation.* Bloomington, Ind.: Indiana University Press, 1971.

____. "Studies in the Book of Amos." *Proceedings of the American Academy for Jewish Research* 46/47 (1979–80): 201–64.

____. "Amos, Edom and Israel—An Unrecognized Source for Edomite History." *Essays on the Occasion of the Seventieth Anniversary of the Dropsie University*, eds. A. Katsh and L. Nemoy. Philadelphia: Dropsie University Press, 1979, 109–32.

Görg, M. "Der *nabi'*—'Berufener' oder 'Seher'?" *BN* 17 (1982): 23–25.

Gossai, H. "*Ṣaddîq* in Theological, Forensic and Economic Perspectives." *SEÅ* 53 (1988): 7–13.

Gosse, B. "Le recueil d'oracles contre les nations du livre d'Amos et l'histoire deutéronomique'." *VT* 38 (1988): 22–40.

Gottlieb, H. "Amos und Jerusalem." *VT* 17 (1967): 430–63.

Gottwald, N. K. *The Tribes of Yahweh: A Sociology of the Religion of Liberated Israel, 1250–1050 B.C.E.* Maryknoll: Orbis, 1979, 512–34.

Gowan, D. E. "The Use of *y'n* in Biblical Hebrew." *VT* 21 (1971): 168–85.

____. "The Beginnings of Exile-Theology and the Root *glh*." *ZAW* 87 (1987): 204–7.

Graesser, C., Jr. "Righteousness, Human and Divine." *CurTM* 10 (1983): 134–41.

Graetz, H. *Emendationes in plerosque Sacrae Scripturae Veteris Testamenti Libros*, ed. G. Bacher. 3 vols. Breslau: Schottlaender, 1893.

Gray, J. "The Day of Yahweh in Cultic Experience and Eschatological Prospect." *SEÅ* 39 (1974): 5–37.

Grayson, A. K. "Studies in Neo-Assyrian History: The Ninth Century." *BO* 33 (1976): 134–45.

____. " Assyria: Ashur-dan II to Ashur-Nirari V (935–745 B.C.)." *CAH* 3/1 (1982): 238–82.

Grech, P. "Interprophetic Re-Interpretation and Old Testament Eschatology." *Augustinum* 9 (1969): 235–65.

Greene, J. T. *The Old Testament Prophet as Messenger in the Light of Ancient Near Eastern Messengers and Messages*. Unpubl. Ph.D. diss., Boston University, 1980.

Greenfield, J. C. "Un rite araméen et ses parallèles." *RB* 80 (1973): 46–52.

____. "The *Marzeah* as a Social Institution." *Acta Antiqua* 22 (1974): 451–55.

Grether, H. G. "Some Problems of Equivalence in Amos 1:3." *BT* 22 (1971): 116–17.

Grosch, H. *Der Prophet Amos*. Gütersloh: Gerd Mohn, 1969.

Gross, W. "Die Herausführungsformel. Zum Verhältnis von Formel und Syntax." *ZAW* 86 (1974): 425–53.

____. "Verbform und Function. *Wayyiqtol* für die Gegenwart." *Münchener Universitätsschriften. Arbeiten zu Text und Sprache im Alten Testament* 1. St. Ottilien, 1976, 99–104.

Grossberg, D. "Noun/Verb Parallelism: Syntactic or Asyntactic." *JBL* 99 (1980): 481–88.

____. "Canticles 3:10 in the Light of a Homeric and Biblical Poetics." *BTB* 11 (1981): 74–76.

Grossfeld, B. "The Translation of the Biblical Hebrew *dqp* in the Targum, Peshitta, Vulgate and Septuagint." *ZAW* 96 (1984): 83–101.

Guiterrez, R. C. *La justicia social en los profetas del siglo VIII: Amos, Oseas, Isaias, y Miqueas*. Fribourg, 1970.

Gunkel, H. "IIB. The Israelite Prophecy from the Time of Amos." *Twentieth Century in the Making*, vol. 1, *Themes of Biblical Theology*, ed. J. Pelikan. London: William Collins Sons; New York: Harper & Row, 1969, 48–75.

Gunneweg, A. H. J. "Religion oder Offenbarung. Zum hermeneutischen Problem des Alten Testaments." *ZTK* 74 (1977): 151–78.

____. "Erwägungen zu Amos 7,14." *ZTK* 57 (1960): 1–16.

Gunning, J. H. *De Godspraken van Amos, Vertaald en Verklaard*. Leiden: E. J. Brill, 1885.

Guthe, H. "Der Prophet Amos." *Die Heilige Schrift des Alten Testaments*, eds. E. Kautzsch and H. Bertholet. 4th ed. Tübingen: J. C. B. Mohr [Paul Siebeck], 1921.

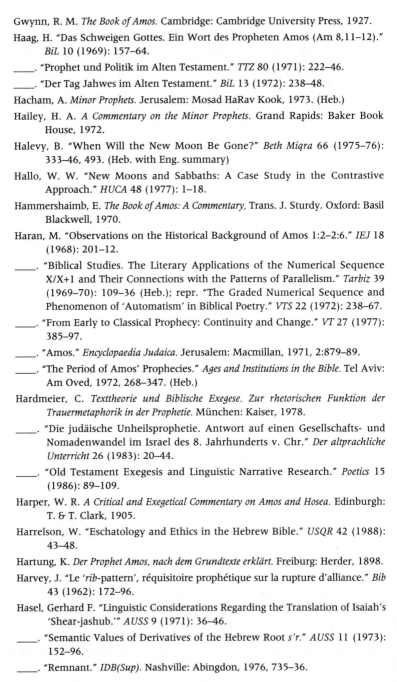

Gwynn, R. M. *The Book of Amos.* Cambridge: Cambridge University Press, 1927.

Haag, H. "Das Schweigen Gottes. Ein Wort des Propheten Amos (Am 8,11–12)." *BiL* 10 (1969): 157–64.

____. "Prophet und Politik im Alten Testament." *TTZ* 80 (1971): 222–46.

____. "Der Tag Jahwes im Alten Testament." *BiL* 13 (1972): 238–48.

Hacham, A. *Minor Prophets.* Jerusalem: Mosad HaRav Kook, 1973. (Heb.)

Hailey, H. A. *A Commentary on the Minor Prophets.* Grand Rapids: Baker Book House, 1972.

Halevy, B. "When Will the New Moon Be Gone?" *Beth Miqra* 66 (1975–76): 333–46, 493. (Heb. with Eng. summary)

Hallo, W. W. "New Moons and Sabbaths: A Case Study in the Contrastive Approach." *HUCA* 48 (1977): 1–18.

Hammershaimb, E. *The Book of Amos: A Commentary,* Trans. J. Sturdy. Oxford: Basil Blackwell, 1970.

Haran, M. "Observations on the Historical Background of Amos 1:2–2:6." *IEJ* 18 (1968): 201–12.

____. "Biblical Studies. The Literary Applications of the Numerical Sequence X/X+1 and Their Connections with the Patterns of Parallelism." *Tarbiz* 39 (1969–70): 109–36 (Heb.); repr. "The Graded Numerical Sequence and Phenomenon of 'Automatism' in Biblical Poetry." *VTS* 22 (1972): 238–67.

____. "From Early to Classical Prophecy: Continuity and Change." *VT* 27 (1977): 385–97.

____. "Amos." *Encyclopaedia Judaica.* Jerusalem: Macmillan, 1971, 2:879–89.

____. "The Period of Amos' Prophecies." *Ages and Institutions in the Bible.* Tel Aviv: Am Oved, 1972, 268–347. (Heb.)

Hardmeier, C. *Texttheorie und Biblische Exegese. Zur rhetorischen Funktion der Trauermetaphorik in der Prophetie.* München: Kaiser, 1978.

____. "Die judäische Unheilsprophetie. Antwort auf einen Gesellschafts- und Nomadenwandel im Israel des 8. Jahrhunderts v. Chr." *Der altsprachliche Unterricht* 26 (1983): 20–44.

____. "Old Testament Exegesis and Linguistic Narrative Research." *Poetics* 15 (1986): 89–109.

Harper, W. R. *A Critical and Exegetical Commentary on Amos and Hosea.* Edinburgh: T. & T. Clark, 1905.

Harrelson, W. "Eschatology and Ethics in the Hebrew Bible." *USQR* 42 (1988): 43–48.

Hartung, K. *Der Prophet Amos, nach dem Grundtexte erklärt.* Freiburg: Herder, 1898.

Harvey, J. "Le 'rib-pattern', réquisitoire prophétique sur la rupture d'alliance." *Bib* 43 (1962): 172–96.

Hasel, Gerhard F. "Linguistic Considerations Regarding the Translation of Isaiah's 'Shear-jashub.'" *AUSS* 9 (1971): 36–46.

____. "Semantic Values of Derivatives of the Hebrew Root *s'r.*" *AUSS* 11 (1973): 152–96.

____. "Remnant." *IDB(Sup).* Nashville: Abingdon, 1976, 735–36.

____. *The Remnant: The History and Theology of the Remnant Idea from Genesis to Isaiah.* Berrien Springs, Mich.: Andrews University Press, 1980.

____. "'Remnant' as a Meaning of *'acharith.*" *The Archaeology of Jordan and Other Studies,* eds. L. T. Geraty and L. G. Herr. Berrien Springs, Mich.: Andrews University Press, 1986, 511–24.

____. "*palaṭ, malaṭ, paliṭ, paleṭ, peleṭah, peleṭah, miplaṭ.*" *TWAT* 6 (1987): 589–606.

____. "Remnant." *International Standard Bible Encyclopedia.* Grand Rapids Eerdmans, 1988, 4:130–34.

Hauan, M. J. "The Background and Meaning of Amos 5:17B." *HTR* 79 (1986): 337–48.

Haupt, P. "Was Amos a Sheepman?" *JBL* 35 (1916): 288–90.

Hauret, C. *Amos et Osée.* Paris: Beauchesne, 1970.

____. "La vocation d'un prophète (Am 7,12–15)." *AsSeign* [Bruges] 46 (1974): 30–35.

Hausmann, J. *Israels Rest. Studien zum Selbstverständnis der nachexilischen Gemeinde.* Stuttgart: W. Kohlhammer, 1987.

Hawkins, J. D. "The Neo-Hittite States in Syria and Anatolia." *CAH* 3/1 (1982): 374–441.

Hayes, J. H. *The Oracles Against the Nations in the Old Testament: Their Usage and Theological Importance.* Unpubl. diss., Princeton Theological Seminary, 1964.

____. "The Usage of the Oracles Against the Foreign Nations in Ancient Israel." *JBL* 87 (1968): 81–92.

____. *Amos, His Time and His Preaching: The Eighth Century Prophet.* Nashville: Abingdon, 1988.

Hayes, J. H., and J. Maxwell Miller. *Israelite and Judean History.* Philadelphia: Westminster; London: SCM, 1977.

Heisksen, H. "Tekoa: Historical and Cultural Profile." *JETS* 13 (1970): 81–89.

Held, M. "Studies in Biblical Homonyms in the Light of Akkadian." *JANESCU* 3 (1970–71): 47–55.

Hélewa, F. J. "L'origine du concept prophétique du 'Jour de Yahvé." *ECarm* 15 (1964): 3–36.

Hellberg, J. L. "Disillusionment on the Day of Yahweh with Special Reference to the Land (Amos 5)." *OTE* 1 (1988): 31–46.

Helter, M. *The Rural Community in Ancient Ugarit.* Wiesbaden: O. Harrassowitz, 1976.

Henderson, E. *The Book of the Twelve Minor Prophets.* Andover, Mass.: W. F. Draper; New York: Sheldon, 1846.

Henry, M. L. *Prophet und Tradition. Versuch einer Problemstellung.* Berlin: W. de Gruyter, 1969.

Hermando, E. "Pueblo de Dios y convivencia humana (Amos–Oseas)." *LU VITOR* 24 (1975): 385–411.

Hermisson, H. J. *Sprache und Ritus im altisraelitischen Kult.* Neukirchen-Vluyn: Neukirchener Verlag, 1965.

Herntrich, V. *Amos der Prophet Gottes.* Göttingen: Vandenhoeck und Ruprecht, 1941.

Hermann, S. *A History of Israel in Old Testament Times*. Philadelphia: Fortress, 1975.

Herrmann, W. "Jahwes Triumph über Mot." *UF* 11 (1979): 371–77.

Heschel, A. J. *The Prophets*. 2 vols. New York: Harper & Row, 1962, 1:27–38.

Hesse, F. "Amos 5, 4–6, 14f." *ZAW* 68 (1956): 1–17.

Hesselberg, H. *Die zwölf Kleinen Propheten ausgelegt*. Königsberg: A. W. Unzer, 1838.

Hillers, D. R. *Treaty Curses and the Old Testament Prophets*. Rome: Pontifical Biblical Institute Press, 1964.

_____. "*Hôy* and *Hôy*-Oracles: A Neglected Syntactic Aspect." *The Word of the Lord Shall Go Forth: Essays in Honor of David Noel Freedman in Celebration of His Sixtieth Birthday*, eds. C. L. Meyers and M. O'Connor. Winona Lake, Ind.: Eisenbrauns, 1983, 185–88.

_____. "Amos 7:4 and Ancient Parallels." *CBQ* 26 (1964): 221–25.

Hindson, E. *The Philistines and the Old Testament*. Grand Rapids: Baker Book House, 1971.

Hirota, K. *An Interpretation of Amos 5,18–20*. Tokyo: Rikkyo University, 1978.

Hirth, V. "Der Dienst fremder Götter als Gericht Jahwes." *BN* 45 (1988): 40–41.

Hitzig, F., and H. Steiner. *Die zwölf Kleinen Propheten erklärt*. 4th ed. Leipzig: Hirtzel, 1881.

Hobbs, T. R. "Amos 3,1b and 2,10." *ZAW* 81 (1969): 384–87.

Hockenhull, B. R. *The Use of Series in the Book of Amos*. Unpubl. Th.D. diss., New Orleans Baptist Theological Seminary, 1987.

Höffken, P. *Untersuchungen zu den Begründungselementen der Völkerorakel des Alten Testaments*. Unpubl. Th.D. diss., University of Bonn, 1977.

_____. "Zu den Heilszusätzen in der Völkerorakelsammlung des Jeremiabuches." *VT* 27 (1977): 398–412.

_____. "Eine Bemerkung zum 'Haus Hasaels' in Amos 1,4." *ZAW* 94 (1982): 413–15.

Hoffmann, H. W. "Form-Funktion-Intention." *ZAW* 82 (1970): 341–46.

_____. "Zur Echtheitsfrage von Amos 9,9f." *ZAW* 82 (1970): 121–22.

Hoffmann, Y. "Did Amos Regard Himself as a *nabi'*?" *VT* 27 (1977): 209–12.

_____. "The Day of the Lord as a Concept and a Term in the Prophetic Literature." *ZAW* 93 (1981): 37–50.

_____. "From Oracle to Prophecy: The Growth, Crystallization and Disintegration of a Biblical *Gattung*." *JNES* 10 (1982): 75–81.

_____. "A North Israelite Typological Myth and a Judean Historical Tradition: The Exodus in Hosea and Amos." *VT* 39 (1989): 169–82.

_____. *The Prophecies Against Foreign Nations in the Bible*. Tel Aviv: Kibbutz Hameuhad, 1977. (Heb.)

Hogg, H. W. "The Starting Point of the Religious Message of Amos." *Transactions of the Third Congress of the History of Religions*, eds. P. S. Allen and J. DeM. Johnson. Oxford, 1908, 1:325–27.

Holladay, J. S. "Assyrian Statecraft and the Prophets of Israel." *HTR* 63 (1970): 29–51.

_____. "Once More, *'anak* = tin, Amos VII,7–8." *VT* 20 (1970): 492–94.

_____. "Amos VI 16b: A Suggested Solution." *VT* 22 (1972): 107–10.

Holm-Nielsen, S. "Die Sozialkritik der Propheten." *Denkender Glaube. Festschrift Carl Heinz Ratschow,* ed. Otto Kaiser. Berlin/New York: W. de Gruyter, 1976, 7–23.

Horine, S. "A Study of the Literary Genre of the Woe Oracle." *Calvary Baptist Theological Journal* 5 (1989): 74–97.

Horn, S. H. "The Amman Citadel Inscription." *BASOR* 193 (1969): 2–13.

Honeycutt, R. L. *Amos and His Message. An Expository Commentary.* Nashville: Broadman, 1963.

Hoppe, L. J. *Being Poor: A Biblical Study.* Wilmington: M. Glazier, 1987.

Horst, F. "Die Doxologien im Amosbuch." *ZAW* 47 (1929): 45–54; repr. *Gottes Recht. Studien zum Recht im Alten Testament,* ed. H. W. Wolff. Munich: Kaiser, 1961, 155–61.

Horton, R. F., and S. R. Driver. *The Minor Prophets.* Edinburgh: T. C. & E. C. Jack, 1904–6.

Houtman, C. "De jubelzang van de struiken der wildernis in Psalm 96:12b." *Loven en geloven, FS N. H. Ridderbos.* Amsterdam: Ton Bolland, 1975, 151–74.

How, J. C. H. *Joel and Amos.* Cambridge: Cambridge University Press, 1910.

Howard, G. "Some Notes on the Septuagint of Amos." *VT* 20 (1970): 108–12.

_____. "The Quinta of the Minor Prophets: A First Century Septuaginta Text?" *Bib* 56 (1974): 15–22.

_____. "Revisions toward the Hebrew in the Septuagint Text of Amos." ErIsr 16 (1982): 125*–33*.

Howington, N. P. "Toward an Ethical Understanding of Amos." *RevEx* 63 (1966): 405–12.

Hubbard, D. A. *Joel and Amos: An Introduction and Commentary.* Leicester: Inter-Varsity, 1989.

Huey, F. B., Jr. "The Ethical Teachings of Amos: Its Content and Relevance." *SWJT* 9 (1966): 57–67.

Huffmon, H. B. "The Covenant Lawsuit in the Prophets." *JBL* 78 (1959): 285–95.

_____. "The Treaty Background of Hebrew *yada'*." *BASOR* 181 (1966): 31–37.

_____. "The Social Role of Amos' Message." *The Quest for the Kingdom of God: Studies in Honor of G. E. Mendenhall,* eds. H. B. Huffmon et al. Winona Lake, Ind.: Eisenbrauns, 1983, 109–16.

Huidberg-Hansen, O. "Die Vernichtung des Goldenen Kalbes und der ugaritische Ernteritus." *Acta Orientalia* 33 (1971): 5–46.

Hulst, A. R. "Over de betekenis van het woord sod." *Vruchten van het Uithof. Fs. H. A. Brongers.* Utrecht, 1974, 37–48.

Hunter, A. V. *Seek the Lord! A Study of the Meaning and Function of the Exhortations in Amos, Hosea, Isaiah, Micah, and Zephaniah.* Baltimore: St. Mary's Seminary and University Press, 1982, 56–105.

Hyatt, J. P. "The Translation and Meaning of Amos 5:23–24." *ZAW* 68 (1956): 17–24.

_____. *The Prophetic Criticism of Israelite Worship.* Cincinnati: Hebrew Union College, 1963.

Igleheart, J. H. *Education and Culture in the Book of Amos*. Unpubl. diss., University of Kentucky, 1974.

Isbell, C. D. "A Note on Amos 1.1." *JNES* 36 (1977): 213–14.

_____. "Another Look at Amos 5:26." *JBL* 97 (1978): 97–99.

Ishida, T. "'The People of the Land' and the Political Crises in Judah." *AJBI* 1 (1975): 23–38.

Jackson, J. "Rhetorical Criticism and the Problem of Subjectivity." *PEGLBS* 2 (1982): 34–45.

_____. "Amos and His Environment." *PEGLBS* 5 (1985): 81–86.

_____. "Amos 5,13 Contextually Understood." *ZAW* 98 (1986): 434–35.

Jacob, E. "Prophètes et intercesseurs." *De la Tôrah au Messie, Mélanges H. Cazelles.* Paris: Desclée, 1981, 205–17.

Jacobs, P. F. "'Cows of Basan'—A Note on the Interpretation of Amos 4:1." *JBL* 104 (1985): 109–10.

Jagersma, H. "The Tithes in the Old Testament." *OTS* 21 (1981): 116–28.

Jansen, H. "Amos of Amasja." *Schrift* 52 (August 1977): 132–37.

Janssen, H. *Voorliefde en verantwoordeliijkheid—Een eksegetische studie over Amos 3,1–2 en 9:7.* Utrecht: Theological Institute, 1975.

Janzen, W. "*Ašre* and *Hoi* in the Old Testament." *HTR* 62 (1969): 432–33.

Jenson, J. K. R. *Amos og Hosea.* Kopenhagen, 1914.

Jeppesen, K., and B. Otzen. *The Productions of Time: Tradition History in Old Testament Scholarship.* Sheffield: Almond, 1984.

Jepsen, A. *Das Zwölfprophetenbuch übersetzt und ausgelegt.* Leipzig/Hamburg: G. Schloessmann, 1937.

Jeremias, J. "Die Vollmacht des Propheten im Alten Testament." *EvTh* 31 (1971): 305–22.

_____. *Die Reue Gottes. Aspekte Alttestamentlicher Gottesvortellung.* Neukirchen-Vluyn: Neukirchener Verlag, 1975.

_____. "Amos 3–6: From the Oral Word to the Text." *Canon, Theology, and Old Testament Interpretation. Essays in Honor of Brevard S. Childs,* eds. G. M. Tucker, D. L. Peterson, and R. R. Wilson. Philadelphia: Fortress, 1988, 220–21.

_____. "Amos 3–6. Beobachtungen zur Entstehungsgeschichte eines Prophetenbuches." *ZAWSuppl* 100 (1988): 123–38.

_____. "Völkersprüche und Visionsberichte im Amosbuch." *Prophet und Prophetenbuch. Festschrift für Otto Kaiser zum 65. Geburtstag,* eds. Volkmar Fritz, K.-F. Pohlmann, and H-C. Schmitt. Berlin/New York: W. de Gruyter, 1989, 82–97.

Jimenez, J. *Relecturas de Amos-Isaias.* Unpubl. diss., Jerusalem, 1973.

Jones, G. H. *An Examination of Some Leading Motifs in the Prophetic Oracles Against Foreign Nations.* Phil. diss., University of Wales, Bangor, 1970.

Jongeling, B. "*Laken* dans l'Ancien Testament." *OTS* 21 (1981): 190–200.

Jozaki, S. "The Secondary Passages of the Book of Amos." *Kwansei Gakuin University Annual Studies* 4 (1956): 25–100.

Justi, K. W. *Amos neu übersetzt und erläutert.* Leipzig: Hitzig, 1820.

Juynboll, T. G. J. *Disputation de Amoso.* Leiden: Brill, 1828.

Kahlert, H. "Zur Frage nach der geistigen Heimat des Amos. Eine Prüfung der These von H. W. Wolff." *Dielheimer Blätter zum AT* 4, Dielheim (1973): 1–12.

Kaiser, O. "Gerechtigkeit und Heil bei den israelischen Propheten und griechischen Denkern des 8.-6. Jahrhunderts. Rudolf Bultmann zum 85. Geburtstag." *N Z Sys Th* 11 (1969): 312–28.

Kaiser, W. C. "The Davidic Promise and the Inclusion of the Gentiles (Amos 9:9–15 and Acts 15:13–18): A Test Passage for Theological Systems." *JETS* 20 (1977): 97–111.

Källstad, T. E. "(Amos 4:11; Zech 3:2) 'A Brand Snatched out of Fire.'" *Archiv für Religionspsychologie* 14 (1980): 237–45.

Kalluveettil, P. *Declaration and Covenant. A Comprehensive Review of Covenant Formulae from the Old Testament and the Ancient Near East.* Rome: Pontifical Biblical Institute Press, 1982, 7–16.

Kapelrud, A. S. *Central Ideas in Amos.* 2d ed. Oslo: Oslo University Press, 1961.

____. "God as Destroyer in the Preaching of Amos." *JBL* 71 (1952): 33–38.

____. "New Ideas in Amos." *VTS* 15 (1965): 193–206.

____. "Israel's Prophets and Their Confrontation with the Canaanite Religion." *Sincretism.* Stockholm, 1969, 162–70.

____. "Amos og hans omgivelser. Opposisjonsinnlegg ved Hans M. Barstads doktor-disputas." *NorTT* 84 (1983): 157–66.

Katzenstein, H. J. *The History of Tyre, from the Beginning of the Second Millennium B.C.E. until the Fall of the Neo-Babylonian Empire in 538 B.C.E.* Jerusalem: Schoecken Institute for Jewish Research of the Jewish Theological Seminary of America, 1973, 193–205.

Katzoff, L. "Noblesse Oblige." *Dor le dor* 16 (1987–88): 213–16.

Kaufmann, Y. *The Religion of Israel. From Its Beginnings to the Babylonian Exile.* New York: Schocken, 1972.

Keddie, G. J. *Lord Is His Name.* Philadelphia: Presbyterian & Reformed, 1986.

Kee, A. "Amos and Affluence." *Furrow* 38 (1987): 151–61.

Keel, O. "Rechttun oder Annahme des drohenden Gerichts? Erwägungen zu Amos, dem frühen Jesaja und Micha." *BZ* 21 (1977): 200–218.

Keil, C. F. *Minor Prophets.* 2d ed. Grand Rapids: Eerdmans, 1882, 10:233–336.

Kellermann, U. "Der Amosschluss als Stimme deuteronomistischer Heilshoffnung." *EvTh* 29 (1969): 169–83.

Kelley, P. H. *Amos: Prophet of Social Justice.* Grand Rapids: Baker Book House, 1973.

____. "Contemporary Study of Amos and Prophetism." *RevEx* 63 (1966): 375–85.

Kelly, J. G. "The Interpretation of Amos 4,13 in the Early Christian Community." *Essays in Honor of Joseph P. Brennan,* ed. R. F. McNamara. New York, 1977, 60–77.

Kessler, R. "Die angeblichen Kornhändler von Amos VIII,4–7." *VT* 39 (1989): 13–22.

Kida, K. *Die Entstehung der Prophetischen Literatur bei Amos.* Unpubl. diss., München, 1973.

Kilian, R. "Gott und Gottesbilder in Alten Testament." *Erbe und Auftrag* 50 (1974): 339–54.

Kilpatrick, G. D. "Some Quotations in Acts, Les Actes des Apôtres. Tradition, rédaction, théologie." *BETL* 48 (1979): 81–97.

Kinet, D. *Der aufhaltbare Untergang. Hosea-Joel-Amos-Micha.* Stuttgart, 1981.

King, D. M. "The Use of Amos 9:11–12 in Acts 15:16–18." *Ashland Theological Journal* 21 (1989): 8–13.

King, P. J. *Amos, Hosea, Micah: An Archaeological Commentary.* Philadelphia: Westminster, 1988.

_____. "Amos." *The Jerome Biblical Commentary*, eds. R. E. Brown et al. 2d ed. Englewood Cliffs, N.J.: Prentice-Hall, 1971, 655–73.

_____. "The *Marzeah* Amos Denounces—Using Archaeology to Interpret a Biblical Text." *BAR* 15 (1988): 34–44.

_____. "The Great Eighth Century." *Bible Review* 5 (1989): 22–33, 44.

Kipper, J. B. "A evoluÿo econômico-social em Israel e a pregaÿao dos profetas." *RevCultBibl* 20 n/f 1 (1977): 309–51.

_____. "A mensagem social dos profetas de Israel." *Perspectiva Teologica* 11 (1979): 247–66.

Kitchen, K. A. "The Philistines." *Peoples of the Old Testament Times*, ed. D. J. Wiseman. London/New York: Oxford University Press, 1973, 53–78.

Klausner, J. *The Book of Amos.* Tel Aviv: Jizreel, 1943. (Heb.)

Klein, R. W. "The Day of the Lord." *CTM* 39 (1968): 517–25.

Klein, S. "Tekoa in Galilee." *Monatsschrift für Geschichte und Wissenschaft des Judentums* 67 (1922): 270–73.

Knabenbauer, J. *Commentarius in prophetes Minores.* Paris: Lethielleux, 1886.

Knapp, C. *Amos and His Age.* London: T. Murby, 1923.

Knauf, E. A. "Beth Aven." *Bib* 65 (1984): 251–53.

Knierim, R. P. "'I Will Not Cause It to Return' in Amos 1 and 2." *Canon and Authority: Essays in the Old Testament Religion and Theology*, eds. G. W. Coats and B. O. Long. Philadelphia: Fortress, 1977, 163–75.

Koch, K.. *Amos. Untersucht mit den Methoden einer strukturalen Formgeschichte.* 3 vols. Kevelaer: Butzon & Bercker, 1976.

_____. *Die Propheten I. Assyrische Zeit.* Stuttgart: Kohlhammer, 1978.

_____. *The Prophets.* 2 vols. Philadelphia: Fortress, 1983–84.

_____. "Die Rolle der hymnischen Abschnitte in der Komposition des Amos-Buches." *ZAW* 86 (1974): 504–37.

_____. "Die Entstehung der sozialen Kritik bei den Propheten." *Probleme biblischer Theologie, FS Gerhard von Rad.* Munich: Kaiser, 1971, 236–57.

_____. "Origin and Effect of the Social Critique of the Pre-Exilic Prophets." *Bangalore Theological Forum* 11 (1979): 91–108.

Köhler, L. *Amos. Der älteste Schriftprophet.* Zurich: Rascher, 1920.

_____. "Amos-Forschungen von 1917 bis 1932." *TRu* 4 (1932): 195–213.

Koenig, A. *Die Profeet Amos: Koort Verklarings oor die Ou Testament.* Kaapstad: N. G. Kerk-Uitgewers, 1974.

Kohata, F. "A Stylistic Study of the Metaphors of Amos." *Festschrift für M. Sekine.* Tokyo, 1972, 147–61.

Koizumi, T. "Toward the Establishment of a Scientific History of Israel—From Nomadic Period to the Organization of the Four Leading Tribes." *AJBI* 12 (1986): 29–76.

Kolbusz, S. F. "Amos 1983." *TBT* 21 (1983): 406–8.

Körner, J. "Die Bedeutung der Wurzel *br'* im Alten Testament." *OLZ* 64 (1969): 533–40.

Kornfeld, W. "Die Gesellschafts- und Kultkritik altestamentlicher Propheten." *Leiturgia-Koinonia-Diakonia. Fs. Kardinal F. Koenig.* Wien/Freiburg/Basel: Herder, 1980, 181–200.

Kraeling, E. G. *Commentary on the Prophets.* 2 vols. Camden, N.J.: T. Nelson, 1966.

Kraft, C. "The Book of Amos." *The Interpreter's One Volume Commentary on the Bible,* ed. C. Laymon. Nashville: Abingdon, 1971, 465–76.

Krasovec, J. "Merism-Polar Expression in Biblical Hebrew." *Bib* 64 (1983): 231–39.

Kraus, H.-J. "Die prophetische Botschaft gegen das soziale Unrecht Israels." *EvTh* 15 (1955): 295–307.

Krause, H.-J. "*hôj* als prophetische Leichenklage über das eigene Volk im 8. Jahrhundert." *ZAW* 85 (1973): 15–46.

Krause, M. *Das Verhältnis von sozialer Kritik und kommender Katastrophe in der Unheilsprophezeiungen des Amos.* Unpubl. diss., University of Hamburg, 1972.

Kroeker, J. *Die Prophetie oder das Reden Gottes. Die vorexililschen Propheten, I. Amos und Hosea.* Giessen/Basel, 1932.

Kselman, J. S. "The ABCB-Pattern: Further Examples." *VT* 32 (1982): 224–29.

Kugel, J. F. *The Idea of Biblical Poetry.* New Haven: Yale University Press, 1981.

———. "Two Introductions to Midrash." *Proof* 3 (1983): 131–55.

Kuntz, M. *Ein Element der alten Theophanieüberlieferung und seine Rolle in der Prophetie des Amos.* Unpubl. diss., University of Tübingen, 1968.

Kutal, B. *Libri prophetarum Amos et Abdiae.* Olmütz: Lidové, Zavody Tiskarskéé Nakladatelské, 1933.

Kutscher, E. Y. *A History of the Hebrew Language.* Ed. R. Kutscher. Jerusalem: Magnes; Leiden: E. J. Brill, 1972.

L'Heureux, C. E. "Understanding the Old Testament Prophecies." *TBT* (1985): 51–59.

Laetsch, T. F. K. *The Minor Prophets.* St. Louis: Concordia, 1956.

Landsberger, B. "Tin and Lead: The Adventures of Two Vocables." *JNES* 24 (1965): 285–96.

Landy, F. "Vision and Poetic Speech in Amos." *HAR* 11 (1987): 223–46.

Lang, B. "Messias und Messiaserwartung im alten Israel." *Bibel und Kirche* 33 (1978): 110–15.

———. "Sklaven und Unfreie im Buch Amos (II 16, VIII 6)." *VT* 31 (1981): 482–88.

———. "The Social Organisation of the Peasant Poverty in Biblical Israel." *JSOT* 24 (1982): 47–63.

_____. *Monotheism and the Prophetic Minority*. Sheffield: Almond, 1983.

Lang, N. "Prophetie und Oekonomie im Alten Israel." *Vor Gott sind Alle Gleich. Soziale Gleichheit, Soziale Ungleichheit und die Religionen*, ed. G. Kehrer. Düsseldorf, 1983, 53–73.

Leeuwen, C. van. "The Prophecy of the *yôm YHWH* in Amos V 18–20." *OTS* 19 (1974): 113–34.

_____. "Quelques problèmes de traduction dans les visions d'Amos chapitre 7." *Übersetzung und Deutung. Studien zum Alten Testament und seiner Umwelt. A. R. Hulst gewidmet von Freunden und Kollegen*, eds. H. A. Brongers et al. Nijkerk: Callenbuch, 1977, 103–12.

Lehmann, M. R. "Biblical Oaths." *ZAW* 81 (1969): 74–92.

Lehming, S. "Erwägungen zu Amos." *ZAW* 55 (1958): 145–69.

_____. *Offenbarung und Verkündigung. Studien zur theologiegeschichtlichen Bedeutung des Verhältnis von Berufung und Theologie bei Amos und Hosea*. Unpubl. diss., University of Kiel, 1953.

Lehrman, S. M. "Amos." *The Twelve Prophets*. London/Jerusalem/New York: Soncino, 1974.

Leiman, S. Z. *The Canon and Masorah of the Hebrew Bible*. New York: Arno, 1974.

Leinberg, W. "Language Consciousness in the Old Testament." *ZAW* 92 (1980): 185–204.

Lemaire, A. "Le sabbat a l'epoque royale Israelite." *RB* 80 (1973): 161–85.

Lemaire, A., and J.-M. Durand. *Les inscriptions araméennes de Sfiréet l'Assyrie de Shamshi-ilu*. Genéve/Paris: Droz, 1984.

Lemche, N. P. *Early Israel*. Leiden: E. J. Brill, 1985, 108–12.

Lenhard, H. "Über den Unterschied zwischen *lkn* und *'l kn*." *ZAW* 95 (1983): 269–72.

Levenson, J. D. "The Hebrew Bible, the Old Testament, and Historical Criticism." *The Future of Biblical Studies. The Hebrew Scriptures*, eds. R. E. Friedman and H. G. M. Williamson. Atlanta, Ga.: Scholars, 1987, 19–59.

Levey, S. H. "Amos in the Rabbinic Tradition." *Tradition as Openness to the Future. Essays in Honor of Willis W. Fisher*, eds. F. O. Francis and R. P. Wallace. Washington, D.C.: University of America Press, 1984, 55–69.

Levine, L. D. "Menahem and Tiglath-Pileser: A New Synchronism." *BASOR* 206 (1972): 40–42.

Limburg, J. *The Lawsuit of God in the Eighth-Century Prophets*. Unpubl. Ph.D. diss., Union Theological Seminary, 1969.

_____. "Amos 7:4: A Judgement with Fire?" *CBQ* 35 (1973): 346–49.

_____. *The Prophets and the Powerless*. Atlanta: John Knox, 1977.

_____. "Sevenfold Structures in the Book of Amos." *JBL* 106 (1987): 217–22.

_____. *Hosea–Micah*. Atlanta: John Knox, 1988.

Lindblom, J. *Prophecy in Ancient Israel*. Philadelphia: Fortress, 1962.

Lindhagen, C. *Propheten Amos*. Stockholm: Verbum, 1971.

Lindström, F. *God and the Origin of Evil: A Contextual Analysis of Alleged Monistic Evidence of the Old Testament*. Lund: CWK Gleerup, 1983, 199–214.

Lipinski, E. "Sale, Transfer, and Delivery in Ancient Semitic Terminology." *Gesellschaft und Kultur im Alten Vorderasien. Schriften zur Gesellschaft und Kultur des Alten Orients* 15 (1982): 173–85.

Lockert, E. *Le Prophète Amos.* Paris: Coveslant, 1909.

Loewenstamm, S. E. "The Address 'Listen' in the Ugaritic Epic and the Bible." *The Bible World,* ed. G. A. Rendsburg. New York: Ktav, 1981, 123–31.

Lohfink, N. "Die Bedeutungen von Hebr. *yrs* Qal und Hif." *BZ* 27 (1983): 14–33.

Löhr, M. *Untersuchungen zum Buch Amos.* Giessen: Töpelmann, 1901.

Long, B. O. "Reports of Visions among the Prophets." *JBL* 95 (1976): 353–65.

_____. "The Social World of Ancient Israel." *Int* 36 (1982): 243–55.

Loretz, O. "Die Berufung des Propheten Amos (7,14–15)." *UF* 6 (1974): 487–88.

_____. "Die prophetische Kritik des Rentenkapitalismus." *UF* 7 (1975): 271–78.

_____. "Vergleich und Kommentar in Amos 3:12." *BZ* 20 (1976): 122–25.

_____. "Ugaritische und hebräische Lexikographie II." *UF* 13 (1981): 127–35.

_____. "*šlm* in Am. 5.22 und das *šhlmjm* Opfer." *UF* 13 (1981): 127–31.

_____. "Ugaritisch-biblisch *mrzh* 'Kultmahl, Kultverein' in Jer 16,5 und Am 6,7." *Künder des Wortes. Beiträge zur Theologie der Propheten: Josef Schreiner zum 60. Geburtstag,* eds. L. Ruppert, P. Weimar, and E. Zenger. Würzburg: Echter, 1982, 87–93.

_____. "Die babylonischen Gottesnamen *Sukkut* und *Kajjamanu.* Ein Beitrag zur jüdischen Astrologie." *ZAW* 101 (1989): 286–90.

_____. "Amos VI 12." *VT* 39 (1989): 240–42.

Loss, N. M. "Uso e valore dei nomi di Dio e dei nomi del populo nel libro di Amos." *Salesianum* 41 (1979): 425–40.

Lubetski, M. "*šem* as a Deity." *Rel* 17 (1987): 1–14.

Lubsczyk, H. "Der Auszug Israels aus Ägypten. Seine theologische Bedeutung in prophetischer und priesterlicher Überlieferung." *Erfurter Theologische Studien* 11. Erfurt, 1963.

_____. "Amos—Prophet and Wordly Man." *Dor le dor* 10/3 (1982): 183–86.

_____. "The Prophecies unto the Nations in the Book of Amos from the Point of View of History." *Beth Miqra* 54 (1983): 287–301, 421–22. (Eng. summary)

_____. "Who Calls for the Waters of the Sea and Pours Them Out upon the Surface of the Earth? (Am 8:8; 9:6)." *Beth Miqra* 101/2 (1985): 259–62. (Heb.)

Lust, J. "Remarks on the Redaction of Amos V 4–6, 14–15." *OTS* 21 (1981): 129–54.

Maag, V. *Text, Wortschatz und Begriffswelt des Buches Amos.* Leiden: Brill, 1951.

Machinist, P. "Assyria and Its Image in the First Isaiah." *JAOS* 103 (1983): 719–37.

McAlpine, T. H. "The Word Against the Nations." *Studia Biblica et Theologica* 5/1 (1975): 3–14.

McCarthy D. J. "An Installation Genre?" *JBL* 90 (1971): 31–41.

_____. *Treaty and Covenant.* Rome: Pontifical Biblical Institute Press, 1978.

McComiskey, T. E. "The Hymnic Elements of the Prophecy of Amos: A Study of Form-Critical Methodology." *JETS* 30 (1987) 139–57; repr. from *A Tribute to Gleason Archer. Essays on the Old Testament,* eds. W. C. Kaiser, Jr., and R. F. Youngblood. Chicago: Moody, 1986, 105–30.

McCullough, W. S. "Israel's Eschatology from Amos to Daniel." *Studies on the Ancient Palestine World. Fs. F. V. Winnett.* Toronto, 1971, 86–101.

McKane, W. "Poison, Trial by Ordeal and the Cup of Wrath." *VT* 30 (1980): 474–92.

McKay, J. W. *Religion in Judah under the Assyrians, 732–609 B.C.* Naperville, Ill.: Alec R. Allenson, 1973.

McKeating, H. *The Books of Amos, Hosea and Micah.* Cambridge: Cambridge University Press, 1984.

Macpherson, A. *Amos and Hosea. Prophets I.* Chicago: ACTA Foundation, 1971, 1–34.

Maier, J., and K. Schubert. *Die Qumran-Essener, Texte der Schriftrollen und Lebensbild der Gemeinde.* München: Kaiser, 1973.

Maigret, J. "Amos et le sanctuaire de Bethel." *Bible et Terre Sainte* 47 (1962): 5–6.

Malamat, A. "Amos 1:5 in the Light of the Til Barsip Inscription." *BASOR* 129 (153): 25–26.

Malchow, B. V. "The Prophetic Contribution to Dialogue." *BTB* 16 (1986): 127–31.

Mallau, H. H. "Las reacciones frente a los mensajes profetocos y el problema de la distincion entre profetas verdaderos y falsos. A proposito de Amos 7:10–17." *RivB* 34 (1972): 33–39.

Margulis, B. B. *Studies in the Oracles Against the Nations.* Unpubl. diss., Brandeis University, 1967.

_____. "A New Ugaritic Farce (RS 24.258)." *UF* 2 (1970): 131–38.

Markert, L. *Struktur und Bezeichnung des Scheltwortes. Eine gattungskritische Studie anhand des Amosbuches.* Berlin/New York: W. de Gruyter, 1977.

_____. "Amos/Amosbuch." *TRE* (1978): 2:471–87.

Markert, L., and G. Wanke. "Die Propheteninterpretation. Anfragen und Überlegungen." *KD* 22 (1976): 191–220.

Marsh, J. *Amos and Micah. Introduction and Commentary.* London: SCM, 1965.

Marti, K. *Das Dodekapropheton erklärt.* Tübingen: J. C. B. Mohr [Paul Siebeck], 1904.

Martin-Achard, R. "The End of the People of God. A Commentary on the Book of Amos." *God's People in the Crisis.* Grand Rapids: Eerdmans, 1984, 1–71.

_____. *Amos—L'homme, le message, l'influence.* Genève: Labor et Fides, 1984.

Martin-Achard, R., and S. P. Re'emi. *Amos and Lamentations: God's People in Crisis.* Grand Rapids: Eerdmans, 1984.

Mauchline, J. "Implicit Signs of a Persistent Belief in the Davidic Empire." *VT* 20 (1970): 287–303.

Mays, J. L. "Words about the Words of Amos." *Int* 13 (1959): 259–72.

_____. *Amos: A Commentary.* Philadelphia: Westminster, 1969.

_____. "Justice: Perspectives from the Prophetic Tradition." *Int* 37 (1983): 5–17.

Mays, J. L., and P. J. Achtemeier, eds. *Interpreting the Prophets.* Philadelphia: Fortress, 1987.

Mazar, E. "Archaeological Evidence for the 'Cows of Bashan Who Are in the

Mountain of Samaria.'" *Festschrift Reuben R. Hecht. Studies in Honor of His 70th Birthday*, eds. B. Azkin et al. Jerusalem: Koren, 1979, 151–57.

Melugin, R. F. "The Formation of Amos: An Analysis of Exegetical Method." *Society of Biblical Literature 1978 Seminar Papers*, ed. P. J. Achtemeier. Missoula: Scholars, 1978, 369–91.

Mendenhall, G. E. *The Tenth Generation*. Baltimore: Johns Hopkins University Press, 1973.

Mettinger, T. N. D. *The Dethronement of Sabaoth: Studies in the Shem and Kabod Theologies*. Lund: CWK Gleerup, 1982.

Metzger, M. "Lodebar und der Tell el-Mghannije." *ZDPV* 76 (1960): 97–102.

Meyer, R. "Gegensinn und Mehrdeutigkeit in der althebräischen Wort- und Begriffsbildung." *UF* 11 (1979): 601–12.

Michel, D. "Amos." *Israels Glaube im Wandel*. Berlin: Verlag Die Spur Dorbandt, 1968, 179–209.

Michel, W. L. "'*lmwt*, 'Deep Darkness' or 'Shadow of Death'?" *BR* 29 (1984): 5–20.

Miguens, M. "*br*' and Creation in the Old Testament." *SBFLA* 24 (1974): 38–69.

Milgrom, J. *Cult and Conscience: The Asham and the Priestly Doctrine of Repentance*. Leiden: E. J. Brill, 1976.

____. "Concerning Jeremiah's Repudiation of Sacrifice." *ZAW* 89 (1977): 273–75.

Miller, C. H. "Amos and Faith Structures: A New Approach." *TBT* 19 (1981): 314–19.

Miller, J. W. *A Beginner's Guide to the Books of the Biblical Prophets—Their Meaning Then and Now*. New York: Paulist, 1987.

Miller, P. D., Jr. "Animal Names as Designations in Ugaritic and Hebrew." *UF* 2 (1970): 177–86.

____. *Sin and Judgment in the Prophets: A Stylistic and Theological Analysis*. Chico, Calif.: Scholars, 1982, 21–26.

____. "The Absence of the Goddess in Israelite Religion." *HAR* 10 (1986): 239–48.

____. "Moses My Servant: The Deuteronomic Portrait of Moses." *Int* 41 (1987): 245–55.

____. "The *MARZH* Text." *The Claremont Ras Shamra Tablets*, ed. L. R. Fisher. Rome: Pontifical Biblical Institute Press, 1971, 37–49.

Mittmann, S. "Amos 3,12–15 und das Bett der Samarier." *ZDPV* 92 (1976): 149–67.

____. "Gestalt und Gehalt einer prophetischen Selbstrechtfertigung (Am 3,3–8)." *TQ* 151 (1971): 134–45.

Moeller, H. A. "Ambiguity of Amos 3:12." *BT* 15 (1964): 31–34.

Mollat, D. *Zukunft und Gegenwart. Die Apokalypse heute gelesen. Aus dem Französischen übersetzt und herausgegeben von C. Scharfenberger*. Leipzig: St. Benno-Verlag, 1987.

Monloubou, L. *Amos et Osée, Sainteté de Justice, Sainteté d'Amour*. Paris: Cerf, 1964.

____. "Prophètes d'Israël: Amos." *DBS* 8 (1972): 706–24.

Morgenstern, J. "The Address of Amos—Text and Commentary." *HUCA* 32 (1961): 295–350.

_____. *Amos Studies*. Vol 1. Cincinnati: Hebrew Union College Press, 1941.

_____. "Jerusalem–485 B.C.E." *HUCA* 27 (1956): 101–80; 28 (1957): 15–48; 28 (1960): 1–30.

_____. "Amos Studies IV: The Addresses of Amos—Text and Commentary." *HUCA* 32 (1961): 295–360.

Moriarty, F. L. "Preacher and Prophet." *Way* 20 (1980): 3–14.

Motyer, J. A. "Amos." *The New Bible Commentary*, eds. D. Guthrie et al. London: Inter-Varsity, 1972, 3:726–41.

_____. *Le rugissement de Dieu*. Lausanne: Presses Bibliques Universitaires, 1982.

_____. *The Day of the Lion. The Message of Amos*. Leicester: Inter-Varsity, 1974.

Mowinckel, S., and N. Messel. *De Senere Profeter Oversatt*. Oslo: H. Aschehoug, 1944.

Muilenberg, J. "The Office of Prophet in Ancient Israel." *The Bible in Modern Scholarship*, ed. J. P. Hyatt. Nashville: Abingdon, 1965, 74–97.

Mulder, M. J. "Die Partikel ken im Alten Testament." *OTS* 21 (1981): 201–27.

_____. "Ein Vorschlag zur Übersetzung von Amos III 6b." *VT* 34 (1984): 106–8.

Müller, H.-P. "Phönizien und Juda in exilisch-nachexilischer Zeit." *WO* 6 (1971): 189–204.

_____. "Die Wurzeln yq , y'q und 'wq." *VT* 21 (1971): 556–64.

_____. "Mythos-Tradition-Revolution." *Phänomenologische Untersuchungen zum Alten Testament*. Neukirchen-Vluyn: Neukirchner Verlag, 1973.

_____. *Ursprünge und Strukturen alttestamentlicher Eschatologie*. Berlin: W. de Gruyter, 1969.

Müller, W. E., and H. D. Preuss. *Die Vorstellung vom Rest im Alten Testament*. Neukirchen-Vluyn: Neukirchener Verlag, 1973.

Munitingh, L. M. "Political and International Relations of Israel's Neighboring Peoples According to the Oracles of Amos." *Studies in the Books of Hosea and Amos. Die Ou Testamentiese Werkgemeenskap in Suid Afrika, 7th and 8th Congress*. Potchefstroom: Rege-Pers Beperk, 1964–65, 134–42.

Muntag, A. "Amosz Toertenelmi Szerepe." *LP* 49 (1974): 584–91.

Murakoa, T. "On Verb Complementation in Biblical Hebrew." *VT* 29 (1979): 425–35.

_____. "Is the Septuagint Amos VIII 12–IX 10 a Separate Unit?" *VT* 20 (1970): 496–500.

Murray, R. "From Biblical Roots." *Way* 27 (1987): 79–88.

_____. "Prophecy and the Cult." *Israel's Prophetic Tradition. Essays in Honor of P. R. Ackroyd*, eds. R. Coggins et al. Cambridge: Cambridge University Press, 1982, 200–16.

Muszynski, H. "Gott und das Böse in der Bibel." *Dein Wort beachten. Alttestamentliche Aufsätze*, ed. J. Reindl. Leipzig, 1981, 151–79.

Na'aman, N. "Looking for KTK." *WO* 9 (1978): 220–39.

_____. "Historical and Chronological Notes on the Kingdoms of Israel and Judah in the Eighth Century B.C." *VT* 36 (1986): 71–92.

_____. "Beth-aven, Bethel and Early Israelite Sanctuaries." *ZDPV* 103 (1987): 12–21.

Naastepad, T. J. M. *Amos.* Kampen: Kok, 1976.

Nagah, R. "Are You Not Like the Ethiopians to Me (Am 9,7)?" *Beth Miqra* 89/90 (1982): 174–82. (Heb. with Eng. summary)

Neef, H.-D. *Die Heilstraditionen Israels in der Verkündigung des Propheten Hosea.* Berlin/ New York: W. de Gruyter, 1987.

Ne'eman, P. "The Day of the Lord in Literary Prophecy." *Beth Miqra* 34 (1968): 57–70. (Heb.)

Neher, A. *Amos. Contribution à l'étude du profetisme.* 2d ed. Paris: Vrin, 1981.

Nel, W. A. G. "Amos 9:11–15—An Unconditional Prophecy of Salvation during the Period of Exile." *OTE* 2 (1984): 81–97.

Neubauer, K. W. "Erwägungen zu Amos 5,4–15." *ZAW* 78 (1966): 292–316.

Newman, B. M., Jr. "Some Hints on Solving Textual Problems." *BT* 33 (1982): 430–35.

Nicholson, E. W. *Exodus and Sinai in History and Tradition.* Oxford: Oxford University Press, 1973.

_____. *God and His People: Covenant and Theology in the Old Testament.* Oxford: Oxford University Press, 1986.

Niditsch, S. *The Symbolic Vision in Biblical Tradition.* Chico, Calif.: Scholars, 1983.

Nielsen, E. "Om formkritik som hjaelpemiddel i historisk-genetisk forskning, belyst ved eksempler fra Amos 1–2 og Mika 1." *Dansk Teologisk Tidsskrift* 52 (1989): 243–50.

Nishimura, T. *Prophecy and Wisdom in the Old Testament. History, Structure and Interpretation.* Tokyo, 1981, 141–59.

Nishizu, T. J. *Bethel and the Rebellions of Israel: Redactional Elements in the Book of Amos.* Unpubl. Ph.D. diss., University of Chicago, 1982.

Noort, E. *Untersuchungen zum Gottesbescheid in Mari. Die "Mariprophetie" in der alttestamentlichen Forschung.* Kevelaer: Butzon & Bercker; Neukirchen-Vluyn: Neukirchen Verlag, 1977.

_____. "JHWH und das Böse. Bemerkungen zu einer Verhältnisbestimmung." *OTS* 23 (1984): 120–36.

Norquist, M. *How to Read and Pray the Prophets.* Liguori, Mo.: Liguori Publications, 1980.

North, R. "Angel-Prophet or Satan-Prophet?" *ZAW* 82 (1970): 31–67.

Nötscher, F. *Zwölfprophetenbuch oder Kleine Propheten.* 2d ed. Würzburg: Echter Verlag, 1948.

Nowack, W. *Die kleinen Propheten übersetzt und erklärt.* 3d ed. Göttingen: Vandenhoeck und Ruprecht, 1922.

Oded, B. *Mass Deportation and Deportee in the Neo-Assyrian Empire.* Wiesbaden: Reichert, 1976.

Oden, R. A., Jr. *The Bible Without Theology: The Theological Tradition and Alternatives to It.* San Francisco: Harper & Row, 1987.

Ogden, B. "Amos og Afguderne." *NorTT* 84 (1983): 167–85.

Ogden, D. K. *A Geography of Amos.* Unpubl. Ph.D. diss., University of Utah, 1982.

Öhler, A. *Mythologische Elemente im Alten Testament. Eine motivgeschichtliche Untersuchung.* Düsseldorf: Patmos, 1969.

O'Neill, D. *The Attitudes of Amos, Hosea, Jeremiah, and Deutero-Isaiah Concerning the Man/God Relationship: A Study of Hebraic Monotheism.* Unpubl. Ph.D. diss., Michigan State University, 1979.

Oort, H. "De Profeet Amos." *Theologische Tijdschrift* 14 (1880): 114–58.

Orlinsky, H. M., and M. Weinberg. "The Massorah on *ianawîm* in Amos 2.7." *Estudios Massoréticos (V Congreso de la IOMS),* ed. E. Fernandez. Madrid: CSIS Institute, 1983, 25–35.

____. "Notes on Some *Masora Parva* of Amos." *Sefarad* 46 (1986): 381–90.

Osswald, E. *Urform und Auslegung im masoretischen Amostext. Ein Beitrag zur Kritik an der neueren traditionsgeschichtlichen Methode.* Unpubl. diss., University of Jena, 1951. Review in *TLZ* 80 (1955): 179.

____. "Die Botschaft der Propheten des 8. Jahrhunderts v. Chr.-Amos-Hosea-Jesaja-Micha." *Von Bileam bis Jesaja. Studien zum Alttestamentlichen Prophetie von ihren Anfängen bis zur 8. Jh. v. Chr. im Auftrag der Altestamentlichen Arbeitsgemeinschaft in der DDR,* ed. G. Wallis. Berlin: Evangelische Verlagsanstalt, 1984, 84–112.

____. "Aspekte neurer Prophetenforschung." *TLZ* 109 (1984): 641–50.

Osten-Sacken, P. von der. "Die Bücher der Tora als Hütte der Gemeinde—Amos 5:26 in der Damaskusschrift." *ZAW* 91 (1979): 432–35.

Osty, C. E. *Amos-Osée traduits.* Paris: Cerf, 1952.

Osty, E., and J. Trinquet. *Les petits prophètes.* Lausanne, 1972.

Otzen, B. "Amos og afguderne." *NorTT* 84 (1983): 167–85.

Ouellette, J. "The Shaking of the Thresholds in Amos 9:1." *HUCA* 43 (1972): 23–27.

____. "Le mur d'étain dans Amos VII,7–9." *RB* 80 (1973): 321–31.

Overholt, T. W. "Commanding the Prophets: Amos and the Problem of Prophetic Authority." *CBQ* 41 (1979): 517–32.

____. *Prophecy in Cross-Cultural Perspective: A Sourcebook for Biblical Researchers.* Atlanta: Scholars, 1986.

Owens, G. G. "Exegetical Studies in the Book of Amos." *RevEx* 63 (1966): 249–40.

Parmentier, R. "Amos réécrit pour 1978." *Dialogue* 79–80, Paris 1978 (= *Actualisation de la Bible,* Paris, 1982, 49–70).

Patterson, R. "The Widow, the Orphan, and the Poor in the Old Testament and in Extra-Biblical Literature." *Bibliotheca Sacra* 130 (1973): 223–34.

Paul, S. M. "Amos 1:3–2:3: A Concatenous Literary Pattern." *JBL* 90 (1971): 397–403.

____. "Amos III 15—Winter and Summer Mansions." *VT* 28 (1978): 358–60.

____. "Fishing Imagery in Amos 4:2." *JBL* 97 (1978): 183–90.

____. "A Literary Reinvestigation of the Authenticity of the Oracles Against the Nations in Amos." *De la Tôrah au Messie,* eds. M. Carrez et al. Paris: Desclée, 1981, 189–204.

____. "Two Cognate Semitic Terms for Mating and Copulating." *VT* 32 (1982): 492–94.

____. "Amos 3:3–8: The Irresistible Sequence of Cause and Effect." *HAR* 7 (1983): 203–20.

_____. *Amos. A Commentary on the Book of Amos.* Minneapolis: Fortress, 1991.

Peckham, B. "Israel and Phoenicia." *Magnalia Dei: The Mighty Acts of God,* eds. F. M. Cross et al. Garden City: Doubleday, 1976, 224–48.

Pedersen, D. L. *The Roles of Israel's Prophets.* Sheffield: SCM, 1981.

Pelser, H. S. "Amos 3:11–A Communication." *Studies in the Books of Hosea and Amos: Die Ou Testamentiese Werkgemeenskap in Suid Afrika: 7th and 8th Congresses.* Potchefstroom: Rege-Pers Beperk, 1964–65, 153–56.

Perlitt, L. *Bundestheologie im Alten Testament.* Neukirchen-Vluyn: Neukirchener Verlag, 1969.

Peter, R. "*swr* and *pr*: Note de lexicographie Hebraique." *VT* 25 (1975): 486–96.

_____. *The Role of Israel's Prophets.* Sheffield: JSOT, 1981, 51–69.

Pfeifer, C. J. "Amos the Prophet: The Man and His Book." *TBT* 19 (1981): 295–300.

Pfeifer, G. "Denkformenanalyse als exegetische Methode, erläutert an Amos 1:2–2:16." *ZAW* 88 (1976): 56–71.

_____. "Amos und Deuterojesaja denkformanalytisch verglichen." *ZAW* 93 (1981): 439–43.

_____. "Die Denkform des Propheten Amos III 3–8." *VT* 33 (1983): 341–47.

_____. "Unausweichliche Konsequenzen: Denkformenanalyse von Amos III 3–8." *VT* 33 (1983): 341–47.

_____. "Die Denkform des Propheten Amos (III 9–11)." *VT* 34 (1984): 476–81.

_____. "Die Ausweisung eines lästigen Ausländers, Amos 7,10–17." *ZAW* 96 (1984): 112–18.

_____. "'Rettung' als Beweis der Vernichtung (Amos 3.12)." *ZAW* 100 (1988): 269–77.

_____. "Die Fremdvölkersprüche des Amos—spätere *vaticinia ex eventu?*" *VT* 38 (1988): 230–33.

_____. "Das Ja des Amos." *VT* 39 (1989): 497–503.

Phillips, A. "Prophecy and Law." *Israel's Prophetic Tradition. Essays in Honour of P. R. Ackroyd,* eds. R. Coggins et al. Cambridge: Cambridge University Press, 1982, 217–32.

Pitard, W. T. *Ancient Damascus: A Historical Study of the Syrian City-State from Earliest Times until Its Fall to the Assyrians in 732 B.C.E.* Winona Lake, Ind.: Eisenbrauns, 1987.

Pleins, J. D. *Biblical Ethics and the Poor: The Language and Structures of Poverty in the Writings of the Hebrew Prophets.* Unpubl. Ph.D. diss., University of Michigan, 1986.

Polley, M. E. *Amos and the Davidic Empire: A Socio-Historical Approach.* New York: Oxford University Press, 1989.

Pope, M. H. "Seven, Seventh, Seventy." *IDB* (1976): 4:294–95.

_____. "Le *mrzh* à Ougarit et Ailleurs." *Annales Archeologiques Arabes Syriennes* 29/30 (1979–80): 141–43.

Porter, J. R. "*Běnê -hannĕbî 'î m* (Amos 7:14 + 10X)." *JTS* 32 (1981): 423–29.

Prado, J. "Amos, Amos Libro de." *Enciclopedia de la Biblia.* Barcelona: Garriga, 1963, 1:435–40.

Praeger, M. "Amos, der Hirte aus Tekoa." *Bibel und Liturgie* 36 (1962–63): 84–96, 164–72, 243–55, 295–308.

Preuss, H. D. *Jahweglaube und Zukunftserwartung.* Stuttgart: Kohlhammer, 1968.

_____. *Verspottung fremder Religionen im Alten Testament.* Stuttgart: Kohlhammer, 1971.

Priest, J. "The Covenant of Brothers." *JBL* 84 (1965): 400–406.

Prignaud, J. "Caftorim et Kerethim." *RB* 71 (1962): 215–29.

Procksch, O. *Die Geschichtsbetrachtung bei Amos, Hosea und Jeremia.* Königsberg, 1901.

_____. *Die kleinen prophetischen Schriften vor dem Exil.* 2d ed. Stuttgart: Deichert [Scholl], 1929.

Puech, E. "Milkom, le dieu ammonite, en Amos I 15." *VT* 27 (1977): 117–25.

Pusey, E. B. *The Minor Prophets,* vol. 2, *Amos.* London: J. H. & J. Parker, 1906.

Putnam, F. "Historical Amos." *Eternity* 33/11 (1982): 37–38.

Rabin, C. "The Language of Amos and Hosea." *Studies in the Minor Prophets,* ed. B. Z. Luria. Jerusalem: Kiryat Sepher, 1981, 115–36. (Heb.)

Rabinowitz, I. "The Crux at Amos III 12." *VT* 11 (1961): 228–31.

Rad, G. von. "The Origin of the Concept of the Day of Yahweh." *JSS* 4 (1959): 97–108.

_____. "Gerichtsdoxologie." *Schalom. Studien zu Glaube und Geschichte Israels. Alfred Jepsen zum 71. Geburtstag dargebracht,* ed. K.-H. Bernhardt. Stuttgart: Calwer Verlag, 1971, 45–79; repr. *Gesammelte Studien zum Alten Testament.* München: Kaiser, 1973, 245–54.

_____. *Old Testament Theology.* 2 vols. New York/London: Harper & Row, 1975, 2:119–25.

Rahtjen, B. D. "A Critical Note on Amos 8:1–2." *JBL* 83 (1964): 416–17.

Rainey, A. F. "Dust and Ashes." *Tel Aviv* 1 (1974): 77–83.

_____. "The Identification of Philistine Gath. A Problem in Source Analysis for Historical Geography." ErIsr 12. *N. Glueck Memorial Volume.* Jerusalem: Israel Exploration Society, 1975, 63–76.

_____. "The *Sitz im Leben* of the Samaria Ostraca." *Tel Aviv* 6 (1979): 91–94.

Raitt, T. M. "The Prophetic Summons to Repentance." *ZAW* 83 (1971): 30–49.

Ramsey, G. "Amos 4:12—A New Perspective." *JBL* 89 (1976): 187–91.

_____. "Speech-Forms in Hebrew Law and Prophetic Oracles." *JBL* 96 (1977): 45–48.

Randellini, L. "Ricchi e poveri nel libro del profeta Amos." *SBFLA* 2 (1951–52): 5–46.

_____. "Il Profeta Amos Defensore dei Poveri." *Bullettino del l'Anicizia Ebraico-Cristiana de Firenze* 6 (1971): 35–43.

Rappel, D. "'The Day of the Lord' in the Bible." *Studies in the Minor Prophets,* ed. B. Z. Luria. Jerusalem: Kiryat Sepher, 1981, 78–85. (Heb.)

Rattigan, M. T. "Hazor and Its Significance." *TBT* 23 (1985): 44–55.

Rector, L. J. "Israel's Rejected Worship: An Exegesis of Amos 5." *ResQ* 21 (1978): 161–75.

Refer, K. *Amos. Die Worte des Propheten übersetzt und gedeutet.* Munich, 1927.

Reiman, P. A. "Models of Exegesis." *Int* 25 (1971): 198–201.

Renaud, B. "Genèse et Théologie d'Amos 3,3–8." *Festschrift H. Cazelles,* eds. A. Caquot and M. Delcor. Kevelaer: Butzon & Bercker, 1981, 553–72.

Rendtorff, R. "Zu Amos 2,14–16." *ZAW* 85 (1973): 226–27.

_____. *Das Alte Testament. Eine Einführung.* Neukirchen-Vluyn: Neukirchener Verlag, 1983.

Reuss, E. *Das Alte Testament übersetzt, eingeleitet und erläutert. Die Propheten.* Braunschweig: Schwetschke & Sohn, 1892.

Reventlow, H. Graf. *Das Amt des Propheten bei Amos.* Göttingen: Vandenhoeck und Ruprecht, 1962.

Richard, E. "The Creative Use of Amos by the Author of Acts." *NT* 24 (1982): 37–53.

Richardson, H. N. "A Critical Note on Amos 7:14." *JBL* 85 (1966): 89.

_____. "*SKT* (Amos 9:11) 'Booth' or 'Succoth.'" *JBL* 92 (1973): 375–81.

_____. "Amos 2:13–16: Its Structure and Function in the Book." *SBLSP I.* Missoula: Scholars, 1978, 361–67.

_____. "Amos's Four Visions of Judgment and Hope." *Bible Review* 5 (1989): 16–21.

Ridderbos, J. *De Kleine Propheten. Eerste Deel: Hosea, Joel, Amos.* 3 vols. Kampen: Kok, 1932.

_____. "Beschouwingen naar aanleding van Wolffs 'Die Stunde des Amos'." *GTT* 72 (1972): 1–18.

_____. *Het Godswoord der Propheten. I. Van Elia tot Micha.* Kampen: Kok, 1980, 98–159.

Rieger, J. *Die Bedeutung der Geschichte für die Verkündigung des Amos und Hosea.* Giessen: Töpelmann, 1929.

Riessler, P. *Die kleinen Propheten oder das Zwölfprophetenbuch nach dem Urtext übersetzt und erklärt.* Rottenburg a. N.: Bader, 1911.

Rinaldi, G. *I Propheti Minori. Fasc. 1. Introduzione Generale, Amos.* Torino/Roma: Marietti, 1952.

_____. "Sull'uso de '*gdh* ('*agudda*) nell 'AT." *Biblica et Orientalia* 24 (1985): 202–4.

Roberts, J. J. M. "A Note on Amos 7:14 and Its Context." *ResQ* 8 (1965): 175–78.

_____. "Recent Trends in the Study of Amos." *ResQ* 13 (1970): 1–16.

Robinson, H. W. *Amos. Hebrew Text.* London: SPCK, 1923.

Robinson, T. H., and F. Horst. *Die zwölf Kleinen Propheten.* 3d ed. Tübingen: J. C. B. Mohr, 1964.

Robscheit, H. "Die Thora bei Amos und Hosea." *EvTh* 10 (1950): 26–38.

Rohland, E. *Die Bedeutung der Erwählungstraditionen Israels für die Eschatologie der alttestamentlichen Propheten.* Heidelberg: Priv. printed, 1956.

Rosenbaum, S. N. "Northern Amos Revisited: Two Philological Suggestions." *HS* 18 (1977): 132–48.

_____. *Amos of Israel: A New Interpretation.* Macon, Ga.: Mercer University Press, 1990.

Rosenmüller, E. F. K. *Scholia in Vetus Testamentum Partis septimae Prophetas minores continentis,* vol. 2, *Amos, Obadias et Jonas.* Leipzig: J. A. Barthii, 1827.

Roth, W. M. W. "The Numerical Sequence x/x+1 in the Old Testament." *VT* 12 (1962): 300–311.

____. *Numerical Sayings in the Old Testament.* Leiden: E. J. Brill, 1965.

Routtenberg, H. J. *Amos of Tekoa: A Study in Interpretation.* New York: Vantage, 1971.

Rowley, H. H. "Was Amos a Nabi?" *Festschrift für Otto Eissfeldt zum 60, Geburtstag,* ed. J. Fück. Halle: Niemeyer, 1947, 191–98.

Rudolph, W. *Joel-Amos-Obadja-Jona.* Gütersloh: Gerd Mohn/Gütersloher Verlagshaus, 1971.

____. "Amos 4,6–13." *Wort-Gebot-Glaube. Beiträge zur Theologie des Alten Testaments: Walther Eichrodt zum 80. Geburtstag,* ed. H. J. Stoebe. Zurich: Zwingli, 1970, 27–38.

____. "Die angefochtenen Völkersprüche in Amos 1–2." *Schalom. Studien zu Glaube und Geschichte Israels: Festschrift für A. Jepsen zum 70. Geburtstag dargebracht,* ed. K.-H. Bernhardt. Stuttgart: Calwer Verlag, 1971, 45–49.

____. "Schwierige Amosstellen." *Wort und Geschichte. Festschrift für Karl Elliger zum 70. Geburtstag,* eds. H. Gese and H. P. Rüger. Neukirchen-Vluyn: Neukirchener Verlag, 1973, 157–62.

Rüger, H. P. "Die gestaffelten Zahlensprüche des Alten Testaments und aramäischen Achikar 92." *VT* 31 (1981): 229–34.

Ruiz, G. *Don Isaac Abrabarnel y su Commentario al Libro de Amos.* Madrid: UPCM, 1984.

____. *Commentarius hebreos medievalis al libro de Amos. (Rashi, A. 'ibn 'Ezra, Beaugency, D. Kimchi, J. 'ibn Caspi).* Madrid: UPCM, 1984.

____. "Amos 5:13 Prudencia en la denuncia Profetica?" *CuBi* 25 (1973): 347–52.

Rusche, H. "Wenn Gott sein Wort entzieht. Meditationen zu Amos 8,11–12." *BiL* 10 (1969): 219–21.

____. *Das Buch Amos erläutert.* Düsseldorf: Patmos Verlag, 1975.

Ryan, D. *Amos.* London: Nelson, 1969.

Sacon, K. K. "Amos 5:21–27—An Exegetical Study." *The Bible, Its Thoughts, History and Language. Essays in Honor of E. Sekine,* ed. S. Arai. Tokyo: Yamamoto Shoten, 1972, 278–99.

Said, D. H. *Longing for Justice: A Study on the Cry and Hope of the Poor in the Old Testament.* Unpubl. Ph.D. diss., University of Edinburgh, 1987.

Sanders, J. A. *From Sacred History to Sacred Text: Canon as Paradigm.* Philadelphia: Fortress, 1987.

Sansoni, C. "Amos: Uomo del suo Tempo." *BeO* 10 (1968): 253–65.

Sargent, J. E. *Hosea, Joel, Amos, Obadiah and Jonah.* Graded Press, 1988.

Sasowski, B. "Dann wende Ich das Schicksal meines Volkes. Die Verheissung des kommenden Heils." *Gericht und Umkehr. Die Botschaft des Propheten Amos.* 1967, 116–19.

Sawyer, J. F. A. "'Those Priests in Damascus': A Possible Example of Anti-Sectarian Polemic in the Septuagint Version of Amos 3:12." *ASTI* 8 (1970): 123–30.

Scharbert, J. "Die prophetische Literatur. Der Stand der Forschung." *ETL* 44 (1968): 346–406.

____. *Die Propheten Israels bis 700 v. Chr.* Köln: J. P. Bachem, 1965, 91–133.

Schegg, P. *Die kleinen Propheten. Erster Teil: Osee-Michaeas.* Regensburg: G. J. Manz, 1854.

Schenker, A. "Zur Interpretation von Amos 3,3–8." *BZ* 30 (1986): 250–56.

Schlier, J. *Die zwölf kleinen Propheten.* Stuttgart: Liesching, 1861.

Schmid, H. "'Nicht Prophet bin ich, noch bin ich Prophetensohn.' Zur Erklärung von Amos 7, 14a." *Judaica* 23 (1967): 68–74.

Schmid, H. H. "Amos. Die Frage nach der 'geistigen Heimat' des Propheten." *WD* 10 (1969): 85–103.

Schmidt, D. "Critical Note: Another Word-Play in Amos?" *Grace Theological Journal* 8 (1987): 141–42.

Schmidt, H. *Der Prophet Amos.* Tübingen: J. C. B. Mohr, 1917.

Schmidt, W. H. *Old Testament Introduction.* New York: Crossroad, 1984.

____. "Die deuteronomistische Redaktion des Amosbuches." *ZAW* 77 (1965): 168–92.

____. "'Suchet den Herrn, so werdet Ihr leben.' Exegetische Notizen zum Thema 'Gott Suchen" in der Prophetie." *Ex Orbe Religionum. Studia Geo Widengren,* eds. C. J. Bleeker et al. Leiden: E. J. Brill, 1972, 127–40.

Schmitt, G. "Bet-Awen." *Drei Studien zur Archäologie und Topographie Altisraels. Beihefte zum Tübinger Atlas des Vorderen Orients.* Wiesbaden: O. Harrassowitz, 1980, 33–76.

Schmitten, W. Th. in der. "Marginalien zur Restvorstellung im Alten Testament." *BiOr* 30 (1973): 9–10.

Schottroff, W. "Der Prophet Amos. Versuch einer Würdigung unter sozialgeschichtlichem Aspekt." *Der Gott der kleinen Leute. Sozialgeschichte Bibelauslegungen,* eds. W. Schottroff and W. Stegemann. Munich: Kaiser, 1979, 39–66.

____. "The Prophet Amos: A Socio-Historical Assessment of His Ministry." *God of the Lowly: Socio-Historical Interpretations of the Bible,* eds. W. Schottroff and W. Stegemann, trans. M. J. O'Connell. Maryknoll, N.Y.: Orbis, 1984, 27–46.

Schoville, K. "A Note on the Oracles of Amos Against Gaza, Tyre, and Edom." *VTS* 26 (1974): 55–63.

____. "The Sins of Aram in Amos." *Proceedings of the Sixth World Congress of Jewish Studies,* vol. 1, ed. A. Shinan. Jerusalem: Magnes, 1977, 363–75.

Schreiner, J. "Was verheissen Israel's Propheten?" *Erwartung, Verheissung, Erfüllung.* Würzburg, 1969, 86–110.

Schult, H. "Amos 7, 15a und die Legitimation des Aussenseiters." *Probleme biblischer Theologie. Gerhard von Rad zum 70. Geburtstag,* ed. H. W. Wolff. Munich: Chr. Kaiser, 1971, 462–89.

Schultes, J. L. *Herr ist sein Name. Ein Arbeitsheft zum Buch Amos.* Klosterneuburg: Österreichisches Katholisches Bibelwerk, 1979.

____. "Gott redet auch durch sein Schweigen. Bibel Meditationen zu Amos 8,4–7, 11–12." *Bibel und Liturgie* 48 (1975): 256–59.

Schuman, N. A. "Amos on de traditie." *Amos, Een Aanklacht de profeet en Zijn betekenius nu.* Amsterdam: Vrije Universiteit, 1979, 17–29.

Schumpp, M. *Das Buch der zwölf Propheten.* Freiburg: Herder, 1950.

Schüngel-Straumann, H. *Gottessbild und Kultkritik vorexilischer Propheten.* Stuttgart: Katholisches Bibelwerk, 1972.

Schunk, K. "Strukturlinien in der Entwicklung der Vorstellung vom 'Tag Jahwes.'" *VT* 14 (1964): 319–30.

____. "Der 'Tag Jahwes' in der Verkündigung der Propheten." *Kairos* 11 (1969): 14–21.

Schwantes, M. *Das Recht der Armen.* Frankfurt am M.: Peter Lang, 1977, 87–99.

____. "Profecia e Organizaÿao: Anotaÿes àluz de um texto (Am 2,6–16)." *EstBib* 5 (1985): 26–39.

Schwantes, S. J. "Note on Amos 4:2b." *ZAW* 79 (1967): 82–83.

Segert, S. "Zur Bedeutung des Wortes *noqed.*" *Hebräische Wortforschung. Festschrift zum 80. Geburtstag von Walter Baumgartner,* eds. B. Hartmann et al. Leiden: E. J. Brill, 1967, 279–83.

____. "A Controlling Device for Copying Stereotype Passages (Amos I 3–II 8, VI 1–6)." *VT* 34 (1984): 481–82.

Seidel, M. "Four Prophets Who Prophesied at the Same Time." *Hiqre Mikra.* Jerusalem: Mosad HaRav Kook, 1978, 195–238. (Heb.)

Seidel, T. "Heuschreckenschwarm und Prophetenintervention. Textkritische und syntaktische Erwägungen zu Amos 7,2." *BN* 37 (1987): 129–38.

Seierstad, I. P. *Die Offenbarungserlebnisse der Propheten Amos, Jesaja und Jeremia.* 2d ed. Olso: Dybwad, 1965.

____. "Oplenelse oglydiget hosprofeten Amos." *Budskapet: Et utvalg au gammeltestamentlige artikler.* Oslo: Universitets forlaget, 1971, 77–97.

Seilhamer, F. H. "The Role of Covenant in the Mission and Message of Amos." *A Light unto My Path. Old Testament Studies in Honor of Jacob M. Myers,* eds. H. N. Bream et al. Philadelphia: Temple University Press, 1974, 435–51.

Sekine, M. "Das Problem der Kultpolemik bei den Propheten." *EvTh* 28 (1968) 605–9.

Sellin, E. *Das Zölfprophetenbuch übersetzt und erklärt.* 2 vols. 3d ed. Leipzig: Deichert [Scholl], 1930.

Selms, A. van. "Isaac in Amos." *Studies in the Books of Hosea and Amos. Die Ou Testamentiese Werkgemeenskap in Suid Afrika 7th and 8th Congresses.* Potchefstroom: Rege-Pers Beperk, 1964–65, 157–65.

Semen, P. "Sensul expresiei 'Iom Iahwe.'" *StTh* 30 (1978): 149–61.

Seybold, K. *Das davidische Königtum im Zeugnis der Propheten.* Göttingen: Vandenhoeck und Ruprecht, 1972.

Shapiro, D. S. "The Seven Questions of Amos." *Tradition* 22 (1982): 327–31.

Shea, W. "Amos' Geographic Horizon." *Studies in the Books of Hosea and Amos.* Potchefstroom: Rege-Pers Beperk, 1964–65, 166–69.

Shoot, W. B., Jr. *The Fertility Religions in the Thought of Amos and Hosea.* Unpubl. diss., University of California, 1951.

Sicre, J. L. *Los dioses olvidados. Poder y riqueza en los profetas de Israel.* Madrid, 1979.

Sieve, J. "Weissage über mein Volk Israel. Der Prophet Amos—Zeit, Persöhnlichkeit, Botschaft." *Gericht und Umkehr. Die Botschaft des Propheten Amos.* 1967, 110–23.

Sievers, E., and H. Guthe. *Amos, metrisch bearbeitet.* Leipzig: Teubner, 1907.

Sinclair, L. A. "The Courtroom Motif in the Book of Amos." *JBL* 85 (1966): 351–53.

Smalley, W. A. "Translating the Poetry of the Old Testament." *BT* 26 (1975): 201–11.

_____. "Recursion Patterns and the Sectioning of Amos." *BT* 30 (1979): 118–27.

Smelik, K. A. D. "Dag der Wrake of Dag des Heren?" *Schrift* 89 (1983): 174–79.

_____. "The Meaning of Amos V 18–20." *VT* 36 (1986): 246–48.

Smend, R. "'Das Ende ist Gekommen'. Ein Amoswort in der Priesterschrift." *Die Botschaft und die Boten. Festschrift für Hans Walter Wolff.* Neukirchen-Vluyn: Neukirchener Verlag, 1981, 67–72.

_____. "Das Nein des Amos." *EvTh* 23 (1963): 404–23.

Smith, B. K. *Layman's Bible Book Commentary,* vol. 13. *Hosea, Joel, Amos, Obadiah, Jonah.* Nashville: Broadman, 1982.

Smith, G. A. *The Book of the Twelve Prophets.* 2 vols. 2d ed. New York: Armstrong, 1928.

Smith, G. V. *Amos: A Commentary.* Grand Rapids: Zondervan, 1989.

_____. "Amos 5:13—The Deadly Silence of the Prosperous." *JBL* 107 (1988): 289–91.

Smith, R. "Amos." *Broadman Bible Commentary.* Nashville: Broadman, 1972, 7:81–141.

Snaith, N. H. *Notes on the Hebrew Text of Amos.* 2 vols. London: Epworth, 1945–46.

_____. *Amos, Hosea, and Micha.* London: Epworth, 1956.

Snyder, G. "Law and Covenant in Amos." *ResQ* 25 (1982): 158–66.

Soggin, J. A. "Das Erdbeben von Amos 1:1 und die Chronologie der Könige Ussia und Jotham." *ZAW* 82 (1970): 117–21.

_____ . "Amos VI, 13–14 und I,3 auf dem Hintergrund der Beziehungen zwischen Israel und Damaskus im 9. Jahrhundert." *Near Eastern Studies in Honor of W. F. Albright,* ed. H. Goedicke. Baltimore: Johns Hopkins Univiversity Press, 1971, 433–41.

_____. *The Prophet Amos: A Translation and Commentary.* London: SCM, 1987.

Soper, B. K. "A New Interpretation of Amos 1:3, etc." *ExpTim* 71 (1959–60): 86–87.

Sowada, J. "Let Justice Surge Like Water." *TBT* 19 (1981): 301–5.

Speidel, K. "Hunger nach Gottes Wort—Meditation zu Amos *, 11–12." *Gericht und Umkehr. Die Botschaft des Propheten Amos.* Neukirchen-Vluyn: Neukirchener Verlag, 1967, 120–22.

Sperber, D. "Varia Midrashica IV." *REJ* 137 (1978): 149–57.

Spiegel, S. "Amos vs. Amaziah." *The Jewish Expression,* ed. J. Goldin. New Haven: Yale University Press, 1976, 38–65.

Spreafico, A. "Amos: structura formale e spunti per una interpretazione." *RivB (Italiana)* 29/2 (1981): 147–76.

Staerk, W. *Amos-Nahum-Habakuk herausgegeben*. Leipzig: Hinrichs, 1908.

Stager, L. E. "The Finest Oil in Samaria." *JSS* 28 (1983): 241–45.

Stamm, J. J. "Der Name des Propheten Amos und sein sprachlicher Hintergrund." *Prophecy: Essays Presented to Georg Fohrer on His Sixty-fifth Birthday, 6 September 1980*, ed. J. A. Emerton. Berlin: W. de Gruyter, 1980, 137–42.

Staples, W. E. "Epic Motifs in Amos." *JNES* 25 (1966): 106–12.

Stave, E. *De Mindre Proferterna*. Uppsala, 1912.

Steck, O. H. "Die Gesellschaftskritik der Propheten." *Christentum und Gesellschaft*, eds. W. Lohff and B. Lohse. Göttingen: Vandenhoeck und Ruprecht, 1969, 46–62.

Steinle, W. *Amos, Prophet in der Stunde der Krise*. Stuttgart: J. F. Steinkopf, 1979.

Stephenson, F. R. "Astronomical Verification and Dating of Old Testament Passages Referring to Solar Eclipses." *PEQ* 107 (1975): 107–20.

Stiles, M. *The Historical Background of the Times of Isaiah the Prophet*. Aptos, Calif.: Self-published, 1979.

Stoebe, H. J. "Überlegungen zu den geistlichen Voraussetzungen der Prophetie des Amos." *Wort-Gebot-Glaube, Fs. W. Eichrodt*. Zürich: Verlag, 1970, 209–25.

———. "Noch einmal zu Amos VII 10–17." *VT* 39 (1989): 342–54.

———. "Der Prophet Amos und sein bürgerlicher Beruf." *WD* 5 (1957): 160–81.

Stolz, F. "Aspekte religiöser und sozialer Ordnung im alten Israel." *ZEE* 17 (1973): 145–59.

Story, C. K. I. "Amos—Prophet of Praise." *VT* 30 (1980): 67–80.

Strange, J. *Caftor/Keftiu. A New Investigation*. Leiden: E. J. Brill, 1980.

Strange, M. *The Books of Amos, Osee and Micah, with a Commentary*. New York: Paulist, 1961.

Strobel, A. *Der spätbronzezeitliche Seevölkersturm. Ein Forschungsüberblick mit Folgerungen zur biblischen Exodusthematik*. Berlin/New York: W. de Gruyter, 1976.

Strus, A. "Interpretation des noms propres dans les oracles contre des nations." *VTS* 36 (1985): 272–85.

Stuart, D. K. *Studies in Early Hebrew Meter*. Missoula: Scholars, 1976, 197–212.

———. "The Sovereign's Day of Conquest. A Possible Ancient Near Eastern Reflex of the Israelite 'Day of Yahweh.'" *BASOR* 221 (1976): 159–64.

———. *Hosea–Jonah*. Waco, Tex.: Word, 1987.

Stuhlmueller, C. *Amos, Hosea, Micah, Nahum, Zephaniah, Habakkuk*. Collegeville, Minn.: Liturgical Press, 1987.

———. "Amos. Desert-Trained Prophet." *TBT* 1 (1962–63): 224–30.

Super, A. S. "Figures of Comparison in the Book of Amos." *Semitics* 1 (1970): 67–80.

Sutcliffe, E. F. *The Book of Amos*. London: Burns, Oates & Washbourne, 1939.

———. "A Note on *'al, le*, and From." *VT* 5 (1955): 436–39.

Synder, G. "The Law and the Covenant in Amos." *ResQ* 25 (1982): 158–66.

Szabp, A. "Textual Problems in Amos and Hosea." *VT* 25 (1975): 500–524.

Szwarc, U. "Thirst after God's Word—Exegetical-Theological Analysis of the Text of Amos 8,11–12." *RTK* 27 (1980): 43–51.

Tadmor, H. "Azriyau of Yaudi." *Scripta Hierosolymitana* 8 (1961): 232–71.

____. "The Historical Inscriptions of Ada-Nirari III." *Iraq* 35 (1973): 141–50.

____. "Assyria and the West: The Ninth Century and Its Aftermath." *Unity and Diversity: Essays in the History, Literature and Religion of the Ancient Near East,* eds. H. Goedicke and J. J. M. Roberts. Baltimore: Johns Hopkins University Press, 1975, 36–48.

Talmon, S. "The Gezer Calendar and the Seasonal Cycle of Ancient Canaan." *JAOS* 83 (1963): 177–87.

____. "The Ugaritic Background of Amos 7:4." *Tarbiz* (1965–66): 301–3. (Heb.)

Talstra, E. "The Use of *ken* in Biblical Hebrew. A Case Study in Automatic Text Processing." *OTS* 21 (1981): 22–39.

Tatford, F. *Prophet of Social Justice: An Exposition of Amos.* Eastbourne: Prophetic Witness, 1974.

Terrien, S. "Amos and Wisdom." *Israel's Prophetic Heritage. Essays in Honor of James Muilenburg,* eds. B. W. Anderson and W. Harrelson. New York: Harper & Brothers, 1962, 108–15.

Theis, J., and J. Lippl. *Die zwölf Kleinen Propheten.* 2 vols. Bonn: P. Hanstein, 1937.

Thiele, E. R. *The Mysterious Numbers of the Hebrew Kings.* 3d. ed. Grand Rapids: Zondervan, 1983.

Thomas, D. W. "Note on *nô'adû* in Amos 3:3." *JTS* 7 (1956): 69–70.

Thompson, C. L. *The Ideological Background and an Analysis of Economic Injustice in the Book of Amos.* Unpubl. diss., Southern Baptist Theological Seminary, 1956.

Thorogood, B. *A Guide to the Book of Amos, with Thema Discussions on Judgement, Social Justice, Priest and Prophet.* London: SPCK, 1971.

Tietsch, A. "Die Botschaft des Amos." *Die Zeichen der Zeit* 26 (1972): 211–17.

Timm, S. *Die Dynastie Omri.* Göttingen: Vandenhoeck und Ruprecht, 1982, 270–73.

Tolk, J. *Predigtarbeit zwischen Text und Situation.* München: Kaiser, 1972.

Toll, C. "Die Wurzel *prm* im Hebräischen." *Orientalia Suecana* 21 (1972): 73–86.

Tourn, G. *Amos, profeta della giustizia,* ed. J. A. Soggin. Torino: Claudiana, 1972.

Touzard, J. *Le livre d'Amos.* Paris: Bloud, 1909.

Toy, C. H. "The Judgement of Foreign Peoples in Amos 1:3–2:3." *JBL* 25 (1906): 25–28.

Trapiello, J. G. "Situacion Historica del Profeta Amos." *EstBib* 26 (1967): 249–74.

____. "La nocien del 'Dia de Yahve' en el Antiguo Testamento." *CuBi* 26 (1969): 331–36.

Treu, U. "Amos 7,14, Schenute und der Physiologus." *NT* 10 (1968): 234–40.

Trochon, M. *Les petites Prophètes.* Paris: Lethielleux, 1883.

Tromp, N. J. *Amos. Profetie als Kritische Funktie.* 1971, 294–302.

____. "Vraagtekens bij Amos." *Amos. Een Aanklacht.* Amsterdam, 1979, 30–40.

____. "Amos V 1–17. Toward a Stylistic and Rhetorical Analysis." *OTS* 33 (1984): 56–84.

Tromp, N. J., and D. Deden. *De Prophet Amos.* Boxtel, 1971.

Tsumura, D. T. "'Inserted Bicolon,' The AXYB Pattern, in Amos i 5 and Psalm IX 7." *VT* 38 (1988): 234–36.

Tucker, G. M. "Prophetic Authenticity: A Form-Critical Study of Amos 7:10–17." *Int* 27 (1973): 423–34.

_____. "Prophetic Superscription and the Growth of the Canon." *Canon and Authority: Essays in Old Testament Religion and Theology,* eds. G. W. Coats and B. O. Long. Philadelphia: Fortress, 1977, 56–70.

_____. "Prophetic Speech." *Int* 32 (1978): 31–45.

_____. "Prophecy and Prophetic Literature." *The Hebrew Bible and Its Modern Interpreters,* eds. D. A. Knight and G. M. Tucker. Philadelphia: Fortress; Chico, Calif.: Scholars , 1985, 325–68.

Tur-Sinai, N. H. *Peshuto shel Miqra.* 6 vols. Jerusalem: Kiryat Sepher, 1967, 3/2, 450–77. (Heb.)

Turner, P. D. M. "'anoikodomein and Intra-Septuagintal Borrowing." *VT* 27 (1977): 492–93.

_____. "Two Septugintalisms with STHRIZEIN." *VT* 28 (1978): 481–82.

Tuschen, W. *Die historischen Angaben im Buche des Propheten Amos.* Unpubl. diss., Universität Freiburg, 1951.

Uehlinger, C. "Der Herr auf der Zinnmauer. Zur dritten Amos-Vision (Am 7,7–8)." *BN* 48 (1989): 89–104.

Uffenheimer, B. *Commentary to Amos,* ed. S. L. Gordon. Tel Aviv: Gordon, 1968. (Heb.)

_____. "Amos and Hosea—Two Directions in Israel Prophecy." *Dor le dor* 5/3 (1977): 101–10. (Heb.)

_____. "Mythological and Rationalistic Thought in Hosea and Amos." *Studies in the Minor Prophets,* ed. B. Z. Luria. Jerusalem: Kiryat Sepher, 1981, 155–79.

Ulrichsen, J. H. "Oraklene i Amos 1:3ff." *NorTT* 85 (1984): 39–54.

Umbreit, F. W. C. *Practischer Commentar über die Propheten des alten Bundes: Kleine Propheten.* Hamburg: R. Perthes, 1843.

Unterman, J. *From Repentance to Redemption. Jeremiah's Thought in Transition.* Sheffield: JSOT, 1987.

Utzschneider, Helmut. "Die Amazjaerzählung (Am 7,10–17) zwischen Literatur und Historie." *BN* 41 (1988): 76–101.

Valeton, J. J. P. *Amos und Hosea.* Trans. F. K. Echternacht. Giessen: J. Ricker, 1898.

Van Andel, J. *De Kleine Profeten.* 2d ed. Kampen: Kok, 1912.

Van Gelderen, C. *Het Boek Amos.* Kampen: Kok, 1933.

Van Gemeren, W. A. *Interpreting the Prophetic Word.* Grand Rapids: Zondervan, 1990, 127–40.

Van Hoonacker, A. *Les douze petits Prophètes traduits et commentés.* Paris: Gabalda, 1908.

van der Wal, A. "The Structure of Amos." *JSOT* 26 (1983): 107–13.

_____. "Background and Rhetorical Function of Amos 3:1–2." *Amsterdamse Cahiers voor Exegese en Bijbelse Theologie* 6 (1985): 83–90.

_____. "Amos 5:13—Een omstreden tekst." *NedTT* 41 (1987): 89–98.

_____. "Amos, Een Paar Notities." *Amos. Een Aanklacht.* Amsterdam: Vrije Universitet, 1979, 5–26.

van der Woude, A. S. "Bemerkungen zu einigen umstrittenen Stellen im Zwölfprophetenbuch. Amos 5:25–26." *Mélanges bibliques et orientaux en l'honneur de M. Henri Cazelles.* Kevelaer: Butzon & Bercker, 1981; Neukirchen-Vluyn: Neukirchener Verlag, 1981, 483–99.

_____. "Three Classical Prophets: Amos, Hosea and Micah." *Israel's Prophetic Tradition: Essays in Honor of Peter R. Ackroyd,* eds. R. Coggins, A. Phillips, and M. Knibb. Cambridge: Cambridge University Press, 1982, 32–57.

van Dyne, J. *Amos–Haggai.* Kansas City: Beacon Hill, 1988.

van Leeuwen, C. "De 'Lofprijzingen' in Amos." *Rondom het Woord* 13 (1971): 255–67.

_____. "De 'Kleine Propheten' in Het Onderzoek van de Laatste Tien Jaar." *NedTT* 28 (1974): 113–29.

_____. "De heilsverwachting bij Amos." *Vruchten van de Uithof. Studies B. A. Brongers.* Utrecht: Theological Institute, 1974, 71–87.

_____. "The Prophecy of the *yom yhwh* in Amos V 18–20." *OTS* 19 (1974): 113–34.

_____. "Amos 1:2, Epigraphe du livre entier ou introduction aux oracles des chapitres 1-2?" *Verkenningen in een Stromgebied. Proeven van oudtestamentisch Onderzoek. Festschrift M. A. Beek,* ed. M. Boertien. Amsterdam: Theologisch Institut van de Universiteit van Amsterdam, 1974, 93–101.

_____. "Quelques problèmes de traduction dans les visions d'Amos chapitre 7." *Übersetzung und Deutung.* Nijkerk: Uitgeverij G. F. Callenbach, 1977, 103–12.

_____. *Amos.* Pot Nijkerk, 1985.

Vanhorn, W. W. *An Investigation of YOM YAHWEH as It Relates to the Message of Amos.* Unpubl. Ph.D. diss., New Orleans Baptist Theological Seminary, 1987.

van Wyk, W. C. "Die Kusiete in Amos 9:7." *Hervormde Teologiese Studies* 22 (1967): 38–45.

Varadi, M. *Il profeta Amos.* Florence: Casa Editrice Israel, 1947.

Varro, R. "Amos: les justes, les pauvres et le prophète." *Masses Ouvrières* 297 (1973): 24–37.

Vattioni, F. "La terminologie dell'alleanza." *Riblos Press* 6/4 (1965): 112–16.

Vaux, R., de. "The Remnant of Israel According to the Prophets." *The Bible and the Ancient Near East.* Trans. J. McHugh. Garden City: Doubleday, 1971, 15–30.

Vawter, B. *Amos, Hosea, Micah, with an Introduction to Classical Prophecy.* Wilmington: Glazier, 1981; Dublin: Gill and Macmillan, 1981.

_____. "The God of Hebrew Scriptures." *BTB* 12 (1982): 3–7.

_____. "Were the Prophets *nabi's.*" *Bib* 66 (1985): 206–20.

Vegas Montaner, L. *Biblia del Mar Muerto: Profetas Menores.* Madrid, 1980.

Veijola, T. "Zu Ableitung und Bedeutung von *he'îi* I im Hebräischen." *UF* 8 (1976): 343–51.

_____. "Die Propheten und das Alter des Sabbatgebots." *Prophet und Prophetenbuch.*

Festschrift für Otto Kaiser, eds. V. Fritz, K.-F. Pohlmann, and H.-C. Schmitt. Berlin/New York: W. de Gruyter, 1989, 246–64.

Veldkamp, H. *De Boer van Tekoa.* Franeker: T. Wever, 1940.

Vermeylen, J. *Du prophète Isaïe à l'apocalyptique.* Paris: Gabalda, 1978, 2:519–69.

_____. "Les prophètes de la conversion faces aux tradition sacrales de l'Israël ancien." *RTL* 9 (1978): 5–32.

Vesco, J.-L. "Amos de Teqoa, défenseur de l'homme." *RB* 87 (1980): 481–513.

Vischer, W. "Amos, citoyen de Téqoa." *ETR* 50 (1975): 133–59.

Vogels, W. "Restauration de l'Egypte et universalisme en Ez 29,13–16." *Bib* 53 (1972): 473–94.

_____. "L'alliance primitive universelle." *Eglise et Theologie* 3 (1972): 291–322.

_____. "Invitation à revenir à l'alliance et universalisme en Amos IX 7." *VT* 22 (1972): 223–39.

Vogt, E. "Zur Geschichte der hebräischen Sprache." *Bib* 52 (1971): 72–78.

Vollborn, W. *Innerzeitliche oder endzeitliche Gerichtserwartung: Ein Beitrag zu Amos und Jesaja.* Kiel: Schmidt & Klaunig, 1938.

Vollmer, J. *Geschichtliche Rückblicke und Motive in der Prophetie des Amos, Hosea und Jesaja.* Berlin/New York: W. de Gruyter, 1971, 8–54.

von Orelli, C. *Die zwölf kleinen Propheten.* 3d ed. Munich: C. H. Beck, 1908.

von Waldow, H. E. "Social Responsibility and Social Structure in Early Israel." *ZAW* 32 (1970): 182–204.

Vriezen, Th. C. "Erwägungen zu Amos 3, 2." *Archäologie und Altes Testament: Festschrift für Kurt Galling,* eds. A. Kuschke and E. Kutsch. Tübingen: J. C. B. Mohr [Paul Siebeck], 1970, 255–58.

Wagner, S. "Überlegungen zur Frage nach den Beziehungen des Propheten Amos zum Südreich." *TLZ* 96 (1971): 653–70.

_____. "*drš.*" *TDOT,* 1978, 3:293–307.

Waldmann, N. M. "The Wealth of Mountain and Sea. The Background of a Biblical Image." *JQR* 71 (1981): 176–80.

Walker, L. L. "The Language of Amos." *SWJT* 9 (1966): 37–48.

Waller, H. S. *The Unity of the Book of Amos.* Unpubl. diss., Southern Baptist Theological Seminary, 1948.

Wanke, G. "Zu Grundlagen und Absicht prophetischer Sozialkritik." *KD* 18 (1972): 2–17.

Ward, J. M. *Amos and Isaiah: Prophets of God's Word.* Nashville: Abingdon, 1969, 92–112.

_____. "Amos." *IDB(Sup).* Nashville: Abingdon, 1976, 21–23.

_____. *Amos and Hosea.* Atlanta: Abingdon, 1981.

_____. *The Prophets.* Nashville: Abingdon, 1982.

_____. "The Eclipse of the Prophet in Contemporary Prophetic Studies." *USQR* 42 (1988): 97–104.

Warmuth, G. *Das Mahnwort. Seine Bedeutung für die Verkündigung der vorexilischen Propheten Amos, Hosea, Micha, Jesaja und Jeremia.* Frankfurt am M./Bern: Peter Lang, 1976.

Watson, W. G. E. "David Ousts the City Rulers of Jebus." *VT* 20 (1970): 501–2.

———. *Classical Hebrew Poetry: A Guide to Its Techniques.* Sheffield: JSOT, 1984.

———. "Internal Parallelism in Classical Hebrew Verse." *Bib* 66 (1985): 365–84.

———. "A Critical Analysis of Amos 4:1ff." *SBLSP* (1972): 489–500.

Watts, J. D. W. "An Old Hymn Preserved in the Book of Amos." *JNES* 15 (1956): 33–39.

———. "The Origin of the Book of Amos." *ExpTim* 66 (1954–55): 109–12.

———. *Vision and Prophecy in Amos.* Grand Rapids: Eerdmans, 1958.

———. "Amos, the Man and His Message." *SWJT* 9 (1966): 21–26.

———. *Studying the Book of Amos.* Nashville: Broadman, 1966.

———. "A Critical Analysis of Amos 4:1ff." *SBLSP* 108. Missoula: Scholars, 1972, 489–500.

———. "Commentaries on Amos." *Religious Studies Review* 7/2 (1981): 128–32.

Weber, H.-R. "Prophecy in the Ecumenical Movement. Ambiguities and Questions." *Prophetic Vocation in the New Testament and Today*, ed. J. Panagopoulos. Leiden: E. J. Brill, 1977, 218–28.

Weimar, P. "Der Schluss des Amos-Buches. Ein Beitrag zur Redaktionsgeschichte des Amos-Buches." *BN* 16 (1981): 60–100.

Weimar, P., and E. Zenger. *Exodus. Geschichten und Geschichte der Befreiung Israels.* Stuttgart: Katholisches Bibelwerk, 1975.

Weinfeld, M. "The Extent of the Promised Land—Status of Transjordan." *Das Land Israel in biblischer Zeit*, ed. G. Strecker. Göttingen: Vandenhoeck und Ruprecht, 1983, 59–75.

———. "The Worship of Molech and the Queen of Heaven and Its Background." *UF* 4 (1972): 133–54.

———. *Deuteronomy and the Deuteronomic School.* London: Oxford University Press, 1972.

———. "The Concept of the Day of the Lord and the Problem of Its *Sitz im Leben*." *Studies in the Minor Prophets*, ed. B. Z. Luria. Jerusalem: Kiryat Sepher, 1981, 55–76. (Heb.)

———. "Aspirations for the Kingdom of God in the Bible and Their Reflections in Jewish Liturgy—The Essence of the Concept of the 'Day of the Lord.'" *Studies in the Bible*, ed. S. Japhet. Jerusalem: Magnes, 1986, 341–72.

Weippert, H. "Amos: Seine Bilder und ihr Milieu." *Beiträge zur Prophetischen Bildsprache in Israel und Assyrien.* Fribourg: Universitätsverlag, 1985, 1–29.

Weippert H., K. Seybold, and M. Weippert. *Beiträge zur prophetischen Bildsprache in Israel und Assyrien.* Freiburg (Switzerland): Universitätsverlag; Göttingen: Vandenhoeck und Ruprecht, 1985.

Weiser, A. *Die Profetie des Amos.* Giessen: Töpelmann, 1929.

———. *Das Buch der zwölf Kleinen Propheten. I. Die Propheten Hosea, Joel, Amos, Obadja, Micha.* 5th ed. Göttingen: Vandenhoeck und Ruprecht, 1967.

Weisman, Z. "Muster und Konstruktionen in den Visionen des Amos." *Beth Miqra* 39 (1969): 40–57. (Heb. with Eng. summary)

———. "Patterns and Structure in the Visions of Amos." *Beth Miqra* 39 (1970): 40–57. (Heb.)

____. "Stylistic Parallels in Amos and Jeremiah: Their Implications for the Composition of Amos." *Shnaton* 1 (1975): 129–49.

Weiss, M. "The Origin of the 'Day of the Lord'—Reconsidered." *HUCA* 37 (1966): 29–72.

____. "'Because Three . . . and Because Four' (Amos 1–2)." *Tarbiz* 36 (1967): 307–18. (Heb. with Eng. summary)

____. "The Pattern of Numerical Sequence in Amos 1–2: A Re-Examination." *JBL* 86 (1967): 416–23.

____. "The Pattern of the 'Execration Texts' in the Prophetic Literature." *IEJ* 19 (1969): 150–57.

____. "These Days and the Days to Come According to Amos 9:13." ErIsr *H. L. Ginsberg Volume* 14 (1978): 69–73. (Heb. with Eng. summary)

____. *The Bible from Within: The Method of Total Interpretation.* Jerusalem: Magnes, 1986.

Weitz, Y. "Amos—*Noqed, Boker,* and *Boleš Shikmim.*" *Beth Miqra* 33 (1968): 141–44. (Heb.)

Wellhausen, J. *Die Kleinen Propheten übersetzt und erklärt.* 3d ed. Berlin: Reiner, 1898; 4th ed. Berlin: W. de Gruyter, 1963.

Wendland, E. R. "The 'Word of the Lord' and the Organization of Amos." *OPTAT* 2/4 (1988): 1–51.

Westermann, C. *Basic Forms of Prophetic Speech.* Philadelphia: Westminster, 1967.

____. "Amos 5, 4–6. 14. 15: Ihr Werdet Leben!" *Erträge der Forschung am Alten Testament. Gesammelte Studien III.* München: Kaiser, 1984, 107–18.

Whybray, R. N. *The Intellectual Tradition in the Old Testament.* Berlin/New York: W. de Gruyter, 1974.

____. "Prophecy and Wisdom." *Israel's Prophetic Tradition. Fs. P. R. Ackroyd,* eds. J. Collins et al. Cambridge: Cambridge University Press, 1982, 181–99.

Wilcke, D. W. "Two Perspectives (Amos 5:1–17)." *CurTM* 13 (1986): 89–96.

Wildberger, H. "*š'r* übrig sein." *Theologisches Handwörterbuch zum Alten Testament,* eds. Ernst Jenni and Claus Westermann. München: Kaiser, 1976, 2:844–55.

Williams, A. J. "A Further Suggestion about Amos IV 1–3." *VT* 29 (1979): 206–11.

____. *Joel and Amos. The Minor Prophets Unfolded.* Cambridge: Cambridge University Press, 1918.

Williams, D. L. "The Theology of Amos." *RevEx* 63 (1966): 393–403.

Williams, J. G. "The Alas-Oracles of the Eighth Century." *HUCA* 38 (1967): 75–91.

____. "Irony and Lament: Clues to Prophetic Consciousness." *Semeia* 8 (1977): 51–74.

Willi-Plein, I. *Vorformen der Schriftexegese innerhalb des Alten Testaments.* Berlin/New York: W. de Gruyter, 1971, 15–69.

Willis, J. T. "Redaction Criticism and Historical Reconstruction." *Encounter with the Text,* ed. M. Buss. Philadelphia: Fortress, 1979.

Wilson, R. R. *Prophecy and Society in Ancient Israel.* Philadelphia: Fortress, 1980, 266–92.

Witaszek, G. *I profeti Amos et Michea nella lotta per la giusticia sociale nell'VIII secolo A.C.* Unpubl. diss., Roma, Gregorianae Pontifical University, 1986, 38–61.

Wittenberg, G. H. "Amos 6: 1–7: 'They Dismiss the Day of Disaster but You Bring Near the Rule of Violence.'" *J Th So Africa* 58 (1987): 57–69.

Wolff, H. W. *Amos the Prophet: The Man and His Background.* Philadelphia: Fortress, 1973.

_____. *Dodekapropheton 2. Joel und Amos.* Neukirchen-Vluyn: Neukirchener Verlag, 1975.

_____. *Joel and Amos.* Philadelphia: Fortress, 1977.

_____. *Die Stunde des Amos, Prophetie und Protest.* München: Chr. Kaiser, 1969.

_____. "Das Ende des Heiligtums in Bethel." *Archäologie und Altes Testament. Festschrift für Kurt Galling,* eds. A. Kuschke and E. Kutsch. Tübingen: J. C. B. Mohr [Paul Siebeck], 1970, 287–98.

_____. "Die eigentliche Botschaft der klassischen Propheten." *Beitrage zur Alttestamentlichen Theologie. Fs. W. Zimmerli.* Göttingen: Vandenhoeck und Ruprecht, 1977, 547–57.

_____. "Prophets and Institutions in the Old Testament." *CurTM* 13 (1986): 5–12.

_____. "The Irresistible Word (Amos)." *CurTM* 10 (1983): 5–13.

_____. "Prophecy from the Eighth Through the Fifth Century." *Interpreting the Prophets,* eds. James L. Mays and Paul J. Achtemeier. Philadelphia: Fortress, 1987, 14–26.

Wolters, A. "Wordplay and Dialect in Amos 8:1–2." *JETS* 31 (1988): 407–10.

Wonderly, W. L. "Poetry in the Bible: Challenge to Translators." *BT* 38 (1987): 206–13.

Woodward, B. F. *A Study of the Norms of Indictment in Amos.* Unpubl. Ph.D. diss., Union Theological Seminary, 1970.

Wright, T. J. "Did Amos Inspect Livers?" *ABR* 23 (1975): 3–11.

_____. "Amos and the Sycamore Fig." *VT* 26 (1976): 362–68.

Würthwein, E. "Kultpolemik oder Kultbescheid?" *Wort und Existenz. Studien zum Alten Testament.* Göttingen: Vandenhoeck und Ruprecht, 1970, 144–60.

_____. "Amos-Studien." *ZAW* 62 (1950): 10–52; repr. in *Wort und Existenz. Studien zum Alten Testament.* Göttingen: Vandenhoeck und Ruprecht, 1970, 68–110.

_____. "Amos 5:21–27." *Wort und Existenz. Studien zum Alten Testament.* Göttingen: Vandenhoeck und Ruprecht, 1970, 55–67.

Wyszowadzki, W. *The Conception of Justice in the Book of Amos.* Unpubl. diss., University of Warsaw, 1982. (Polish)

Yadin, Y. "The Archaeological Sources for the Period of the Monarchy." *The World History of the Jewish People,* eds. A. Malamat and I. Eph'al. Jerusalem/London: Massada, 1979, 4:187–235.

_____. "Beer-Sheba. The High Place Destroyed by King Josiah." *BASOR* 222 (1976): 5–15.

Yadin, Y., et al. *Hazor II: An Account of the Second Season of Excavations, 1956.* Jerusalem: Magnes, 1960.

Yamashita, T. "Noqed." *Ras Shamra Parallels: The Texts from Ugarit and the Hebrew Bible,* ed. L. Fisher. Rome: Pontifical Biblical Institute Press, 1975, 2:63–64.

Yamauchi, E. M. "Cultic Prostitution. A Case Study in Cultural Diffusion." *Orient and Oxident. Festschrift in Honor of C. H. Gordon.* Kevalaer: Butzon & Bercker, Neukirchen-Vluyn: Neukirchener Verlag, 1973, 213–23.

Yeivin, S. "The Divided Kingdom." *The World History of the Jewish People,* ed. A. Malamat. Jerusalem: Magnes, 1979, 4:164–65.

____. "The Social, Economic, and Political Situation According to Amos and Hosea." *Studies in the Minor Prophets,* ed. B. Z. Luria. Jerusalem: Kiryat Sepher, 1981, 97–111. (Heb.)

Yeo, K.-K. "Amos (4:4–5) and Confucius: The Will (Ming) of God (Tien)." *Asia Journal of Theology* 4 (1990): 472–88.

Yoshida, H. "Prophecy and Salvation, in the Case of Amos." *Kiyo: Meiji Gakuin University Christian Research Institute Bulletin* 14 (1981): 27–47.

Youngblood, R. "LQRT in Amos 4:12." *JBL* 90 (1971): 98.

Zakovitch, Y. *"For Three . . . and for Four." The Pattern of Numerical Sequence in the Bible.* 2 vols. Jerusalem: Mekor, 1979. (Heb.)

Zalcman, L. "Piercing the Darkness at *boqer* (Amos VII 14)." *VT* 30 (1980): 252–55.

____. "Astronomical Allusions in Amos." *JBL* 100 (1981): 53–58.

Zerafa, P. "Il Resto d'Israele nei profeti preesilici." *Angelicum* 49 (1972): 3–29.

Zevit, Z. "A Misunderstanding at Bethel—Amos VII 12–17." *VT* 25 (1975): 783–90.

____. "Expressing Denial in Biblical Hebrew and Mishnaic Hebrew, and in Amos." *VT* 29 (1979): 505–9.

Ziegler, J. "Die Einheit der Septuaginta zum Zwölfprophetenbuch." *Sylloge. Gesammelte Aufsätze zur Septuaginta.* Göttingen: Vandenhoeck und Ruprecht, 1971, 29–42.

Zimmerli, W. *Studien zur alttestamentlichen Theologie und Prophetie, Gesammelte Aufsätze II.* München: Kaiser, 1974.

____. "Vom Prophetenwort zum Prophetenbuch." *TLZ* 104 (1979): 481–96.

____. "Das Gottesrecht bei den Propheten Amos, Hosea und Jesaja." *Werden und Wirken des Alten Testaments. Festschrift für Claus Westermann zum 70. Geburtstag.* Göttingen: Vandenhoeck und Ruprecht, 1980; Neukirchen-Vluyn: Neukirchener Verlag, 1980, 216–35.

____. "The Word of Divine Self-manifestation (Proof-Saying): A Prophetic Genre." *I Am Yahweh,* ed. W. Brueggemann. Atlanta: John Knox, 1982, 99–110.

Ziv, Y. "'Bôper Ubôlesh Shikmîm—b'Teqoa'?" *Beth Miqra* 92 (1982): 49–51. (Heb.)

Zobel, H.-J. "Prophet in Israel und in Judah. Das prophetische Verständnis des Hosea und Amos." *ZTK* 82 (1985): 281–99.

____. "*hôj.*" *Theologisches Wörterbuch zum Alten Testament,* 2:382–88; "*hôy.*" *Theological Dictionary of the Old Testament.* Grand Rapids: Eerdmans, 1978, 359–64.

Zyl, A. H. van. "Die Sondebesef bij Amos." *NGGT* 9 (1968): 69–82.

____. *The Moabites.* Leiden: E. J. Brill, 1971.

Index